STUDIES IN
IMPERIA·

general editor John M.

Established in the belief that imp
phenomenon had as significant an e
as on the subordinate societies, Stu   ...sm
seeks to develop the new socio-cultu ₋ approach which
has emerged through cross-disciplinary work on popular
culture, media studies, art history, the study of education
and religion, sports history and children's literature.
The cultural emphasis embraces studies of migration and
race, while the older political and constitutional,
economic and military concerns are never far away.
It incorporates comparative work on European and
American empire-building, with the chronological focus
primarily, though not exclusively, on the nineteenth and
twentieth centuries, when these cultural exchanges were
most powerfully at work.

The Victorian soldier in Africa

Published in our
centenary year
≈ **2004** ↫
MANCHESTER
UNIVERSITY
PRESS

The Victorian soldier in Africa

Edward M. Spiers

MANCHESTER UNIVERSITY PRESS
Manchester and New York

distributed exclusively in the USA by Palgrave

Published by Manchester University Press
Oxford Road, Manchester M13 9NR, UK
and Room 400, 175 Fifth Avenue, New York, NY 10010, USA
www.manchesteruniversitypress.co.uk

Distributed in the United States exclusively by
Palgrave Macmillan, 175 Fifth Avenue,
New York, NY 10010, USA

Distributed in Canada exclusively by
UBC Press, University of British Columbia, 2029 West Mall,
Vancouver, BC, Canada V6T 1Z2

British Library Cataloguing-in-Publication Data is available

Library of Congress Cataloging-in-Publication Data is available

ISBN 978 0 7190 9127 8 paperback

First published by Manchester University Press in hardback 2004

This paperback edition first published 2013

Printed by Lightning Source

CONTENTS

LIST OF MAPS

GENERAL EDITOR'S INTRODUCTION

Visit almost any military or regimental museum and you will find mementos of individual lives. These take many forms: medals, uniforms, bibles, letters, diaries, paintings, photographs; or sometimes collected 'ethnic' materials, both the weaponry of opponents and the artefacts of their peaceful activities. The relatives of soldiers, NCOs and officers usually find solace in donating such materials to the museums where they feel they will be cherished, will be useful to those wishing to study military history, or will be displayed for public view. Sometimes, the donations happen after their owner's death in action; sometimes at the end of a full life of survival and return to 'civvy street'. Naturally, much of this material relates to the two World Wars of the twentieth century, but, given Britain's imperial past, it is striking that a high proportion of these donations relate to the imperial campaigns of the nineteenth and early twentieth centuries. This is also true of so many of the colours and battle honours that hang in churches, testimony to a communal pride, or to the large numbers of memorials, brass plaques and gravestones to be found around the country. For the observant visitor, colonial campaigns have a habit of turning up almost anywhere, not only in the museums, churches and graveyards of the imperial power, but also in the landscape, memories and preserved artefacts among the peoples against whom these campaigns were fought.

Although there has been a plethora of many different types of military history, this book is one of the first to consider the lives and attitudes of individuals both in the officer corps and in the ranks, in this case exclusively on the British side. Each war also stimulates a small wave of publications, something apparent again in the Falklands, Gulf and Iraq wars of the last quarter century. Soldiers still write letters, keep diaries (now sometimes audio diaries) and occasionally write books, all with an eye both to their relatives and to a wider public. Each war throws up its criticisms and its controversies and after each there is a sort of 'appeal to the ancestors' as a means of modifying policy, improving conditions or equipment, and as testimony to bravery and incompetence, political strategy and military tactics.

This book takes a sequence of colonial campaigns in Africa and sets out to illuminate them from the materials left by British combatants. These men were taken from familiar surroundings to highly unfamiliar ones, to 'small wars' that Sir Charles Callwell described as 'campaigns against nature'. 'Nature' in this instance was not just the environment, but the nature of conventional warfare, the nature of opponents who often turned out to be more competent than any over-confident imperialist expected, and indeed the nature of the British soldiery who had to cope with climatic conditions, disease, and indigenous tactics such as they had never imagined. Inevitably, the soldiers reflected on all of these in their letters and diaries, in their judgments of the situations in which they found themselves, and in their attitudes to superiors and the 'enemy' which were often severely tested and modified in the course of campaigns.

In doing so, they invariably kept people at home informed in ways that were not always possible in the press. For, after all, the writings and materials that went home were all part of the manner in which an imperial society tried to make sense of the warfare into which its elite led it. The materials that are revealed and analysed in this book were part of the reciprocal character of the imperial experience: warfare was not just some 'distant noise'. Through its combatants' connections with families and friends, it was, in some senses, a set of surprising, often disorientating, and sometimes tragic events, which were also experienced by those at home.

John M. MacKenzie

ACKNOWLEDGEMENTS

Quotations from material in the Royal Archives appear with the gracious permission of Her Majesty Queen Elizabeth II. Other use of Crown copyright material in the National Archives (Public Record Office) or other repositories is by permission of Her Majesty's Controller of Stationery. I should like to acknowledge permission of the Trustees of the National Library of Scotland, the Trustees of the Royal Gloucestershire, Berkshire and Wiltshire (Salisbury) Museum, the Trustees of the Military Museums of Devon and Dorset, the Trustees of the Duke of Cornwall's Light Infantry Museum and the Trustees of the Liddell Hart Centre for Military Archives to quote from papers in their archives. I am particularly grateful to Mr A. Massie for permission to quote from numerous archival collections in the National Army Museum and for every effort made to trace the owner of the copyright of Sergeant Hooper's typescript diary (and, if the latter makes himself known, his assistance will be acknowledged in any future edition of this book). I am also obliged to Mr Nick Russel for permission to quote from the correspondence of Sir Archibald Hunter in the Sudan Archive, University of Durham, and to Mr James Methuen Campbell for permission to quote from the papers of 3rd Baron Methuen in the Wiltshire and Swindon Record Office.

I should also like to acknowledge the assistance of Dr P. B. Boyden (National Army Museum), Ms Samantha J. McNeilly (Royal Archives), Richard Childs (county archivist, West Sussex Record Office), Lieutenant-Colonel P. A. Crocker (Royal Welch Fusiliers Museum, Caernarfon Castle), Mr R. McKenzie (Argyll and Sutherland Highlanders Museum), Mr T. B. Smyth (The Black Watch Archive), Lieutenant-Colonel A. A. Fairrie (Highlanders Museum), Lieutenant-Colonel D. Eliot (Light Infantry Office, Taunton), Lieutenant-Colonel R. A. Leonard (The Keep Military Museum, Dorchester), Lieutenant-Colonel D. Chilton (Royal Gloucestershire, Berkshire and Wiltshire Regiment Museum, Salisbury), Major M. Everett and Mrs C. Green (Royal Regiment of Wales Museum, Brecon), Mrs J. Hogan (assistant keeper, Archives and Special Collections, University of Durham), Mr Robin Harcourt Williams, (librarian and archivist to the Marquis of Salisbury), Mrs A. S. Elsom (Museum of the Staffordshire Regiment), Major L. H. White (Duke of Cornwall's Light Infantry Museum), Mr Tony Cox (Devonshire and Dorset Regimental Headquarters), Mr Norman Newton (Inverness Library), Ms S. Malone and Mr B. Smith (Gordon Highlanders Museum), Mr G. C. Streatfeild (Soldiers of Gloucestershire Museum), Miss Judith Hodgkinson, Mr Durrant and Ms Jacqueline A. Minchinton (Northampton Museums), Mr P. Donnelly (King's Own Royal Regiment Museum, Lancaster), Ms M. Lindsay Roxburgh (Royal Engineers Library), Mr Terry Knight (Cornish Studies Library, Redruth, Cornwall), Ms J. Brown (Plymouth Central Library), Ms Janet Williams (Lichfield Library), Mrs V. Allnutt (Bristol Central Library), Mr Wilf. Deckner (Somerset Studies

Library), Ms P. M. Robinson (Reference Library, Salisbury), Mr N. Kingsley (Gloucestershire Record Office), Ms Z. Lubowiecka (Hove Reference Library), Mr A. Crookston (Wiltshire and Swindon Record Office) and the staff of: Inter-Library Loans (Brotherton Library, University of Leeds); Education Department (Aberdare Library); Local Studies (Central Library, Bradford); Local Studies (Cardiff); Local Studies (Chichester Public Library); Local Studies (Dorchester); Reference Library (Hereford); Reference Library (Newport); Reference Library (Leeds); Liverpool Record Office; the British Library Newspaper Collection (Colindale); the British Library Asia Pacific and Africa Collections; the Liddell Hart Centre for Military Archives, King's College London; and the National Library of Scotland.

I am also grateful for a Small Research Grant from the British Academy, a University of Leeds Study Leave Award in the Humanities and a Research Leave Award from the Arts and Humanities Research Board.

Finally, I should like to express my thanks to various colleagues who have assisted me in this project, namely: Professors F. R. Bridge, J. Gooch, R. D. Black and P. Hammond of Leeds University; Professor B. J. Bond, formerly of King's College, University of London; Professor I. F. W. Beckett, formerly of the University of Luton; and Professor K. Jeffery of the University of Ulster at Jordanstown. I am grateful to David Appleyard for the services of the Graphics Support Unit, Leeds University, in preparing the maps; and to Peter Harrington, Anne S. K. Brown Military History Collection, Brown University, Rhode Island, for his assistance in finding an image for the cover of the book. I am most grateful to Fiona, my wife, for her helpful proof-reading and to Robert and Amanda for bearing with their father during the writing of this book.

Edward M. Spiers
July 2003

ABBREVIATIONS

1/, 2/	1st, 2nd Battalion
AHC	Army Hospital Corps
APA	Asia Pacific and Africa Collections (British Library)
ASHM	Argyll and Sutherland Highlanders Museum
BWA	Black Watch Archive
CIV	City of London Imperial Volunteers
DCLI	Duke of Cornwall's Light Infantry
FLH	Frontier Light Horse
GHM	Gordon Highlanders Museum
GRO	Gloucestershire Record Office
HHM	Hatfield House Muniments
HLI	Highland Light Infantry
JRSF	*Journal of the Royal Scots Fusiliers*
JSAHR	*Journal of the Society for Army Historical Research*
LHCMA	Liddell Hart Centre for Military Archives, King's College London
NAM	National Army Museum
NLS	National Library of Scotland
NRMC	Northamptonshire Regimental Museum Collection
PP	Parliamentary Papers
PRO	Public Record Office
QOHC	Queen's Own Highlanders Collection
RA	Royal Artillery
RAMC	Royal Army Medical Corps
REJ	*Royal Engineers Journal*
REL	Royal Engineers Library
RGBWM	Royal Gloucestershire, Berkshire and Wiltshire Regiment Museum (Salisbury)
RPLM	Royal Pavilion Libraries and Museums
RRWM	Royal Regiment of Wales Museum (Brecon)
SAD	Sudan Archive, University of Durham
SGM	Soldiers of Gloucestershire Museum
SLIA	Somerset Light Infantry Archive
SMR	Sudan Military Railway
SRM	Staffordshire Regiment Museum (Lichfield)
VC	Victoria Cross
WRO	Wiltshire and Swindon Record Office
WSRO	West Sussex Record Office

GLOSSARY

ansar	armed followers of the Mahdi
assegai	a slender spear of hard wood used in South Africa
commando	a Boer military body
donga	a gully
drift	a ford
fellahin	an Egyptian peasant
impi	a body of armed natives
kaffir	a name applied to African natives
Khedive	the Sultan of Turkey's viceroy in Egypt
khor	a dry watercourse
knoll	a round hillock
kop or kopje	a small hill
kraal	a native village or corral for animals
laager	a defensive ring of ox-wagons
nek	a depression or pass in a mountain range
Porte, the	the Turkish imperial government
sangar	a stone breastwork
Sirdar	commander-in-chief of the Egyptian Army
spruit	a small deepish watercourse, dry except during and after rains
veld	open, unforested grass country
zareba	a fortified camp or defensive perimeter made of mimosa bush in the Sudan

INTRODUCTION

Since the 1970s our understanding of the late Victorian army has benefited from a diverse and burgeoning array of scholarship. There have been major works on civil–military relations, the army and society, army reform, and imperial defence, buttressed by biographies of senior commanders, studies of war correspondents and the role of the army in imperial propaganda.[1] Yet the human experience of Victorian warfare has been less well documented – an oversight that contrasts sharply with a profusion of recent studies on human experience in twentieth-century warfare. Quite reasonably the authors of twentieth-century studies claim that their works shed light on the demands and burdens of campaigning, especially the ordeal of battle, perceptions of enemies, allies and warfare itself, relations between officers and men (and between various units fighting along side each other) as well as insights on tactics, morale, discipline, weaponry, and combat motivation.[2] These historical inquiries have benefited from the extent of twentieth-century warfare – total wars in two cases, involving millions of protagonists, many of whom were literate and left testimony about their experiences (not merely letters, poems and diaries but also oral testimony on tape and in film). There is obviously less scope for examining the military experience of the British soldier in the late nineteenth century when the numbers involved, the degree of literacy and the facilities for recording opinions were less extensive. Nevertheless, Victorian soldiers wrote letters to family and friends at home, kept diaries, composed poems, and occasionally gave interviews in far greater numbers than is often realised. This was particularly true of the soldiers who left bases in Britain and the Mediterranean to serve in the relatively short campaigns in Africa before returning (or expecting to return) home. From their writings retained in national and regimental archives, with even more recorded in the metropolitan and provincial press and some in articles and memoirs, insights can be gleaned about campaigning in Africa as well as about the values, priorities and perceptions of the soldiers themselves.

In his study of the South African War (1899–1902), Thomas Pakenham argues that 'the ordinary soldiers took time off to write letters back to England in reply to those thousands of letters from home that littered the veld at every camp site. It was the first dramatic test of the new mass literacy, this orgy of letter writing by the working class.'[3] Tabitha Jackson concurs; she claims that Forster's Education Act of

1870 had provided a framework for compulsory elementary education, and that the literacy rate had grown from 63.3 per cent in 1841 to 92.2 per cent in 1900. The war, she asserts, had produced a 'new outpouring of writing' and 'an equal appetite for reading' about it, hence the dispatch of 58 newspaper correspondents with the main British army to South Africa.[4] Yet in *The Red Soldier* (1977), and in *Marching Over Africa* (1986), the late Frank Emery revealed that Victorian soldiers had written numerous letters from earlier campaigns. He confirmed that letter-writing was not an exclusive preserve of regimental officers,[5] and that many shrewd and observant commentaries were written by non-commissioned officers (NCOs) and private soldiers. Emery, though, spread his work over much of the Victorian period, including odd letters from the Crimea, India and Afghanistan, and so covered several campaigns in a perfunctory manner – one letter from the Asante War (1873–74), six from the reconquest of the Sudan (1896–98) and a mere three from the South African War. More recent writing indicates that there is an abundance of material to sustain more focused research and writing on particular campaigns.[6] Utilising such evidence should not only add to our understanding of these operations but may also provide corroborating testimony for critical or contentious issues, supply a greater range of perspectives from soldiers in different regiments or corps, and yield insights from soldiers engaged in different aspects of the same campaigns (particularly those in front-line, reserve or supporting roles). In seeking to test these assumptions, this work will concentrate on the later African campaigns from the Asante War (1873–74) to the South African War, and, in the last campaign, review the experience of regular soldiers from two distinctive parts of the United Kingdom – Scotland and the west country.

Emery rightly argued that the Victorian soldiery, despite being recruited primarily from the labouring classes in town and country, was more literate than often imagined.[7] If educational improvements flowed from Forster's Education Act and the 1872 Scottish Education Act, they varied from locality to locality, hardly applied to the poverty-stricken masses in Ireland, and required the addition of free and compulsory elementary education in the early 1890s.[8] Meanwhile the army developed its own educational requirements. In 1861 the possession of an army certificate of education was made a condition of promotion – a third-class certificate for promotion to corporal, a second-class certificate for promotion to sergeant, and a first-class certificate for a commission from the ranks. From 1871 compulsory attendance of five hours per week was required for new recruits and a new fourth-class certificate of education – a minimum intended for all soldiers – was introduced. Superficially the growth in educational attainment levels, as monitored by the director-general of military education, appeared meteoric, with 48.8 per cent of the rank-and-file described as 'possessing a superior level of education' by 1878, 85.4 per cent by 1889.[9]

These claims, like all educational statistics, have to be interpreted with care. By 1888, over 60 per cent of the other ranks were unable or unwilling to pass the examination for a fourth-class certificate of education (that is, simple reading and an ability to complete a few easy sums – a level purportedly attainable by an 8-year old child). So limited were these achievements that the army abolished the fourth-class certificate in 1888 and terminated compulsory schooling. Henceforth it relied upon persuasion and inducement to raise educational standards. It made the possession of a first-class certificate one of the conditions for promotion to sergeant and the possession a second-class certificate a condition for promotion to corporal. It also expected that the regiments would make provision for voluntary schooling. Nevertheless, genuine improvements in educational standards occurred: the proportion of the rank-and-file in possession of third-class certificates of education rose by nearly 30 per cent from 1870 to 1896, and illiteracy – defined as an inability to read or write one's own name – diminished sharply (from an affliction of 90 per cent of rankers in 1860 to virtual elimination by the end of the century). By the 1890s, fewer than 40 per cent of men had achieved more than the barest levels of literacy, and the proportion attaining first-class certificates of education remained persistently small. In short, the improvements were genuine but limited; as Alan Skelley perceptively observes, neither the national system of education nor the provisions made by the army were particularly effective by the late 1890s, and 'the standard reached by the majority of those in the ranks was elementary at best'.[10]

A literary aptitude, therefore, was perhaps not as common in the late Victorian army as some have supposed, but it was far from rare. However, an aptitude to write and the inclination and/or opportunity to do so did not always coincide. When a campaign was underway some found all too little time to write or too little inclination to do so. An engineer serving with Colonel Henry Evelyn Wood's column in Zululand apologised to friends in Sheffield: 'I have very little time for writing. We are working all day, and have not time for anything, we are so pushed', while an officer writing from Suakin in March 1885 was equally apologetic: 'You must not expect many letters, as unless I get a spare day like this I have no time or place to write.'[11] This may have been special pleading, at least as regards the lengthy Anglo-Zulu War where, as Archibald Forbes (the veteran reporter of the *Daily News*) recalled, letter-writing appeared to be the chief relaxation of the men in their encampments.[12] When Sergeant Josh S. Hooper (2/Buffs) was appointed as his regiment's letter carrier, crossing the Tugela River with mail in the morning and later re-crossing with stamps from the post office on the Natal side, he found himself 'in great demand from Colonel to Private' as 'they all want to receive letters or send some off'.[13]

During the Egyptian campaign of 1882, Lieutenant Charles B. Balfour (1/Scots Guards) was extremely fortunate inasmuch as he possessed ample supplies of paper and had the use of a table that his servants built for him.[14] Many others shared the anxieties of Lieutenant H. W. Seton-Karr (1/Gordon Highlanders): 'I have not been able to write for some time as materials are short and there is nothing to write on.'[15] Yet officers and men struggled to overcome these difficulties: Seton-Karr kept an extensive diary of his experiences in Egypt, and many soldiers borrowed paper and pencils or paid exorbitant amounts for materials (6d a sheet for ruled paper in some instances). Some pleaded for paper to be sent from home, while others scribbled letters on the back of knapsacks, leaving the lines of cloth visible in one or two erasures, or liberated supplies from enemy quarters. A Bishopshire youth found paper in a sheikh's tent after the battle of Ginnis (30 December 1885) that was described 'as coarse in texture and crossed by dark and thick horizontal lines'.[16] Even so, writing as a sedentary exercise could be a daunting experience. Colonel H. S. Jones, in command of the Royal Marine battalion in Egypt, complained that 'the flies must be seen to be realised. They literally make everything black. I am writing under great difficulties, lying on the ground, and tormented beyond belief by these pests.'[17] In writing from Ambigol Wells during the Gordon relief expedition, a Cornish officer serving in the West Kent Regiment apologised for his 'penmanship, but the flies are doing their best to carry my nose and mouth by assault; they are simply awful'.[18]

Some soldiers had additional incentives to persevere with their literary activities. Quite apart from an understandable desire to reassure family and friends that the writer had survived the campaign or a particular battle, several staff and regimental officers wrote for leading newspapers and journals during the Asante War and in many, if not all, of the subsequent campaigns. By its sheer prevalence, military journalism set a context for letter-writing from the front and provided a further impulse, if only in the desire to get personal versions of events to an audience at home (or sometimes to one in the colonies). Major-General Sir Garnet (later Field Marshal Viscount) Wolseley had already written extensively in *Blackwood's Magazine* about his exploits in the Red River expedition of 1870. He regarded the Magazine's payments, in excess of '£25 a month', as 'a nice addition to one's half pay'.[19] Two of his staff officers in the Asante campaign, Captain (later General Sir)

Henry Brackenbury and Lieutenant (later Major-General Sir) John F. Maurice also wrote for newspapers and journals. Brackenbury, the author of a two-volume history of the campaign, readily accepted £300 from Blackwood for the work as he was a 'poor man' who needed recompense for 'the loss of my appointment which I gave up when I went with Sir Garnet, and the heavy expense of the campaign, and other matters . . .'.[20] Financial gain remained a powerful incentive: when Brackenbury wrote for the *Illustrated London News* in the summer of 1877, he was allowed 25 columns at four guineas per column of 1,100 words; when he wrote for the *Daily Telegraph*, he received £5 per column of 1,500 words.[21] Twenty years later the *Morning Post* paid Winston Churchill £10 per column for the 15 articles that he wrote from the Sudan – articles that spanned some 140 manuscript pages.[22]

In spite of the increasing presence of 'special' correspondents and war artists in these campaigns – some 30-odd in the Sudan (1896–98) and at least 70 accredited journalists with the British army in South Africa by early 1900[23] – the serving officer remained much in demand. When Charles Fripp, the *Graphic*'s correspondent, fell ill and had to leave Zululand, he persuaded Lieutenant Edward Hutton (60th Rifles) to make sketches for him and send them to his newspaper for publication.[24] Journalists sometimes missed key episodes in battles, such as the charge of the 21st Lancers at Omdurman (2 September 1898), and so required soldiers to provide the crucial insights. Just as Captains Edward Stanton and Sir Henry Rawlinson, as well as Corporal John Farquharson (1/Seaforth Highlanders), provided sketches from the earlier battle of Atbara (8 April 1898), Lieutenant John Brinton (2/Life Guards), who was attached to the 21st Lancers and was wounded in the charge, may have supplied details for René Bull's sketch of the charge. Brinton, according to his friend Churchill, served as a correspondent for Bull's paper *Black and White*.[25]

Neither the Horse Guards nor the War Office welcomed this profusion of writing for the press. In November 1872 Edward Cardwell, the secretary of state for war, ruefully quoted the adjutant general, General Sir Richard Airey, as stating: 'Three years ago no one was allowed to talk shop: now every one wants to write a Book.'[26] Similarly, in the festering relations between Wolseley and the Duke of Cambridge, who was the officer commanding-in-chief, the duke claimed that he dreaded Wolseley's 'connection with the Press'.[27] Even if the War Office came to appreciate that military correspondents were likely to be less critical than their civilian counterparts, some senior officers, including Sir Horatio Herbert Kitchener, remained profoundly suspicious of soldiers (such as Winston Churchill) who used their reporting to prepare for a political or another career once they left the service.[28]

Letter-writing from the front, which was mainly passed on by the *recipient* to metropolitan or local newspapers, with or without the agreement (or the name, rank and military affiliation) of the writer concerned, came into a different category. The army appreciated that soldiers wanted to receive correspondence from family and friends, and that a two-way flow of correspondence could sustain morale during an overseas campaign. Concessionary rates for postage persisted since the late eighteenth century (1*d* for soldiers' letters and 6*d* each for officers'), and elaborate arrangements were made with colonial postal services to support the flow of mail to and from the soldiers in Zululand and later the Transvaal. When the army was sent to Egypt in 1882 an Army Post Office Corps (APOC) was formed of volunteers from the 24th Middlesex (Post Office) Rifle Volunteers, and during the campaign six army post offices were opened (two in Alexandria, one in Port Said, one in Ismailia, and two accompanying the march of the 1st and 2nd Divisions), with another 15 staff manning five field post offices to service the needs of the 7,000 men sent from India to Egypt. There were similar arrangements in support of the Suakin expedition of 1885, and during the South African War, a vastly expanded APOC (396 all ranks by May 1901) sustained the massive war effort. If troops on the march could not obtain stamps, the letters were charged to the addressees at the rate which would have been prepaid. By the end of September 1902, APOC had delivered 68.9 million letters and newspapers and 1.4 million parcels to the troops.[29]

Nevertheless, the War Office remained anxious about information from a campaign finding its way into the public domain. On 7 March 1881 Ralph Thompson, the permanent under-secretary at the War Office, warned newspaper editors not to reveal information, particularly if sent by telegraph, that could assist the enemy. He evinced concern about revealing the dates when reinforcements were due to arrive, all movements of troops, the numbers of guns and garrisons, details of transport and where collected, and information about temporary bridges and posts.[30] Understandable as these anxieties were, what was published in Britain was probably of less importance than what was written in Africa and either published locally (a section of the Egyptian press remained hostile to the British policy in Egypt and the Sudan)[31] or went astray. The *Daily Chronicle*'s extensive reports of the battle of Abu Klea (17 January 1885) went missing for several weeks, and other reports and sketches from the same battle never reached their destination. Some 2,000 bags of mail were also seized, ransacked and burnt by the Boers when they captured the Roodewal Railway Station on 7 June 1900.[32] Beleaguered British forces went to extraordinary lengths to protect their correspondence: in the Transvaal, in 1881, dispatches were written on tissue paper, folded small and hard, and then placed in quills which native runners concealed in their hair. All too often, though, the runners discarded their messages lest the Boer patrols discover them. During the Sudan campaign of 1898 when the expedition moved beyond the railway terminus, correspondents sent their letters, sketches, and telegrams down river by native swimmers.[33]

From the Egyptian campaign onwards, the military authorities moved beyond exhortation and censored telegrams from the front. On the subsequent Nile expedition Bennet Burleigh, the correspondent of the *Daily Telegraph*, complained that the excised copy concerned both well-understood military details and the feelings of officers and men about the news of Khartoum's capture and the death of Gordon. 'For that black day', he wrote, 'very few of those who formed part of the Nile Valley expeditionary force will ever forgive the officials responsible.'[34] While information on the troops' morale might have been of interest to the Mahdi, its suppression served political purposes. 'Special' correspondents faced even more difficulties when the obsessively secretive Kitchener was in charge of the Sudan campaign of 1896–98. He treated most of the press with contempt, rarely gave interviews, limited their telegraphic allowance to 200 words a day, and required Major (later Major-General Sir) F. Reginald Wingate to act as censor. As Wingate, assisted by Brevet-Colonel (later Major-General) Leslie Rundle and Major (later Major-General) Hector Macdonald, had to read thousands of words daily, this meant delays and cuts, often without telling the writers.[35] Apart from irritating the 'special' correspondents, this censorship enhanced the value of uncensored communications from the front, namely the letters of officers and men.

Generally letters from soldiers (and sometimes from civilians accompanying the expeditionary forces) leant colour, corroboration at times, and often particular insights to the reports from 'special' correspondents. Their style varied enormously, ranging from highly personalised, graphic and blood-curdling descriptions to more detached, detailed and factual accounts. Even if the letters were perforce limited in perspective, often blinkered by regimental loyalty, and frequently inaccurate in assessing distance, casualties and numbers of the enemy, they had a lasting value. They described the hardships, dangers, fears and exhilaration of active service in a way rarely conveyed in the official dispatches. Sometimes they constituted the only first-hand record of particular engagements, that is, if the vast majority of officers were killed, as in the ambush at Bronkhorst Spruit (20 December 1880) or if journalists were not present, as in the siege of Wakkerstroom (1880–81).[36]

Their value was further enhanced by the ability of editors to identify the authors, exploit their local appeal, and highlight the element of human interest. Letters passed on by recipients to the metropolitan or, more commonly, local newspapers might or might not carry the author's name, rank, and regimental affiliation. Traditionally, serving officers who wrote directly for newspapers or journals had to be discreet. Sir John Adye feared that any revelation of his name 'would injure me professionally', while Brackenbury insisted: 'The authorship [of an article on the Royal Artillery] must be kept secret . . . They may *guess* as much as they like, but they must not be able to *assert* who is the writer.'[37] A fortnight later he urged that Blackwood should 'not send me a cheque for RA article, lest it should be traced, – unless it is without my name, payable to bearer, and not crossed'.[38] Similarly, during the South African War, when writing for the newspapers had become so prevalent that officers and men sent letters directly for publication in the 'Letters from the Front' columns of many newspapers, these letters were often anonymous,[39] unlike those passed on by friends and family to the press.

Provincial newspapers, especially those who could not afford to send their own 'specials' or employ officers to cover a campaign, reproduced reports from the central press agencies or from those in the major London newspapers. Like the London press, they also printed letters passed on from the family and friends of serving soldiers, especially as these were a cheap and distinctive form of news. When the *South Wales Daily News* received its first letter describing the battlefield at Isandlwana, it stated that 'We shall be glad to publish any letters from soldiers at the seat of war, which may be received by their friends in South Wales and Monmouthshire.'[40] It was inundated with letters thereafter. Provincial weeklies (and evening dailies) exploited the potential of this correspondence by emphasising the local provenance of the writer, or by highlighting the regional or county connections of certain regiments, or by publishing material that was new and different from the reports already published in the metropolitan press. For most of the South African War, the *Somerset County Gazette* ran a weekly column entitled 'Our Country's Share in the War' in which it published letters from the front and commented on the activities of the Somerset Light Infantry. If local newspapers could hardly claim that soldiers' letters were 'scoops', they welcomed the correspondence as a means of enhancing their coverage of contemporary campaigns and of sustaining their readers' interest in the fate of soldiers overseas. Their headlines capitalised on the local dimension, with phrases such as 'A Barnstaple Man at Ulundi', 'A Wiganer in South Africa', 'Letters from Bury Lads', 'A Pitlochry Soldier's Baptism of Fire', or 'Letter from a Leeds Man' – even in the last instance, where the correspondent was later described as 'formerly of Leeds, but now of central Africa'![41]

If editors knew the writer personally, they could vouch for his integrity, especially if he commented upon contentious issues (such as the killing of retreating Zulus after the battle of Ulundi).[42] They printed letters recounting the bravery of local soldiers, notably the death of Private Donald Cameron, 79th (Cameron Highlanders), who was reportedly the first man to enter the enemy trenches at Tel-el-Kebir (13 September 1882) and was immediately dubbed a 'Perthshire Hero'.[43] They also printed letters which informed family and friends about the survival and good health of local soldiers: after Tel-el-Kebir, a Royal Marine sent a letter to his parents in Stirling in which he mentioned meeting another nine men from his home town, (naming three rankers from the 42nd (1/Black Watch), another three from the 72nd (1/Seaforth Highlanders), two from the 74th (2/Highland Light Infantry) and one from the 79th (Queen's Own Cameron Highlanders).[44] Editors relished the opportunity of exposing errors in official reports that listed certain soldiers as missing or dead. The *Wigan Observer* printed a letter from Private John Stevens, a ranker in the ill-fated 1/24th that was annihilated at Isandlwana (22 January 1879), explaining that he had been posted elsewhere before the battle. While recounting his own survival, Private Stevens reported that his friend and fellow Wiganer Private Dyer was among the slain.[45] The *Dover Express* was even more caustic over a perfunctory letter sent by the War Office to a 60-year old widow, stating that her youngest son had perished in the same battle. When Private James Holland wrote to her subsequently, the paper asserted: 'One may imagine the joy of the mother on the receipt of the letter, but one may also imagine from this what the life of a British soldier is thought of at headquarters.'[46]

Human interest aside, editors and sometimes journalists (where the letters or interviews were incorporated as part of longer reports) commended the letters to their readers. The *South Wales Weekly and Daily Telegraph* praised the correspondence of private soldiers from Monmouthshire in Zululand and *en route* to Afghanistan as 'replete with interest and are creditable specimens of the progress of education in the army'.[47] The *Midland Counties Express* lauded an 'interesting letter' from Lieutenant-Colonel the Hon. Reginald Talbot (1/Life Guards) in Egypt as 'Its style contrasts very favourably with the high-flown descriptions of certain special correspondents.'[48] The *Natal Witness* reproduced a lengthy report from a journalist of the *Free State Express*, who had interviewed two soldiers – Sergeant Jeremiah Madden (King's Dragoon Guards) and Private Joseph Venables (58th Regiment) – captured by the Boers after the battle of Laing's Nek (28 January 1881). The journalist reported their stories verbatim, including accounts of how they had been well-treated by their captors, and claimed that they were 'told in good faith'.[49]

More substantively editors drew their readers' attention to letters that contained vivid or 'graphic' accounts, sometimes of fierce hand-to-hand fighting or the formidable effects of British fire-power or simply the immense and varied hardships of campaigning in African conditions.[50] In these respects, editors were not only selecting letters of particular interest but were also extracting passages that might appeal to their readership. The editorial role, therefore, went beyond Emery's claim that newspaper editors simply 'tidied up spelling, improved grammar and punctuation, and possibly corrected the proper names appearing in their raw copy. . . [even if] their substance and content would appear unchanged'.[51] Although many editors published letters in their entirety, especially when they were short but even on occasion when they spanned a couple of columns of newsprint, they also selected key passages for publication and excised others. Oliver Borthwick, son of the owner of the *Morning Post,* and its editor J. N. Dunn excised and amended the lengthy correspondence of Winston Churchill from the Sudan, which certainly contained superfluous material.[52]

Editors were not always scrupulous in their printing of soldiers' letters. They sometimes misspelt surnames (during the Anglo-Zulu War, the 2/24th had neither a Corporal Samuel Miles nor a Sergeant W. Maule, as the *Bristol Observer* and the *Brecon County Times* alleged, but it did have a Corporal Samuel Wiles and a Sergeant W. Morley).[53] They occasionally reported an involvement in battles where none had occurred; indeed, they had little opportunity to corroborate the veracity of authors who stated or implied that they had been present at famous battles, notably Isandlwana and the defence of Rorke's Drift.[54] The late Norman Holme, in his substantive study *The Noble 24th,* correctly observed that 'spurious claims' were made by several soldiers, 'possibly to increase their standing within the community, or with members of their family' and that these are now 'firmly embedded in family folklore'.[55] Soldiers sometimes retracted comments made in correspondence sent immediately after a battle. Lieutenant Henry Curling, RA, psychologically shaken after escaping from Isandlwana, later conceded: 'When I was ill, I wrote such a stupid letter: I think I must have been off my nut when I wrote it.'[56] Accordingly any usage of soldiers' letters as historical sources has to be corroborated, wherever possible.

Nevertheless, editors correctly described the content of most letters as intrinsically 'interesting' or of 'great interest' inasmuch as they provided timely commentary on matters that would catch the attention of their readers. If pride of place went to detailed descriptions of major battles and vivid accounts of hand-to-hand fighting,[57] there were plenty of reports on the hardships of campaigning, descriptions of native allies and adversaries, comments on other fighting units, newspaper reporting, and, in some letters, even critical remarks about commanding officers. Whether these letters were intended for publication (and some were),[58] they were often frank and forthright in their mode of expression and sometimes raised issues of controversy at home. In doing so, they contributed to debates about the terms and conditions of military service, the effectiveness of weapons, support services and military leadership, and the strategy and tactics employed in African campaigns.

The letters have a longer term value as eyewitness accounts of the British Army on active service, and as testimony to the values, motives, concerns and aspirations of Victorian soldiers. As sources, these letters have their limitations; only a small proportion remain in their original form, often deposited in national or regimental museums, and most survive as printed material in nineteenth-century newspapers. Although editors reproduced some letters fully and accurately, their intervention, as already described, devalued many of the originals. Where comparisons with original letters can be made, as in the correspondence of Churchill and a few others, the excisions appear to be mainly personal and family asides, lengthy narratives, some florid writing and occasionally assertions too sweeping to print.[59] So material has been lost but even the original letters did not always reveal the innermost thoughts of the authors. Like the sepoy letters of the Great War, selected for publication by David Omissi, the correspondence evolved through 'layers of filtration'.[60] Soldiers exercised a degree of self-censorship as they were writing to friends and family at home, and so tended to express themselves correctly (avoiding swearwords) and to dwell upon socially acceptable matters (rarely referring to any sexual liaisons). As with the sepoy letters, there was 'scribal intervention' if authors, like Private James Price (2/24th), required a literate 'chum' to write their letters for them.[61] Where scribes were involved, this could produce a somewhat stilted and conformist prose, reflecting either standard phrases suggested by the scribes or the inhibitions of the author as he expressed himself in a semi-public arena.[62] Yet the proportion of Victorian soldiers who relied upon scribes was probably far smaller than in the overwhelmingly illiterate sepoy army, and, unlike the sepoys, the Victorian soldiers could express opinions without fear of censorship at regimental or more senior levels.

As a consequence, their views remain unique as a commentary upon the course and conduct of particular campaigns. While general points can be drawn from this correspondence and are summarised in the Epilogue, the letters are used, first and foremost, within the context and chronology of specific campaigns. Each chapter of the book focuses upon a different campaign, using the letters to indicate how feelings evolved from the hopes and optimism at the outset, through periods of acclimatisation and adjustment to the rigours and pace of campaigning, to the sensations of excitement and relief (or sometimes shock and horror) at surviving major battles, and ultimately to moments of reflection as the hostilities drew to a close. They provide breadth of coverage from all arms and services,[63] comment on all the major events and battles, and address the principal issues of each campaign. They proffer important insights from the regimental level, from officers and other ranks, on the course and conduct of colonial warfare.

During the campaigns, soldiers wrote letters from troop-ships, camps, bivouacs, and occasionally from forts or barracks (as in Egypt), but generally in surroundings quite different from the confines of British barracks where noise, profanity and bustling camaraderie were commonplace. Soldiers found themselves frequently in open, thinly populated country, sometimes quite isolated from the nearest township, and periodically under threat from a hostile foe. During moments of repose they reflected upon the strains of campaigning and the realities of war, composing and writing their letters in privacy (or in confidence with a literate friend). Letter-writing flourished, argued Alexander Forbes, because life in camp enabled the best qualities of the soldier to emerge: they used 'less foul speech, . . . were more kindly to one another, and more Godly than in garrison'.[64] Although these observations were purely impressionistic, active service probably had some effect inasmuch as rankers (unlike the officers) had less access to drink (other than the occasional rum issued at night) and the risks of battle placed a premium on comradeship and fatalism about the future.

Yet the sheer quantity of the correspondence indicates that the Victorian army was possibly not as remote from the rest of society as is sometimes supposed. Although the army attracted the bulk of its recruits from casual labourers and the urban poor – young men seeking a refuge from hunger and unemployment or an escape from their domestic circumstances, especially from amatory mistakes – it had a broader appeal. It attracted those who were impressed by military bands and uniform as recruiting parties marched through their locality, or were ready on a whim or fancy to travel abroad, join friends in the ranks, and seek a life of adventure instead of a tedious menial occupation. Admittedly many of these recruits, unless they came from military families, probably enlisted without the blessing and support of their families. Few families had a positive image of the army as a career, that is, living in barracks and serving under military discipline, tales of drunken and licentious soldiery, lengthy periods of overseas service, and limited prospects on returning to civilian life. As Lord Wavell recollected, 'There was in the minds of the ordinary God-fearing citizen no such thing as a good soldier; to have a member who had gone for a soldier was for many families a crowning disgrace.'[65] This correspondence indicates, nonetheless, that many soldiers kept in touch with families and friends. They either reconciled with relatives after the trauma of enlistment or kept in touch with them or, in some cases, forged new relationships through marriage.[66] In letters from Africa they expressed concerns about the health and welfare of family, asked to be remembered to old friends, and passed on messages about comrades from the same locality.[67]

The authors may have taken the Queen's shilling, and left their domestic surroundings, but they knew that there would be interest at home in how they fulfilled their military commitments. In this respect the letters testify to the motivations of the authors, as well as to their morale, attitudes to death in battle, and their warrior ethos – values that distinguished them from many of their civilian readers (other than those with a service background). Campaigning in Africa, as the writers indicated, afforded an opportunity to serve 'Queen and country', to do their duty, and to earn honours for their regiment (or their company, frequently described as 'the pride of the regiment'), promotions in the field, and medals for themselves.[68] Highly motivated, these soldiers usually exuded confidence in their leaders (at least initially, and often throughout their campaigns); recorded few instances of ill-discipline on active service (other than in the protracted South African War); and appreciated the efforts expended on their logistic support, including the postal services and the supply of food and provisions (which rarely broke down). If these feelings were expressed in a somewhat formulaic language, the letters indicate that most soldiers began (and sometimes ended) these campaigns positively motivated, with a strong sense of comradeship and robust morale. Nor does it seem that they were simply writing in this vein to impress their readers. They could be frank, and the letters are particularly revealing when they describe the flagging of morale after serious defeats, or when units found themselves besieged and the toll of sick and wounded began to mount. As a Gordon Highlander reflected on the siege of Ladysmith: 'The authorities may keep much in the dark, but the fearful truths connected with this part of the misery of the siege remain all the same . . . I know what the pinch of hunger is.'[69] Many soldiers, nonetheless, remained fatalistic about the risks of battle and, whether actively religious or not, frequently claimed that survival was a matter of God's will. If they were to die, they expected to do so by fighting 'bravely' at their 'post' or by fighting and dying 'like a faithful English soldier'. Such sentiments car-

[13]

ried credibility when the authors had just observed the sacrifice of comrades at Isandlwana and the sight of corpses strewn over the battlefield.[70] They chimed with fervent desires to engage their foes, to gain revenge for fallen comrades and to close with the enemy. As soldiers they were imbued with a warrior ethos, a code by which they would assess adversaries and allies alike.

The attractions of active service, though, ranged beyond military matters. Campaigning in Africa fulfilled desires for adventure and foreign travel that were among the more positive attractions of military service. These young soldiers saw sights in an exotic continent that many of their families and friends would never do; they visited places in Egypt that they had only learned about from sermons and Biblical readings. Their writings, if not remotely on a par with those of contemporary missionaries and explorers,[71] sustained the growing popular interest in Africa generally, and in Egypt in particular. For Drummer George Paterson (1/Black, Watch), Cairo was as 'pretty a city as ever I saw. The streets are lined with tall, shady trees on each side, while the houses (in the principal part of the city) are magnificent. No wonder then Cairo is called the mother of the world.' Tel-el-Kebir, he informed his friend, was 'situated in the Land of Goshen, a land, I am sure, you have often read about as well as myself'.[72]

The letters reveal, too, that Egypt (and to a lesser extent the other campaigns in Africa) had more prosaic attractions. Egyptian service offered the prospect of earning khedival medals and a khedival allowance which, if added to the field allowance, almost doubled the daily pay of regimental officers.[73] Given the relatively low rates of pay endured by officers and other ranks, another facet of army life that hardly enhanced its image at home, active service had its compensations. This was especially true for the rank-and-file, some of whom earned gratuities for distinguished service in the field. Although soldiers regularly grumbled about the charges for sea-kit and the cost of goods supplied by local traders, they no longer suffered many of the stoppages that could reduce their pay to as little as a penny a day in Britain; and, if serving on 'dry' campaigns, soldiers had little incentive to spend money anyway. As Sergeant J. F. Bolshaw (17th Lancers) wrote from Zululand: 'If I ever do return again I shall be quite a rich man, as we cannot spend any money here. All our pay is saved.'[74]

The linkage between the attractions and opportunities of active service and the image or reputation of the army at home underpins much of the correspondence from the African campaigns. Soldiers, if despatched from Britain on expeditionary forces, anticipated that they would return home relatively quickly. They reckoned that the campaigns would be short and decisive affairs, and, in writing about their exploits, were either preparing for their homecoming or at least leaving a record in case they failed to do so. This context had less significance for soldiers drawn from garrisons in the Mediterranean, Natal and Cape Colony, or from the army of occupation when it was formed in Egypt, or from India, but the turnover of men in a short-service army always ensured that many were anticipating a return to Britain (not least the reservists who rejoined the colours for a specific conflict, like the 80,000 who served in the South African War). Facing the prospect (or possibility) of an early return to Britain, soldiers had every incentive to write about their own experiences, as well as the achievements of their unit, the mission as a whole, and any likely rewards. Lance Corporal J. A. Cosser wanted not merely to earn a medal but to 'come into the street and show off a medal'.[75] If positive accounts of service in Africa could enhance the status of individual soldiers in their own communities, they could also boost the reputation of the army generally.

Where matters went awry in African campaigns, soldiers were even more anxious about the manner in which they were reported at home. In extreme calamities their letters might provide crucial evidence, but normally they anticipated that official despatches and the reports of 'special' correspondents were likely to precede the receipt of correspondence from themselves. Explaining any reverses and apportioning blame seemed crucial requirements, and some soldiers were quick to explain events from their own point of view. In these circumstances the writing was often forthright, whether occasioned by apparent paranoia – as in the case of Lance-Corporal Cosser: 'They do not let the people of England know half of what goes on here'[76] – or worried by press censorship in later campaigns, or incensed by the perceived failings of command or of the government. Although many soldiers remained deferential, defending embattled commanders from outside critics, some broke ranks to criticise commanders, and others readily denounced their respective governments. Those who expressed political opinions may or may not have been representative of fellow soldiers, but they were often blunt in their assertions – as Sergeant Bolshaw wrote from Zululand: 'There is no mistake about the English Government's fault in sending so few men as they did.'[77]

In short, the letter-writing of Victorian soldiers remains valuable because of its range and scope. Despite the factual errors, limited perspectives, and editorial intrusion, these letters contain a wealth of detail, some unique insights and highly revealing commentary about the army on active service. If the chronology and events of specific campaigns establish a context for each group of letters, the relationship between soldiers and their local communities, the image of the army at home and the process of conveying news from Africa provide a broader framework for the correspondence as a whole. The letters may contain few literary flourishes, but they are written with vigour and clarity, are often conversational in character and are sometimes passionate in expression. They reflect all too well the feelings and tensions of soldiers operating in an alien environment, with their values, discipline and training periodically stretched to the limits.

Notes

1 E. M. Spiers, 'The British Army: Recent Writing Reviewed', *Journal of the Society for Army Historical Research (JSAHR)*, 63:256 (1985), 194–207; E. M. Spiers, *The Late Victorian Army 1868–1902* (Manchester: Manchester University Press, 1992), pp. 340–61.

2 H. Cecil and P. H. Liddle (eds), *Facing Armageddon: The First World War Experienced* (London: Leo Cooper, 1996), pp. xviii–xxiii; J. Keegan, 'Towards a Theory of Combat Motivation', and H. Strachan, 'The Soldiers' Experience', in P. Addison and A. Calder (eds), *Time to Kill: The Soldier's Experience of War in the West, 1939–1945* (London: Pimlico, 1997), pp. 7 and 371.

3 T. Pakenham, *The Boer War* (London: Weidenfeld & Nicolson, 1979), p. 376.

4 T. Jackson, *The Boer War* (London: Channel 4 Books, 1999), pp. 80–1.

5 F. Emery, *The Red Soldier: Letters from the Zulu War, 1879* (Johannesburg: Jonathan Ball, 1977), p. 262; and F. Emery, *Marching Over Africa: Letters from Victorian Soldiers* (London: Hodder & Stoughton, 1986), pp. 17–32.

6 J. Downham, *Red Roses on the Veldt: Lancashire Regiments in the Boer War, 1899–1902* (Lancaster: Carnegie Publishing, 2000); E. M. Spiers, 'Campaigning Under Kitchener', in E. M. Spiers (ed.), *Sudan: The Reconquest Reappraised* (London: Frank Cass, 1998), pp. 54–81; E. M. Spiers, 'The Scottish Soldier in the Boer War', in J. Gooch (ed.), *The Boer War: Direction, Experience and Image* (London: Frank Cass, 2000), pp. 152–65, 273–7.

7 Emery, *Marching Over Africa*, pp. 18–19.

8 G. Sutherland, *Policy-Making in Elementary Education, 1870–1895* (London: Oxford University Press, 1973), pp. 122–5, 162, 308, 328; J. Lee, *The Modernisation of Irish Society, 1848–1918* (Dublin: Gill & Macmillan, 1973), p. 31; A. R. Skelley, *The Victorian Army at Home: The Recruitment and Terms and Conditions of the British Regular, 1859–1899* (London: Croom Helm, 1977), p. 88.

9 Skelley, *Victorian Army at Home*, pp. 89–90.

10 *Ibid.*, pp. 90, 98.

11 'A Thrilling Incident in the Zulu War', *Sheffield Daily Telegraph*, 24 July 1879, p. 3; 'Letter from an Officer at Suakin', *Oswestry Advertizer*, 22 April 1885, p. 5.

12 'Archibald Forbes' Lecture at Folkestone', *Dover Telegraph*, 1 October 1879, pp. 5–6.

13 National Army Museum (NAM), Acc. No. 2001/03/73, Sergeant (Sgt) J. Hooper, diary, 9 April 1879.

14 S. G. P. Ward (ed.), 'The Scots Guards in Egypt, 1882: The Letters of Lieutenant C. B. Balfour', *JSAHR*, 51 (1973), 80–104.

15 Gordon Highlanders Museum (GHM), PB228, diary of Lt H. W. Seton-Karr, 28 August 1882.

16 'Letter from the Soudan', *Kinross-shire Advertiser*, 23 January 1886, p. 2; see also 'A Soldier's Letter from Korti', *Dover Express*, 30 January 1885, p. 5, Corporal (Cpl) F. W. Licence, letter, *Rugby Advertiser*, 12 March 1879, p. 4; 'A Sheffield Soldier in Zululand', *Sheffield Daily Telegraph*, 17 June 1879, p. 3; 'Another Letter', *Aberystwyth Observer*, 26 July 1879, p. 4.

17 Colonel (Col.) H. S. Jones, letter, *Bradford Observer*, 29 September 1882, p. 3.

18 Letter from 'An officer', *Western Morning News*, 13 January 1885, p. 8.

19 Royal Pavilion Libraries and Museums, Brighton and Hove City Council, Wolseley Collection, 163/4/13/i, G. Wolseley to R. Wolseley, 'December 1870 or January 1871'; National Library of Scotland (NLS), Blackwood MSS, MS 4283, f. 200, G. Wolseley to Blackwood, 7 January 1871.

20 NLS, Blackwood MSS, MS 4315, f. 98, H. Brackenbury to Blackwood, 27 November 1874; see also R. Wilkinson-Latham, *From Our Special Correspondent: Victorian War Correspondents and Their Campaigns* (London: Hodder & Stoughton, 1979), p. 120.

21 NLS, Blackwood MSS, MS 4356, ff. 64–5, Brackenbury to Blackwood, 2 June 1877.

22 K. Wilson, 'Young Winston's Addisonian Conceit: A Note on "The War on the Nile" Letters', Appendix 1 in Spiers (ed.), *Sudan*, pp. 223–8.

23 H. Cecil, 'British Correspondents and the Sudan Campaign of 1896–98', in Spiers (ed.), *Sudan*, pp. 102–27; S. Badsey, 'The Boer War as a Media War', in P. Dennis and J. Grey (eds), *The Boer War: Army, Nation and Empire. The 1999 Chief of Army/Australian War Memorial Military History Conference* (Canberra: Army History Unit, 2000), pp. 70–83.

24 'Some Recollections of the Zulu War, 1879: Extracted from the Unpublished Reminiscences of the late Lieut.-General Sir Edward Hutton, KCB, KCMG', *The Army Quarterly*, 16 (1928), 65–80.

25 P. Harrington, 'Images and Perceptions: Visualising the Sudan Campaign', in Spiers (ed.), *Sudan*, pp. 82–101.

26 The National Archives, Public Record Office (PRO), Cardwell MSS, 30/48/3/21, f. 19, E. Cardwell to Lord Northbrook, 6 November 1872.

27 Royal Archives, VIC/AddE/1/9819, Cambridge MSS, Duke of Cambridge to Queen Victoria, 6 November 1881.

28 J. Pollock, *Kitchener: The Road to Omdurman* (London: Constable, 1998), p. 126; Wilkinson-Latham, *From Our Special Correspondent*, p. 202.

29 P. B. Boyden, *Tommy Atkins' Letters: The History of the British Army Postal Service from 1795* (London: National Army Museum, 1990), pp. 5, 18–25; see also 'The Post Office Corps', *Scotsman*, 25 October 1882, p. 7 and 'The Postage of Letters to Suakim', *Yorkshire Post*, 19 March 1885, p. 7.

30 'The War Office and the Newspapers', *Yorkshire Post*, 8 March 1881, p. 4.

31 Cecil, 'British Correspondents and the Sudan Campaign', p. 108.

32 'The Battle of Abu Klea', *Daily Chronicle*, 25 February 1885, p. 5; Wilkinson-Latham, *From Our Special Correspondent*, p. 190; Boyden, *Tommy Atkins' Letters*, pp. 25–6.

33 'The Boers' Treachery', *Sheffield Daily Telegraph*, 29 March 1881, p. 2; Harrington, 'Images and Perceptions', p. 91.

34 'Press Censorship at Korti', *Western Morning News*, 27 March 1885, p. 8; Wilkinson-Latham, *From Our Special Correspondent*, p. 190.

35 Wilkinson-Latham, *From Our Special Correspondent*, p. 230; Cecil, 'British Correspondents and the Sudan Campaign', pp. 108–12.

36 'A True Statement of the Bronker's Spruit Massacre', *Times of Natal*, 28 February 1881, p. 6; 'The Boers' Treachery', p. 2.

37 NLS, Blackwood MSS, MS 4566, f. 22, Sir J. Adye to Blackwood, 10 February 1891 and MS 4356, f. 47, Brackenbury to Blackwood, 9 April 1877.

38 NLS, Blackwood MSS, MS 4566, f. 58, Brackenbury to Blackwood, 25 April 1877.

39 For example, 'How the Boers Reform. An Officer's Outburst'; 'The Kilt Condemned'; 'The Gordon Volunteers at the Front', *Aberdeen Journal*, 20 December 1900, p. 5; 13 January 1900, p. 6; 1 August 1900, p. 6.

40 'Letter from T. Williams, of the 2–24th Regt', *South Wales Daily News*, 8 March 1879, p. 3.

41 'A Barnstaple Man at Ulundi', *North Devon Herald*, 18 September 1879, p. 5; 'Letter from a Wiganer in South Africa', *Wigan Observer and District Advertiser*, 28 March 1879, p. 5; 'Letters from Bury Lads', *Bury Times*, 10 September 1898, p. 6; 'A Pitlochry Soldier's Baptism of Fire', *Perthshire Constitutional & Journal*, 8 January 1900, p. 3; 'Letter from a Leeds Man', *Yorkshire Post*, 9 September 1879, p. 8.

42 'A Barnstaple Man at Ulundi', p. 5.
43 'A Perthshire Hero at Tel-el-Kebir', *Kinross-shire Advertiser*, 7 October 1882, p. 3.
44 'Letter from a Son of the Rock', *Stirling Observer*, 28 September 1882, p. 4.
45 'Letter from a Wiganer in South Africa', p. 5.
46 'Letters from the Front', *Dover Express*, 28 March 1879, p. 3.
47 'Letters from Monmouthshire Men in the Camps', *South Wales Weekly and Daily Telegram*, 7 March 1879, p. 4.
48 'Letter from a Local Officer of the Guards in Egypt', *Midland Counties Express*, 30 September 1882, p. 7.
49 'Interesting Letter from Lange's [*sic*] Nek', *Natal Witness*, 31 March 1881, p. 3.
50 'The Charge of the "Black Watch" at Tel-el-Kebir', *Irish Times*, 9 October 1882, p. 5; 'The Black Watch at Tamanieb', *Weekly News* (Dundee), 12 April 1884, p. 6; 'A Dingwall Boy's Account', *Ross-shire Journal*, 6 May 1898, p. 7.
51 Emery, *Marching Over Africa*, p. 19.
52 Wilson, 'Young Winston's Addisonian Conceit', pp. 224–8.
53 As soldiers probably did not include their surnames in letters to friends or family, this information may have been passed on to the newspapers concerned by word of mouth, so increasing the possibility of error. See 'A Corporal's Letter', *Bristol Observer*, 19 April 1879, p. 5, and 'The Battles of Isandula & Rorke's Drift', *Brecon County Times*, 29 March 1879, p. 5.
54 Corporal Wiles, reportedly 'one of the few who survived the recent battle at Isandula', does not appear on any of the lists of survivors, and is notably absent from those men who were interviewed afterwards. Compare 'A Corporal's Letter' with F. W. D. Jackson, *Isandhlwana 1879: The Sources Re-Examined* (The Baracks, Brecon: South Wales Borderers and Monmouthshire Regimental Museum, 1999), Appendix B: 'European Survivors of Isandhlwana', pp. 58–9.
55 N. Holme, *The Noble 24th: Biographical Records of the 24th Regiment in the Zulu War and the South African Campaigns 1877–1879* (London: Savannah, 1999), p. 4.
56 Lieutenant H. Curling to Willy, 4 April 1879, reproduced in *The Curling Letters of the Zulu War: 'There Was Awful Slaughter'*, ed. A. Greaves and B. Best (Barnsley: Pen & Sword Books, 2001), p. 118.
57 'A Letter from Private Parry, A Merthyr Man', *South Wales Daily Telegram*, 16 April 1879, p. 3; 'The Attack on Tel-el-Kebir', *Cornish Times*, 14 October 1882, p. 3; 'The Black Watch at Tamai', *Strathearn Herald*, 12 April 1884, p. 2; 'The Charge of the 21st Lancers: A Newark Soldier's Experiences', *Sheffield Daily Telegraph*, 5 October 1898, p. 5.
58 'Boers' Treachery', p. 2.
59 Wilson, 'Young Winston's Addisonian Conceit', pp. 224–7; see comments on the editing of Lt Scott-Stevenson's account of the battle of Tamai in chapter 5.
60 D. Omissi, *Indian Voices of the Great War: Soldiers' Letters, 1914–18* (London: Macmillan, 1999), pp. 4–9.
61 'Letter from a Cwmyoy Man', *Abergavenny Chronicle*, 26 April 1879, p. 3.
62 Omissi, *Indian Voices*, pp. 5, 9.
63 Unlike the sepoy letters from 1916 onwards, which were written mainly by cavalrymen who saw much less action and suffered fewer casualties: Omissi, *Indian Voices*, p. 11.
64 'Mr. Archibald Forbes' Lecture at Folkestone', p. 6.
65 Field Marshal Sir A. Wavell, *Soldiers and Soldiering* (London: Jonathan Cape, 1953), p. 125; see also Spiers, *Late Victorian Army*, pp. 129–33.
66 Only a small proportion – about 6 per cent – of rankers were allowed to marry 'on the strength', but the proportions were higher in the cavalry regiments (which had a higher ratio of sergeants to enlisted men) and in the Guards regiments which did not move about so much. The wives and families of soldiers who married 'off the strength' were not entitled to any welfare provisions. M. Trustram, *Women of the Regiment: Marriage and the Victorian Army* (Cambridge: Cambridge University Press, 1984), pp. 30–2.
67 'Letter from Another Abergavenny Man', *Abergavenny Chronicle*, 26 April 1879, p.

3; 'The Zulu War', *Sheffield Daily Telegraph*, 20 March 1879, p. 3; and 'The Battle of Tel-el-Kebir, *Strathearn Herald*, 21 October 1882, p. 2.

68 'Letters of Monmouthshire Men in the Camps', *South Wales Weekly and Daily Telegram*, 7 March 1879, p. 4; 'Zulu War', p. 3; 'Letter from Another Crieff Soldier', *Strathearn Herald*, 21 October 1882, p. 2.

69 'Letters from Ladysmith', *Strathearn Herald*, 21 April 1900, p. 3.

70 'Letters from Monmouthshire Men in the Camps', p. 4; 'Letter from a Cwmyoy Man', p. 3.

71 T. Pakenham, *The Scramble for Africa* (London: Weidenfeld & Nicolson, 1991), pp. xvi–xvii, 140.

72 'The Late Lieutenant G. Stirling', *Strathearn Herald*, 21 October 1882, p. 2.

73 It increased a captain's daily pay from 6s 6d to 12s (or from 32.5p to 60p): NAM, Acc. No. 8305/55, Cameron MSS, Capt. N. Cameron to Sir W. Cameron, 26 May 1898.

74 *Northampton Mercury*, 26 July 1879, p. 3; see also Skelley, *The Victorian Army at Home*, pp. 182–4.

75 'Sheffield Soldiers in Zululand', *Sheffield Daily Telegraph*, 17 May 1879, p. 3.

76 *Ibid.*

77 *Northampton Mercury*, 26 July 1879, p. 3.

CHAPTER ONE

Fighting the Asante

'Wolseley's march to Kumasi' has been described as 'one of the military dramas of the Victorian age'.[1] Britain exercised an informal protectorate over parts of the Gold Coast from the early 1830s, the fever-ridden region traditionally known as 'a white man's grave'. As two previous British expeditions in 1823 and 1863–64 had suffered serious losses, the Colonial Office resolved not to send another British force to the Gold Coast, even after the Asante (pronounced *Ashanti*) invaded the protectorate in 1873. Although a composite force headed by a detachment of Marines under Colonel Festing thwarted the invasion at Elmina (13 June 1873), panic gripped the authorities at Cape Coast Castle.[2] On 13 August the British Government appointed Sir Garnet Wolseley as administrator and commander-in-chief on the Gold Coast and despatched him, with twenty-seven special-service officers, to work with the local Fante tribesmen to resist the Asante. Following his arrival in September, Wolseley promptly requested British reinforcements, planned a short campaign over the less hazardous months of December, January and February, and then decisively defeated the Asante in battle before sacking their capital, Kumase (6 February 1874). He earned enormous plaudits for this campaign, which cost under £800,000 and involved minimal casualties.[3] Yet the campaign aroused its share of controversy, both at the time and subsequently. While special correspondents, such as Henry M. Stanley and Winwoode Reade, berated the failure of his transport arrangements and the risks involved in a prompt evacuation of Kumase,[4] some modern commentators argue that Wolseley discounted the military worth of the Fante precipitately.[5] Few deny that Wolseley and his forces conducted a remarkable campaign, overcoming formidable natural obstacles while incurring relatively few casualties, and several commentators, taking their cue from Cardwell, regard this campaign as a vindication of his reforms.[6] In reviewing the experiences of some thirty-five officers and men from all the British infantry units and support arms, it will be possible to gauge whether they had any insights on these and other aspects of the campaign.

Wolseley's scepticism about the resolve, reliability and martial prowess of the coastal tribes, particularly if required to fight in the bush, was widely shared by British officers and men. Prior to Wolseley's arrival in September, Colonel Festing (Royal Marine Artillery) had already engaged the Asante near the town of Elmina. With only 300 men, including light infantry, artillery, sailors and some soldiers from the 2nd West India Regiment, he had first suppressed local disaffection in the town and then repulsed an attack by some 3,000 Asantes. Having routed the Asante in about two hours, killing King Kofi Karikari's nephew and four of his six chiefs, Festing lacked the men to mount a counter-offensive. As he said after the battle, 'get me 5,000 native allies at Abbaye, I will undertake to engage the enemy. The native allies were promised me, but they were never forthcoming.'[7] Like Festing, Wolseley quickly concluded that the Fante tribes could not protect themselves: they had become preoccupied with trading, 'grown less warlike and more peaceful than formerly', and their kings could not raise the men required.[8] Hausas were employed in the punitive raids upon the disaffected villages of Essaman, Amquana and Ampenee, but in the raid on Essaman (14 October 1873) they were criticised for a lack of discipline and reckless firing. 'They are plucky fellows', wrote Lieutenant Edward Woodgate, 'probably the best native Auxiliaries we shall get, and it is a pity there are so few of them, their great fault seems to be shyness of bush fighting, and in the difficulty of restraining them in the open when their blood is up.'[9]

Even when the Asantes, suffering losses from smallpox and dysentery, began their retreat to the River Pra, native forces under British command struggled to harass them effectively. Whenever the Fantes gained sight of the enemy or heard their war-drums or even a rumour of their presence, they either broke ranks and ran or cowered at the rear. Officers lamented the fate of 'poor' Lieutenant Eardley Wilmot, RA, who was left at the head of his column when the vast majority of native levies deserted during an action north of Dunkwa (3 November 1873). Severely wounded, he kept fighting with a small group of soldiers from the 2nd West India Regiment until shot through the heart.[10] At least his courageous resistance prevented a rout, but one briefly occurred at Fesu (27 November 1873) when an advance party of Hausas, followed by the company of Kossus, broke under Asante fire and stampeded to the rear for 200 yards, carrying a naval officer 'along in the crowd' unable to feel his feet 'for a long way'. 'That affair', he reckoned, 'will make the Ashantees [sic] very plucky . . . they are no

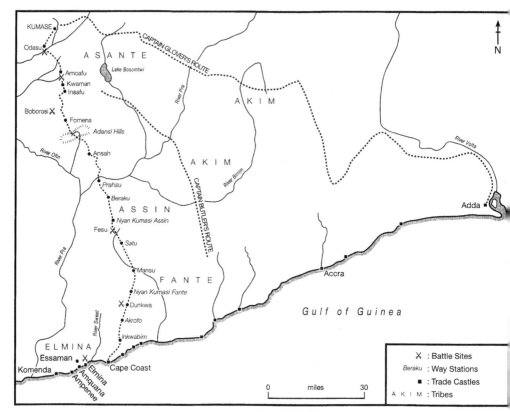

1 Asante War, 1873–74

mean enemies in the bush. Had we had English troops it would have been different; we could have followed them into the bush, and bayoneted them, as it is not so thick here.'[11] These preliminary engagements, if not tactically decisive, gave an early insight into the fighting methods of the Asante. The latter's penchant for decapitating captured enemies prompted one 'bluejacket' from HMS *Decoy* to describe them as 'barbarous wretches', adding: 'but we will give them a lesson they will not forget in a hurry. They are afraid of a white man; one is equal to four of these black fellows.'[12]

Although Wolseley continued to employ native auxiliaries (two native regiments under Major Baker Russell and Colonel H. E. Wood, VC, would accompany his expedition and several others were supposed to be raised by Captains Dalrymple, Butler and Glover in diversionary columns – only one of which materialised), he requested the dispatch of British soldiers. In doing so, he accepted Cardwell's instructions that 'every preparation should be made in advance', that these forces should not be disembarked until the decisive moment occurred, and that they should operate only in the most favourable climatic conditions, namely the four months from December to March.[13] Originally Wolseley hoped to land these forces by mid-December, but delays created by the dilatory retreat of the Asantes, and the problems of securing and retaining the services of native labourers, delayed his plans. As the troop-ships arrived in mid-December, he sent the *Himalaya* carrying the 2nd Battalion, Rifle Brigade, the *Tamar* with the 23rd Fusiliers (Royal Welch Fusiliers) and the *Sarmatian* with the 42nd Highlanders (The Black Watch) back to sea until the end of the year.[14]

Soldiers were bitterly frustrated by the delay in disembarkation irrespective of whether they had endured a miserable journey, like Rifleman George H. Gilham, confined to his bunk for seven days, or had experienced, as Private Robert Ferguson (Black Watch) recalled, 'a grand voyage to the Gold Coast'. Many officers and non-commissioned officers of the Black Watch were so eager to land that they offered to undertake any kind of duties ashore, but in each case they were refused.[15] As in all expeditionary campaigns, the journeys from home had done much more than transport men and equipment. In the case of the Black Watch, soldiers fondly recalled the enthusiastic scenes when the *Sarmatian* left Portsmouth, with Prince Arthur gracing the occasion, and another salute from the Channel Squadron off Gibraltar. They forged cordial relations with the 135 volunteers from the 79th (Cameron) Highlanders, who had brought the battalion up to strength. The Camerons, who served as a distinct company, were regarded as a 'very nice body of men . . . anxious to fall into our way of doing things'. During the voyage all soldiers were vaccinated, and they were able to prepare their equipment, attend lectures on the Gold Coast and try out their 'drab' Gold Coast clothing. The men were 'rather proud' that they were allowed to wear 'a small red buckle fixed on their helmet' in place of the regiment's traditional red hackle. Although discipline had to be enforced at times (Private E. Black received twenty-five lashes for threatening to throw a sergeant overboard[16]),the men were in good heart when they arrived off Cape Coast, and so spending another fortnight aboard ship was remembered by Ferguson as 'the weariest and dullest days of it'.[17]

Meanwhile the Royal Engineers pressed on with their labours, constructing a path along the 74 miles from Cape Coast to Prahsu, with eight camp sites, two hospitals and 237 bridges. Major Robert Home, RE, who was in charge of the task, recalled that it had to be undertaken despite recurrent tropical thunderstorms. Every day he was wet to the skin and he was eventually hospitalised with 'a frightful attack of fever'.[18] On 12 December another officer evaluated these efforts:

The engineers have pioneered the road to the Prah, hacking and hewing it through forests of teak and mahogany and across streams and swamps and over hills and valleys. Their advance will get to the Prah the day after to-morrow . . . The permanent stations for the European troops – nine [sic] in number – are nearly completed, with huts for from 400 to 2,000 men each, with officers' quarters, hospitals, stores, magazines, and defence works. The work has never stopped, and gang after gang of labourers have been worked off their legs. This is a most exhausting service – everything to be done on foot, and I have been moving sometimes twenty to thirty miles in a day, feeling utterly done up at night, not to mention two attacks of fever, during one of which I was delirious for two days.[19]

The Naval Brigade, marching ahead of the main body of infantry, pro-vided invaluable assistance. They helped to build a bridge across the Pra in 3 days and spent 17 days, working 4 hours per day, felling trees, clearing a camp site and building huts. A 'bluejacket' recalled that 'it was blazing hot work . . . felling trees in that latitude'.[20]

When allowed to disembark, British units did so in order and moved immediately into the interior. The Naval Brigade, requiring the least transport, had landed on 27 December, the Rifle Brigade and more engi-neers on New Year's Day, the Black Watch on the 3 and 4 January, and the 23rd Fusiliers on the following day. Soldiers, armed with their short Snider rifles and sword–bayonets, marched in the early mornings, cov-ering some 7–10 miles per day, before resting during the heat of the day and the close, sultry evenings. They found the smell appalling: Lieu-tenant Ernest N. Rolfe, RN, greatly appreciated a bottle of eau de Cologne, 'which, with a bit of camphor in the corner of my handker-chief, I find most useful, as the stench along the road of the newly turned soil and dead Ashantees [sic] beats Paris'. [21] Nevertheless, many marvelled at their first sight of a tropical rain forest. As an officer wrote:

The vegetation is more glorious than anything I have ever seen. As underwood there are groves of plantains with huge green leaves and flow-ers of the most brilliant scarlet, masses of convolvuli of all colours, and palm trees with their trunks covered with exquisite ferns. Shooting up here and there are bamboo plants looking like bunches of huge green ostrich feathers. Above all this tower the gigantic trees, their stems bare for the first 100 or 150 feet, then leaves spreading out above like clouds of bright emerald green.[22]

Sapper Arthur Richards wondered how this 'beautiful green bush' with its 'magnificently coloured birds and butterflies' and an abundance of cocoa nuts, oranges, figs and other fruits could be so unhealthy.[23]

Soldiers and sailors were mightily impressed by the organisation on their behalf, particularly the regular supplies of food (1lb of preserved beef, 1lb of biscuit, tea, sugar and rice each day, with grog at night) and medical support (both preventive measures, such as the periodic issue of quinine and lime juice and the rapid removal of fever-ridden cases[24]). Yet the entire support network depended upon native bearers, whose incapacity continued to bedevil the operation. Lieutenant H. Jekyll, RE, who was in charge of erecting the telegraph, struggled to find labourers despite being 'authorised to spend unlimited money'. 'One difficulty', he wrote, 'is the stupidity and laziness of the natives, who require a great amount of supervision. I thought of giving them piece work, but that won't do, for the nigger doesn't care for money, he only cares for idleness.'[25] Sergeant-Major Benjamin Bennett (23rd Fusiliers) regarded the Fantes as 'the most debased wretches I have ever seen',[26] while another officer feared for the supply system itself 'as the Fantees, who are our carriers, are frightened to death of the Ashantees [sic]', and so had to be placed under 'a very strong guard'.[27] Although the Fante women were much admired for their stoicism, carrying 60lb loads on their heads in addition to children on their hips,[28] the laziness of their menfolk and the recurrent desertions along the line of march gave rise to profound concerns. As the transport system became increasingly problematical, Wolseley had to seek carriers from the 2nd West India Regiment and required most of the Fusilier Battalion and the Royal Artillery still at Cape Coast to re-embark on their ship. Captain A. J. Rait would have to rely on the 60 Hausa gunners that he had trained so well, and only Lieutenant-Colonel the Hon. Savage Mostyn, his adjutant, Lieutenant W. Phibbs, 7 officers and 100 volunteers from the 23rd were retained initially, although another 200 were brought forward later to replace the sick. At the central depot of Mansu 135 Black Watch under Captain Moore volunteered to carry stores, mainly 50lb boxes on their heads and shoulders, over the next 11 miles to Suta.[29]

What really alarmed the soldiers and sailors, however, was the possibility of a premature peace. At Prahsu the sailors were perturbed when 'eleven niggers came down with a message from King Coffee [sic], begging us to stop and palaver a bit'.[30] Once Wolseley had dismissed these emissaries, insisting that he would sign a peace treaty only in Kumase and that King Kofi must release all his prisoners and pay an indemnity of 50,000 ounces of gold, he played a ruse on them by sending the Naval Brigade ahead, so that they would pass the sailors supposedly marching en route north of the Pra. 'Bluejacket' recalled:

> We had a little Gatling gun with us, which, just as the ambassadors hove in sight, we managed to fire off at nothing particular. Either the noise of the gun or the sight of us was too much for one of the ambassadors, for that same night he shot himself dead in his tent, and left the others to carry to the King the news that the Naval Brigade was coming along.[31]

As the news of the meeting filtered back, many soldiers were delighted. Sapper Richards, manning his telegraph office at Dunkwa, relished the prospect of the Union Jack flying 'on the highest house or hovel that Coomassie holds'.[32] When the Black Watch reached Prahsu on 21 January 1874, one of its non-commissioned officers recorded in his diary:

> Met a good number of sick coming down country – mostly seamen and riflemen; many of them look very bad. Our men hanging out very well, but about 40 complaining. They are afraid of being left behind, and say they are better than they really are.[33]

The main body of Wolseley's expedition began its crossing of the Pra on 20 January and proceeded towards the town of Fomena, north of the Adansi Hills, where it planned to create a forward supply depot. Lord Gifford's Assin scouts, followed by the engineers, their labourers and Major Baker Russell's Hausa auxiliaries, had crossed the Pra some fifteen days earlier to cut a path through the undergrowth and establish some camping sites. Captain J. Nicol, one of Russell's officers, recalled: 'our duties are various – road-making, bush clearing, throwing up earthworks, carrying provisions and ammunition, surveying, fighting, making camp, etc'. He found clearing villages particularly time-consuming: in one case, 'I had 150 men with me, and it took us three hours to clean out enough to house the Naval Brigade. One house was a Fetish house; the state of affairs there was remarkably nasty.'[34] Although the following soldiers had to struggle along a rudimentary path, make their own huts and cope with further desertions from their Fante bearers, they found consolations on the line of march. A commissariat officer described the climate as 'much less enervating than on the southern side of the Prah';[35] indeed Captain Nicol found a cooling breeze when he reached the summit of the Adansi Hills, some 1,500 feet above sea level, although there was little to see but a mist-lined canopy of the tropical rain forest.[36] Sergeant Charles Lewis (Rifle Brigade) described the wood as 'not so thick as on the other side of the Prah, but, of course, it is nothing but wood everywhere'. Lewis, like others, was impressed by the signs of civilisation in Asante territory, especially by comparison with the villages south of the Pra: 'the houses', he noted, 'are built in a kind of square, with a court in the centre and open – I mean with no covering – the walls are built and thatched, having the front or side facing the court open . . . the floors are about 3ft. from the ground, and made of red clay'.[37] On the other hand, meeting the prisoners released by the *Asantehene* (King Kofi), including a German missionary, his wife and child, gave a powerful insight into Asante practices. They had been held prisoner for five years, and 'the poor woman', wrote Nicol, 'had been subject to some horrible indignities', while the missionary, as the commissariat officer learned, 'had got little to eat but snails, and was in constant danger of losing his head'. They were delighted to be free.[38]

More Asante envoys, suing for peace, accompanied the released prisoners; they informed Wolseley that the king would agree to all his terms if only he would halt his advance. Entering Kumase, though, had become a *sine qua non* for Wolseley. His reply that he was determined to do so, whether as friend or foe, delighted Captain Nicol, as 'we expect all to be settled in a fortnight'.[39] Sergeant Lewis yearned to engage the enemy and 'soon let King Coffee know what we came here for', and there was apparently 'great glee' among the Black Watch as it became clear that the king was going 'to dispute our entry into Coomassie'.[40] Once Wolseley had accumulated his reserve supplies, he resumed his advance towards Kumase, but had to remove initially a threat to his flank from at least 1,000 Asantes moving towards the village of Boborasi. Colonel John McLeod (Black Watch) led a mixed European and native force against the village, and a sailor from the *Active* described the ensuing engagement. 'As we took them by surprise, and were not aware of their position being so close', he recalled, 'it was a regular set out for a few minutes. Then we went to work in earnest, and after about an hour, we cleared the village'. On the return march the Asantes counter-attacked:

> their dreadful war yells and drums sounded right and left of us, and they made a desperate attack on our rear. But they reckoned rather too soon; and as the Active's company was rear guard, we gave them a warm reception, and their war cry turned to wailing, for they retired cut to pieces. . . . That was the first battle since we landed; and the Naval Brigade consequently had the first rub, as we were first into the village and last out of it.[41]

For the loss of only three men (including Captain Nicol), Mcleod's detachment had routed at least twice its number of Asantes. They had taken fourteen prisoners and captured muskets, powder and the state umbrella of General Asamoa Kwanta. More importantly they had gained valuable experience in bush-fighting and a morale-boosting victory. 'Bluejacket' recollected:

> The Ashantees [sic] stuck to their ground like bricks . . . before we moved them. I don't know in what order we were formed. I only know there was a man of ours on my left and another on my right, and I had orders to keep in line with them, and so I did. As for the Ashantees, you precious seldom got a sight of them, for you couldn't make anything out ahead of you more than a dozen feet. Our orders from the General were to 'fire low – fire slow, and charge home'.[42]

Similar tactics would be employed by the main body of the expedition when it moved on to the village of Insafu (30 January). Acting on information that the enemy were deployed in their thousands nearby (actually in a horseshoe formation along a strong defensive position – a ridge near the village of Amoafo – overlooking a mud-filled swampy ravine into which the only path descended and then ascended on the slope beyond), Wolseley decided on a frontal assault with some 2,200 soldiers while guarding against the enemy's tactic of attacking the flanks and of trying to surround the opposing army. 'The plan of operations', wrote Rolfe,

> was to advance in a hollow square, the 42d Highlanders forming the front face extending 300 yards on either side of the road, where Rait's guns were to move, and the rear face being composed of the Rifles, while the left was composed of 100 sailors and Russell's Regiment, and the right face of 100 sailors and Wood's Regiment . . . In the centre the carriers for hammocks and ammunition were to move. The plan looked excellent on paper, but no one thought it would come off as wished in practice. The Chief of Staff [Colonel John McNeill] added a final order, somewhat in German style – 'If you can't carry out your orders, do the best you can.'[43]

At about 7.40 a.m. on 31 January, the Black Watch under the command of Brigadier Sir Archibald Alison, a one-armed veteran of the Crimea, engaged the enemy. With their pipers playing, company after company descended into the ravine, meeting with a ferocious fire from the Asantes. Private Ferguson recalls:

> This was a trying way for us, young soldiers, to get under fire. The Ashantees [sic] were swarming in advance on our flanks in thousands, and I almost felt my time was up, and that I was to be potted like a rabbit in cover . . . We were fighting in sections, every man in his place, and doing his best. Seldom we got a right shot at a black fellow, they kept so well under cover, but they did keep popping at us! And so close it was too! They were mostly armed with the old flintlocks, and loaded with pieces of ragged lead, rusty iron and stones. Had they been better armed, more of us would have fallen . . . In such circumstances, we kept on firing and advancing as best we could . . . most of our men were getting wounded, but only a few were going to the rear . . . When we had a moment to speak and look at each other we would glance along the files to see who were hit and if any were down. Such is the way we had to fight in the bush; it was all against us, and if a couple of big guns had not been brought to our assistance I doubt we would have fared worse.[44]

Ferguson's account of the battle is only one of several that have survived, and, like all such narratives, is limited in perspective. None of the individual recollections compare with the tactical understanding of Brackenbury's authoritative work, based on all the reports sent to him as Wolseley's assistant military secretary during the twelve-hour engagement.[45] Yet neither Brackenbury nor the unit commanders, nor the special correspondents, who also wrote accounts of the battle, had any overview of how the battle was fought. As Rolfe recalled, all information was 'secondhand, for nobody could see anyone at 50 yards' distance from him'.[46] So the insights of front-line soldiers and sailors have some enduring value, not least when they all pay tribute to the resolute courage and fighting attributes of the Asantes. It took over four hours before the Highlanders broke through the enemy's lines to enter their base at Amoafo. The Asantes had defended all the intervening villages and thereafter redoubled their flank attacks and later mounted several assaults on the baggage train (prompting the Fantes to flee and requiring a redeployment of Riflemen to secure the baggage and the depot at Kwaman). 'The Ashantis', wrote one naval officer, 'fought well, and had to suffer severely before they gave in'; and among the wounded afterwards, 'many were the expressions of admiration of the undaunted courage and good fighting properties of the Ashantees [sic]'.[47]

'British pluck and the Snider' had prevailed, asserted another sailor.[48] Pluck, in the sense of spirit, courage and commitment, was certainly evident on the British side. Many officers and men were wounded but kept on firing as best they could. 'Bluejacket' was close to Wood when he was 'hit full in the chest' but he kept 'blazing away for half an hour after' until he could stand no more.[49] The Highlanders bore the brunt of the casualties, with two dead (one of whom, Private Thomson, became separated from his unit and was decapitated by the enemy) and 129 wounded (nine of whom later died of their wounds) – or about one in four of those engaged. Their discipline, zeal and determination won praise from comrades in other units, even if one thought that they had been too erect and conspicuous at first – 'they got more cautious afterwards, and got more undercover, which is the chief thing in this warfare'.[50] When interviewed after the war, one Black Watch sergeant recalled:

> I got hit twice – once in the neck here, and then in the breast, and thought it was worse than it really was when I saw blood come streaming over my grey coat. Did I fall out? No, sir, I didn't. Lieutenant Mundy [sic, probably Mowbray] got a severe wound on the head close by, and as it didn't seem to occur to him that there was any need to fall out, I stuck by him at the front.[51]

British fire-power was widely regarded as the other key ingredient in the victory. The breech-loading Snider was a far superior weapon to the flintlock muskets possessed by the Asantes, with one sailor even suggesting that it was 'murder, not a fair fight'.[52] That on the following day the Royal Engineers claimed to have buried some 3,010 Asantes, and that those were only the corpses in and around the road,[53] testified to the carnage inflicted. Inevitably in bush warfare, where the square formation, as Rolfe had feared, split apart as it began to manoeuvre (with gaps appearing between the front and both flanks), friendly fire will have added to the confusion. Sailors found themselves 'firing into the 42nd, and they were firing into us, we were in a fix, and had to cease firing. But we soon found our mistake out, and we gave it to them [the Asantes] again; and so we kept on all day.'[54] Although the Gatling machine-gun was not used, Rait's field guns, which had to be manhandled across the swamp and up the path, provided invaluable support for Russell's Hausas, the 42nd and the Rifles. Even a solitary field gun could have a powerful effect on enemy morale; as Gilham observed: 'A small field gun which was got into position did good work among the enemy, as did the rockets which were sent among them, and no doubt astonished them'.[55]

Notwithstanding the victory at Amoafo, officers like Rolfe realised that the Asante had mounted attacks 'all down the line of communications'.[56] With Fante bearers refusing to move from Fomena after the attack on the depot, one officer asserted: 'The chief source of anxiety is now getting supplies along, the convoy which went this morning [2 February] having been stopped yesterday.'[57] Once five companies of the 42nd and the Naval Brigade had cleared some Asantes from a nearby village, the expedition, minus baggage, pressed forward. They swept aside various ambushes and fought another pitched battle on the northern bank of the Oda River. In this six-hour engagement, in which the Asante again 'stood well',[58] Wolseley's forces seized the next village, Odasu, and repulsed three counter-attacks upon it. Thereafter Wolseley sent the Highlanders forward, and they advanced, as described by Dr Troup, surgeon to the 42nd, 'with pipes playing, the men shooting everything before them, and cheering along the whole line'.[59] Having left the artillery and the Rifles trailing in their wake, the Highlanders, after a brief halt, completed the last few miles, whereupon, as Ferguson recalled, 'we entered Coomassie in the grey darking [sic], our pipes playing the 'Highland Laddie'. We gave three cheers for old Scotland after all was over.'[60]

If the soldiers' descriptions of Kumase hardly compare with the evocative accounts of the special correspondents, especially Melton Prior's remarkable drawing 'Sketches From Coomassie: The King's Slaughtering Place',[61] they at least indicated their own priorities. For soldiers, who had been caught in a tropical downpour on the eve of entering the city and had to clamber through a swamp near Kumase, shelter and drinking water were key requirements. In this respect the

42nd were particularly fortunate as they met Asante women on entering the city, and the latter 'could not have been kinder to us, if it had been Edinburgh we were marching into'.[62] They found water for the conquering intruders before disappearing at nightfall. When the Naval Brigade belatedly entered the largely deserted Kumase, they found shelter, if not water, on their arrival.[63] As Wolseley clung to the forlorn hope that the *Asantehene* would return to sign a treaty, he banned looting, and so soldiers had to uphold this order, flogging their Fante bearers whenever they were caught in the act. They also guarded the royal palace, which was described as 'really very fine, full of beautiful things of marvellous sorts, untidy and dirty to a degree, but still fairly large and full of valuable things'.[64] As the Asante did not reappear after a couple of days, and as the weather continued to deteriorate with another thunderstorm, Wolseley chose to abandon the capital. Having seized some royal treasures for auction, he left on 6 February, ordering the engineers and native labourers to burn the city while the Black Watch acted as rear guard.

Within two days the expedition had reached Amoafo, whereupon Dr Troup reflected on the exploits of the Highlanders:

> We have had over 100 wounded, and about 10 officers – the majority, however, slight. We have had the brunt of the whole thing, and the regiment has behaved splendidly. I am proud to have served in the field with it, and to have earned my second medal in its company. I would not be surprised if two or three officers got the Victoria Cross [Lance Sergeant S. McGraw did receive the VC] . . . I have been six days lying in the open, and two days drenched with rain; had to cross a river naked with my clothes over my head, [the Oda had swollen above the bridge across it] and to sleep without a change. It is all over now, and we can scarcely avoid a laugh occasionally.[65]

During the swift return to Cape Coast (units re-embarked from 19 to 27 February), few paused to reflect upon Wolseley's triumph. As several of the letter writers, and those interviewed later by the press, succumbed to fever or dysentery on the return journey, they could hardly comment on the terms accepted by the *Asantehene's* messengers at Fomena on 13 February.[66] Many of the others, all too aware of the burgeoning number of sick, simply wished to reach the coast as quickly as possible. They took credit for a successful campaign, fought on inhospitable terrain against a much more numerous enemy, but did not attribute their success (as some modern scholars have) to Cardwell's recent reforms of the army, notably the abolition of purchase and the introduction of short-service enlistments.[67] As the expedition contained many purchase officers (all but one of the Royal Welch Fusilier officers had purchased their commissions)[68] and long-service soldiers, while many of the youngest, newly enlisted, soldiers remained at home or had never disembarked, Rait challenged the significance of the Carwellian legacy. In accepting the freedom of Arbroath on 18 April 1874, the indefatigable gunner declared:

> With regard to the abolition of purchase, I hope that it will not deter the same class of officers who have always joined the service from continuing to do so . . . I do hope, gentlemen, that the same type of men will still continue to serve Her Majesty for I am sure with such gentlemen in the service the rank and file will always be keen to follow . . . I also think that medical testimony will bear me out when I say that it is a mistake in having soldiers too young. They will not stand the experience of hardships of a campaign in the same way as older men would do.[69]

Notes

1 W. D. McIntyre, 'British Policy in West Africa: The Ashanti Expedition of 1873–4', *Historical Journal*, 5:1 (1962), 19–46.
2 *Ibid.*, 26–31; H. M. Stanley, *Coomassie and Magdala: The Story of Two British Campaigns in Africa* (London: Sampson Low, 1874), pp. 18–19.
3 J. Keegan, 'The Ashanti Campaign, 1873–4', in B. Bond (ed.), *Victorian Military Campaigns* (London: Hutchison, 1967), pp. 163–98.
4 W. Reade, *The Story of the Ashantee Campaign* (London: Smith, Elder & Co, 1874), p. 395; Stanley, *Coomassie and Magdala*, pp. 258–9.
5 McIntyre, 'British Policy in West Africa', 33, 37; F. Agbodeka, *African Politics and British Policy in the Gold Coast 1868–1900* (London: Longman, 1971), p. 51.
6 Sir R. Biddulph, *Lord Cardwell at the War Office* (London: John Murray, 1904), p. 244; Keegan, 'Ashanti Campaign', p. 195; A. Lloyd, *The Drums of Kumasi: The Story of the Ashanti Wars* (London: Longmans, 1964), pp. 151–2.
7 'Colonel Festing's Story of the War', *Morning Post*, 27 March 1874, p. 6.
8 PRO, WO 33/26, Sir G. Wolseley to the War Office, 13 October 1873.
9 King's Own Royal Regiment Museum, Lancaster, KO LIB 137, Lt E. Woodgate, journal, 16 October 1873; see also I. Harvie, 'The Raid on Essaman, 14 October 1873:An Account by Lieutenant Edward Woodgate of an Operation during Wolseley's Ashanti Expedition', *JSAHR*, 77 (1999), 19–27.
10 Surgeon-Major A. A. Gore, 'The Rescue of the Body of Lieutenant Wilmot', *Evening Standard*, 23 February 1874, p. 1; 'Colonel Festing's Story of the War', p. 6.
11 'The Ashantee War', *Army and Navy Gazette*, 3 January 1874, p. 3.
12 'A Sailor's Life on the Gold Coast', *Bridge of Allan Reporter*, 24 January 1874, p. 4.
13 PRO, WO 33/26, Cardwell to Wolseley, 8 September 1873; Wolseley to Cardwell, 13 October 1873.
14 PRO, WO 33/26, Wolseley to Cardwell, 15 December 1873.
15 G. H. Gilham, 'With Wolseley in Ashanti', in E. Milton Small (ed.), *Told from the Ranks* (London: Andrew Melrose, 1877), pp. 76–86; 'A Stirlingshire Soldier's Account of the War', *Stirling Observer and Midland Counties Express*, 2 April 1874, p. 6; 'Letters from the Troops', *Brechin Advertiser*, 13 January 1874, p. 2; *Morning Post*, 29 January 1874, p. 6; 'The 42d Royal Highlanders', *Bridge of Allan Reporter*, 24 January 1874, p. 4.
16 'Diary of a Non-Commissioned Officer of the 42d Regiment', *Kinross-shire Advertiser*, 28 March 1874, p. 2.
17 'A Stirlingshire Soldier's Account of the War', p. 6.
18 'Gold Coast. – Abstract from a letter from Lieut. H. Jekyll, R.E.', *Royal Engineers Journal (REJ)*, 4 (1 February 1874), 9–10.

19 'The Ashantee War', *Weekly Mail*, 10 January 1874, p. 6. There were only eight camping sites: see W. Walton Claridge, *A History of the Gold Coast and Ashanti*, 2 vols, 2nd edn (London: Frank Cass, 1964), vol. 2, pp. 90–2.
20 'A Bluejacket's Campaign in Ashantee', *Daily News*, 25 March 1874, p. 3; see also Commander P. R. Luxmore's journal, 28 November 1873, quoted in R. Brooks, *The Long Arm of Empire: Naval Brigades from the Crimea to the Boxer Rebellion* (London: Constable, 1999), p. 123.
21 'The Ashantee War', *Morning Advertiser*, 28 February 1874, p. 5. Although described as a 'Naval Officer' in the article, Rolfe mentions his appointment as Wolseley's naval *aide-de-camp* and so his identity can be found in Commodore W. N. W. Hewett's despatch of 29 January 1874, Parliamentary Papers (PP), *Gold Coast. Further Correspondence Respecting the Ashantee Invasion*, No. 5, (1874), XLVI, pp. 869–72; see also *Daily News*, 25 March 1874, p. 3.
22 *Morning Post*, 14 February 1874, p. 5.
23 'Letters from Welshmen Engaged in the Ashantee War', *Carnarvon and Denbigh Herald*, 14 March 1874, p. 6.
24 *Ibid.*; *Morning Post*, 14 February 1874, p. 5; and 'Diary of a Non-Commissioned Officer of the 42d Regiment', *Kinross-shire Advertiser*, 4 April 1874, pp. 2–3.
25 'Ashantee War: Extract from a letter from Lieut. H. Jekyll, R.E.', *REJ*, 4 (2 March 1874), 15–16.
26 'Newport Letters from the Gold Coast', *South Wales Evening Telegram*, 24 February 1874, p. 3.
27 *Morning Post*, 14 February 1874, p. 5.
28 'Letters from Welshmen Engaged in the Ashantee War', p. 6.
29 'Newport Letters from the Gold Coast', p. 3; Keegan, 'The Ashanti Campaign', p. 190; 'Pluck of the 42d Highlanders', *Edinburgh Evening News*, 11 March 1874, p. 3; Walton Claridge, *A History of the Gold Coast*, vol. 2, pp. 100–1.
30 'A Bluejacket's Campaign in Ashantee', p. 3.
31 *Ibid.*; see also PP, *Further Correspondence Respecting the Ashantee Invasion*, No. 5 (1874), pp. 869–72, Wolseley to the Earl of Kimberley, 6 January 1873 (sic).
32 'Letters from Welshmen Engaged in the Ashantee War', p. 6.
33 'Diary of a Non-Commissioned Officer of the 42d Regiment', 4 April 1874, p. 2.
34 'The Ashantee War', *The Times*, 7 March 1874, p. 10.
35 'On the March', *Scotsman*, 27 February 1874, p. 5.
36 *The Times*, 7 March 1874, p. 10; see also Gilham, 'With Wolseley in Ashanti', p. 80.
37 'The March Through Ashantee', *The Times*, 6 March 1874, p. 10; see also *The Times*, 7 March 1874, p. 10, and 'Diary of a Non-Commissioned Officer of the 42d Regiment', 4 April 1874, p. 2.
38 *The Times*, 7 March 1874, p. 10; 'On the March', p. 5; 'Diary of a Non-Commissioned Officer of the 42d Regiment', p. 3.
39 'The Late Captain Nicol', *Nuneaton Chronicle*, 7 March 1874, p. 3; PP, *Ashantee Invasion. Latest Despatches from Sir Garnet Wolseley*, No. 6, (1874), XLVI, pp. 888–9.
40 'Diary of a Non-Commissioned Officer of the 42d Regiment', p. 3.
41 'The Services of the Naval Brigade', *Hampshire Telegraph and Sussex Chronicle*, 28 March 1874, p. 8; see also Lt A. McLeod's journal, 31 January 1874, quoted in Brooks, *Long Arm of Empire*, p. 125.
42 'A Bluejacket's Campaign in Ashantee', p. 3; see also Walton Claridge, *A History of the Gold Coast*, vol. 2, pp. 113–15.
43 *Morning Advertiser*, 28 February 1874, p. 5; see also Keegan, 'The Ashanti Campaign', p. 190.
44 'A Stirlingshire Soldier's Account of the War', p. 6.
45 H. Brackenbury, *The Ashanti War*, 2 vols. (Edinburgh: Blackwood, 1874), vol. 2, pp. 160–79.
46 *Morning Advertiser*, 28 February 1874, p. 5.
47 'The Ashantee War – Letters from Officers', *Grimsby News*, 13 March 1874, p. 3; see also 'A Bluejacket's Campaign in Ashantee', p. 3; 'The Services of the Naval Brigade',

Hampshire Telegraph and Sussex Chronicle, 28 March 1874, p. 8; 'Reception of the 42nd Highlanders', *Crieff Journal*, 27 March 1874, p. 4; and Brackenbury, *The Ashanti War*, 2, pp. 175–7.

48 'Services of the Naval Brigade', p. 8.

49 'A Bluejacket's Campaign in Ashantee', p. 8.

50 'Services of the Naval Brigade', p. 8; see also 'A Bluejacket's Campaign in Ashantee', p. 8; *Morning Advertiser*, 28 February 1874, p. 5; Black Watch Archive (BWA) 0683, 'The Advance on Coomassie' (letter from a colour-sergeant in the Rifles, 5 February 1874); and NRA 0080, 'Record of Service of the 42nd Royal Highland Regiment', p. 23.

51 'Reception of the 42nd Highlanders', p. 4.

52 'Letters from Welshmen Engaged in the Ashantee War', p. 6.

53 'Services of the Naval Brigade', p. 8.

54 *Ibid.*; see also Brackenbury, *Ashanti War*, 2, pp. 171–2.

55 Gilham, 'With Wolseley in Ashanti', p. 83; see also Brackenbury, *Ashanti War*, vol. 2, pp. 165–6, 169, 173.

56 *Morning Advertiser*, 28 February, 1874, p. 5.

57 'Ashantee War – Letters from Officers', p. 3; see also Keegan, 'The Ashanti Campaign', p. 193.

58 'Services of the Naval Brigade', p. 3; Gilham, 'With Wolseley in Ashanti', p. 84; 'A Bluejacket's Campaign in Ashantee', p. 3.

59 'Letter from a Surgeon of the 42nd', *Yorkshire Telegraph*, 28 March 1874, p. 3.

60 'A Stirlingshire Soldier's Account of the War', p. 6.

61 *Illustrated London News*, 25 April 1874, pp. 388–9; see also P. Hodgson, *The War Illustrators* (London: Osprey, 1977), pp. 110–11.

62 'Reception of the 42nd Highlanders', p. 4.

63 'A Bluejacket's Campaign in Ashantee', p. 3.

64 'Ashantee War – Letters from Officers', p. 3; see also 'A Stirlingshire Soldier's Account of the War', p. 6; Gilham, 'With Wolseley in Ashanti', pp. 84–5.

65 'Letter from a Surgeon of the 42nd', p. 3.

66 'Reception of the 42nd Highlanders', p. 4; 'A Bluejacket's Campaign in Ashantee', p. 3; 'A Stirlingshire Soldier's Account of the War', p. 6.

67 'Services of the Naval Brigade', p. 8; Gilham, 'With Wolseley in Ashanti', pp. 85–6; 'Letter from a Surgeon of the 42nd', p. 3. Compare with Keegan, 'Ashanti Campaign', p. 195, and Lloyd, *Drums of Kumasi*, pp. 151–2.

68 Royal Welch Fusiliers Museum, 407, 'Digest of Service: Historical Register, 2nd Battalion Royal Welch Fusiliers'; and Major E. L. Kirby, *Officers of the Royal Welch Fusiliers, 16 March 1689 to 4 August 1914*.

69 'Presentation of the Freedom of Arbroath to Major Rait, C.B.', *Arbroath Guide*, 25 April 1874, p. 3.

CHAPTER TWO

Campaigning in southern Africa

Eyewitness accounts are among the many sources used in the voluminous literature on the Anglo-Zulu War of 1879, a major test of British
command, transport arrangements, and the fighting qualities of the
short-service soldier. Quite apart from the writings of the late Frank
Emery, who refers to eighty-five correspondents in *The Red Soldier* and
another twenty-four in his chapter on that campaign in *Marching Over
Africa*,[1] there are invaluable edited collections of letters from individual officers by Sonia Clark[2] and Daphne Child,[3] and by Adrian Greaves
and Brian Best.[4] While the papers and journals of the British commanding officers have been splendidly edited,[5] some perspectives of officers
and other ranks appear in testimony before official inquiries (into the
disasters at Isandlwana and Ntombe, and the death of the Prince Imperial)[6] and among the sources used by F. W. D. Jackson and Ian Knight,
and by Donald Morris in his classic volume *The Washing of the Spears*.[7]
Yet the letters found by Emery – the core of the material used for the
views of regimental officers and other ranks[8] – represent only a fraction
of the material written during the Anglo-Zulu War. Many more officers
and men kept diaries or wrote to friends and family, chronicling their
exploits in that war and its immediate predecessors, the Ninth Cape
Frontier War (1877–78) and the campaign against the Pedi chief,
Sekhukhune (1878). While several soldiers complained about the postal
arrangements or the scarcity of stamps and paper, they still wrote letters, even improvising, as Corporal Thomas Davies (2/24th) did, by
using gunpowder as ink.[9] Their correspondence forms the core of this
Chapter's review of campaigning in southern Africa.

Several of the regiments who fought the Zulus had already served in
southern Africa. The 1/24th (of the 2nd Warwickshires, later South
Wales Borderers) and the 1/13th (Somerset Light Infantry) had served in
southern Africa since 1875; the 2/Buffs, the 80th (2/South Staffordshires) and the 88th (1/Connaught Rangers) had joined them in 1877,

and the 2/24th, largely composed of short-service soldiers, had arrived in March 1878. These forces, coupled with the 90th Light Infantry (Perthshire Volunteers), two batteries of field artillery (N/5 and II/7) and the 7th Company, Royal Engineers, undertook a daunting array of garrison and other duties in Cape Colony, Natal, along the Zululand border, and in the Transvaal. Sir Arthur Cunynghame, the general officer commanding (GOC) South Africa, compensated for his lack of cavalry by forming mounted infantry from the 1/24th in 1875, and raising additional bodies of mounted riflemen, volunteers and mounted police from the colonial communities, as well as native auxiliaries, both before and during the Ninth Cape Frontier War.[10] The Mfengu were willing to fight the Ngqika and the Gcaleka in the Transkei, while the Swazis readily joined in attacking the mountainous strongholds of the Pedi in eastern Transvaal.

The Ninth Cape Frontier War and campaign against Sekhukhune

The campaigns of 1877–78 were a series of largely desultory engagements, often involving small bodies of imperial troops (sometimes half-companies or less) and/or mounted police and their auxiliaries. These bodies repelled raids on police posts and convoys, skirmished in thick bush and periodically mounted reprisal raids – burning villages and seizing cattle. When the Xhosa massed in their thousands and engaged in set-piece battles – at Nyamaga (13 January 1878) and Centane (7 February 1878) – they suffered heavy defeats, breaking before the disciplined fire-power of a few hundred infantry, mounted police, a rocket battery and a few guns. At Nyamaga, recalled Lieutenant Thomas R. Main, (RE), 'our Martini Henrys produced terrible havoc amongst the enemy who, having no opportunity to reload, bolted across the open plain', pursued by the police and Mfengu auxiliaries. Thereafter campaigning over the rolling hills, high plateaus, and bush-covered ravines and valleys became wearisome and tedious: 'We trekked up & down the Transkei', wrote Main, 'but rarely brought the Kafirs [sic] to book'.[11]

Volley-firing was also to the fore when the small force under Colonel H. Rowlands, VC, tried to storm the rocky fastnesses of the Pedi. One soldier of the 1/13th described how the assault was launched on 27 October 1878, with companies deployed in skirmishing formation, supported by artillery, Swazis and the Carrington Horse. 'In a short time', he wrote, 'one thought the gates of hell were let loose and that demons were fighting'. Under continuous fire and periodic counter-attacks, the 1/13th had to charge up a mountain, support the

Carrington Horse who 'were too weak to keep their position', and, despite driving the enemy up the mountain, had to retire 'after six or seven hours hard fighting . . . exhausted from thirst'. Having failed to capture the stronghold of Chief Sekhukhune, Rowlands prudently withdrew as his expedition was crippled by heat, lack of water and horse-sickness. The march back to the camp at Spekboom Drift, as a 1/13th Light Infantryman observed, was a debilitating experience: 'When we got to the river I do not think there was one man but drank four canteens full of water as fast as one could drink, we were so exhausted and thirsty.'[12]

Understandably the abortive campaign against Sekhukhune, undertaken over peculiarly difficult terrain by an under-strength force,[13] had less impact upon British military thinking than did the bush fighting in the Transkei. Many of the commanding officers and regular forces, who would serve in the Anglo-Zulu War, fought in the Ninth Cape Frontier War. In March 1878 Lieutenant-General the Hon. Frederic A. Thesiger, later the second Baron Chelmsford, superseded Cunynghame. He utilised the estimable services of Colonel Evelyn Wood, VC, with the 90th Foot, and Major Redvers Buller in command of the Frontier Light Horse (FLH), to mount systematic drives through the bush to overcome the elusive Ngqikas by the end of May. The campaign repeatedly demonstrated that concentrated fire-power from small bodies of regulars, or sometimes colonials, could disperse much larger bodies of Xhosa, even without the aid of prepared defences. A Tauntonian described such an action when sixty police, supported by four 7-pounder muzzle-loading guns, sent 'between 4,000 and 6,000 niggers running for dear life', but when the trail of one of their guns broke down later they had to withdraw, whereupon the accompanying 400 Mfengus panicked and fled.[14]

When another patrol of forty Connaught Rangers, twenty police and three volunteers was ambushed by about 1,000 Gcaleka (30 December 1877), several police, noted one of the volunteers, jumped 'on their horses and (five or six) galloped through and away'.[15] Major Moore, who earned a VC for leading the patrol, reported more positively: 'The Connaught Rangers, boys though they are – not one of them had ever seen an enemy before – and some of the Frontier Armed Police, behaved admirably.' He criticised only their 'very mild' shooting that accounted for a 'small number of the enemy'.[16] Local volunteers and the native levies had provided invaluable support, especially in pursuit of the enemy and their cattle, but their periodic displays of ill-discipline and unreliability evoked profound misgivings among the regulars.[17]

Although the resistance of the Ngqika and Gcaleka proved unexpectedly stubborn, many soldiers realised that a more challenging war with the Zulus was imminent. While based in King William's Town in the summer of 1878, Lieutenant Main heard 'rumours of unrest among the Zulus with their powerful army of 30,000 trained warriors, a very different foe to the undisciplined Kafirs'.[18] British units were ordered into Natal as war appeared imminent (it was eventually provoked by Cetshwayo's rejection of an ultimatum from Sir Bartle Frere, the high commissioner for South Africa, requiring acceptance of a British resident and the disbandment of the Zulu army). Private George Morris (1/24th) anticipated 'hard fighting' ahead, while his comrade Private John Thomas approved of the strict discipline in Pietermaritzburg: 'I saw six soldiers flogged on Saturday morning, and two this morning, for being drunk on the line of march. They will have to remember that the Zulus have got Martini-Henry rifles as well as we . . .'.[19]

The Anglo-Zulu War: first invasion of Zululand

Chelmsford duly assembled his army of 17,929 officers and men, including over 1,000 mounted colonial volunteers and some 9,000 natives, and amassed a mighty array of transport – 977 wagons, 56 carts, 10,023 oxen, 803 horses and 398 mules.[20] He planned to deploy five columns, two of which (No. 2 under Lieutenant-Colonel A. W. Durnford and No. 5 under Rowlands) were to defend the borders of Natal and the Transvaal, respectively, while the other three were to cross into Zululand on 11 January 1879. Wood's No. 4 Column was to cross the Blood River and subdue the northern areas of the Zulu kingdom; Colonel C. K. Pearson's No. 1 Column was to cross the Lower Drift of the Tugela (Thukela) River and establish a base for future operations at the abandoned mission of Eshowe; and No 3, or Centre, Column, nominally under Colonel Richard T. Glyn, but effectively under Chelmsford's command, would cross into Zululand at Rorke's Drift, where a supply depot was established on 11 January 1879. Soldiers found the country rugged and progress slow: companies of the 2/24th had to make roads for several days before advancing to the temporary camp site at Isandlwana. Even those serving in the lines of communication, like Private M. Gerrotty (2/4th), reported: 'This is bad country to travel in. We marched 150 miles up country, hardly any water, and some of it of the worst description, all climbing up hills.'[21]

Within a day of crossing into Zululand, Chelmsford launched an attack on Chief Sihayo's mountainous kraal above the Batshe River. A corporal of the 24th wrote: 'We were at great disadvantage owing to the rocks and bush, but we managed to rout them out in the long run after about eight hours' fighting.' He admitted that 'it is very hard work travelling after these Zulus. They can run like horses.'[22] This early display of Zulu mobility exposed the shortage of mounted men with the Centre Column, and a week later Chelmsford ordered Durnford, with the Natal Native Horse, a battalion of infantry and a rocket battery, to support his column.[23]

By the time Durnford, with his 250 mounted men, reached Isandl-wana (about 10.30 a.m. on 22 January 1879), Chelmsford had already departed with six companies of the 2/24th, four guns of Harness's battery, a detachment of mounted infantry, and the Natal Native

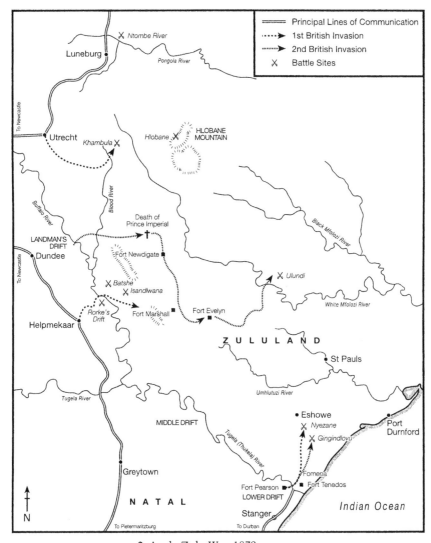

2 Anglo-Zulu War, 1879

Pioneers. He had done so at first light after a reconnaissance party under Major John Dartnell reported 1,000 Zulus some 12 miles eastwards. Fearing lest Dartnell or another reconnaissance party under Commandant Rupert Lonsdale had encountered the main Zulu *impi*, Chelmsford planned to reinforce them but left a substantial force (five companies of the 1/24th, one company of the 2/24th, the two remaining 7-pounder guns, over 100 mounted infantry and four companies of the Natal Native Contingent) under Lieutenant-Colonel Henry Pulleine, 1/24th, to guard the camp. He also required Pulleine to keep his cavalry vedettes advanced, draw in his line of infantry outposts and defend the camp, if attacked. Once Durnford's force arrived, including the rocket battery, there were nearly 1,800 men at Isandlwana; by the early evening, only some 55 Europeans and less than 400 natives survived.

Of the European survivors, most of the British soldiers testified before official inquiries or wrote letters that have been used in accounts of the battle.[24] Captain W. Penn Symons (2/24th) reviewed some of this evidence in a regimental inquiry, including the testimonies of the six survivors of the 1/24th (Privates Grant, Johnson, Trainer, Williams, Bickley and Wilson) and observed: 'It was very remarkable how their accounts afterwards varied. Men forgot what they saw and did amidst great excitement, and mixed up what others told them with their own experiences and reminiscences.'[25]

Some survivors, like Lieutenant Curling, were profoundly shocked by the experience and were not always lucid in their recollections; others embellished their accounts, even in the case of H. C. Young possibly claiming to have escaped from Isandlwana when, according to Lieutenant Higginson, he was in Sandspruit on the day of the battle.[26] Moreover these accounts, as F. W. D. Jackson has observed, 'do little more than hint at the final stages of the battle', where they gave the impression of organised resistance collapsing – an impression contradicted by Zulu testimony and the location of the dead.[27]

Despite these shortcomings, the correspondents corroborated aspects of the battle, not least Colonel Durnford's behaviour on reaching the camp, where he outranked Pulleine. Durnford had already learned from Lieutenant John Chard, RE, whom he had met while the latter was returning to Rorke's Drift, that Zulus were moving on the distant hills,[28] but the reports from outposts and vedettes were of varying accuracy. When Durnford heard subsequently that the enemy were retiring, he determined to pursue them and prevent any reinforcement of the main *impi* that was supposed to be engaging Chelmsford. An 'eyewitness' confirmed Lieutenant W. F. D. Cochrane's claim that Durnford requested the assistance of two companies of the 24th, which Pulleine refused, and Trooper Muirhead (Natal Carabineers) regarded

Durnford as 'the cause of all the disaster' on account of his provocative advance at a time when the camp was not even protected by a laager of wagons.[29] Pulleine had to defend the camp, which sprawled over half a mile of ground, but had neither entrenched it (which would have been difficult on the hard stony ground) nor organised a laager (a time-consuming and skilled task that may have seemed superfluous for a temporary camp site, where wagons were still bringing forward supplies from Rorke's Drift). Although scouts were supposed to give adequate notice of any impending attack, Lieutenant Teignmouth Melvill, 1/24th, and others had warned of the dangers of undefended camps in Zulu territory, and when Captain Edward Essex led survivors back to Helpmekaar, after the battle, he immediately ordered the construction of a wagon laager to afford protection.[30]

As regards the battle itself, Private Edward Evans of the mounted infantry was another survivor (and brought news of the disaster to Rorke's Drift).[31] In a letter to his mother and brother, he hinted at the problem of overextended lines but said nothing about the ammunition supply:

> On the 22nd January 1879, at 4 a.m., General Lord Chelmsford marched out his main column, about 2,000 strong, intending to attack the main body of Cetyawyo's [sic] army. . . and when our column was about 13 miles away from camp we (the men left in camp) could hear the roar of their cannons, and believed everything was going on successfully with them. Now comes the sorrowful history of our camp! About 9 a.m. our company of the 2–24th Regiment was on vidette [sic], or outline picket, on the left flank of ours, when the enemy made his appearance on the left front of our camp. Our picket opened fire on the enemy. We got the order, 'Every man stand to his arms, and be ready for action at a moment's notice.' About 11 a.m. the enemy made its appearance in four large columns, estimated at 15,000 strong. Colonel Durnford, R.E., gave orders for his mounted men to go and flank them on the right, and the rocket party also went to meet them, but had no time to fire more than one rocket when they were cut up. Only one escaped. Then Colonel Pulleen [sic] took out about 500 of the 1-24th, and threw out a line of skirmishers in front of the enemy, when the poor fellows opened a most destructive fire on the enemy, knowing they had to fight for their lives, and intending to sell their lives as dear as possible. They were over numbered more than 20 to one. Two divisions of artillery were also pouring down upon them as fast as shot and shell could be used, but took no effect on the murderous savages. Where 100 would fall 300 would come up and fill up the gap. All the mounted men were guarding the back of the camp, but to no good. Heedless of shot or shell, or bayonet stabs, they kept coming in by thousands, and killed our men like dogs.[32]

A 20-year-old Natal policeman served in support of Durnford's flanking movement and wrote of the Zulus:

we saw the hill black with them, coming on in swarms, estimated at 20,000. We held a ditch as long as possible, but being outnumbered the order was given to get into camp. Well we got there. I went all over the place for a gun, but could not get one. My revolver was broken . . . The Zulus were in the camp, ripping our men up, also the tents and everything they came upon with their assegais.[33]

Only mounted men, like Evans and Muirhead, had any chance of escape: Muirhead described how Surgeon-Major Shepherd was killed in flight after briefly stopping to examine a fallen trooper.[34] One of the escaping Basuto horsemen claimed that their chief had made them concentrate their fire on one spot in the Zulu ranks, mowing 'a lane for the moment through the Zulus' and then dashing through it.[35] 'It was a ride for life', wrote Evans, 'Many of our noble heroes that escaped from the hands of the enemy lost their lives in crossing the Buffalo River. Thank God for learning me to swim. My horse fell in the water, and both of us went down together, and both swam out again – but a very hard struggle.'[36]

The remainder of Chelmsford's Column had apparently marched out, 'full of spirits at the thought of a brush with the enemy', and heard nothing from the camp until the sound of gun-fire about 12.30 a.m. When a horseman brought news of the attack, the readiness of Lieutenant-Colonel Arthur Harness, with his four guns and two companies of 2/24th, to march back contrasted with the incredulity of Major Gosset and other members of Chelmsford's staff.[37] As Harness's soldiers first marched back some 5 miles, then were ordered to rejoin the column before finally being ordered to return to the camp, a colour-sergeant of the 2/24th recalled: 'It was awfully annoying this marching backwards and forwards; but a soldier's first duty is obedience and away we went, though awfully tired.'[38] A few miles from the camp, the general and advance escort returned to explain that the camp had fallen. When Chelmsford, who seemed, according to Private P. Fitzgerald (2/24th), 'very near crying',[39] ordered that the camp should be retaken even at the point of the bayonet, the ranks responded with three cheers.[40] By nightfall (times vary, but probably about 8 p.m.), the column stormed into the camp with fire from guns and volleys, and bayonets fixed. Apart from a few drunken Zulus, who were quickly bayoneted, the soldiers found the camp deserted.[41] They spent a largely sleepless night, punctuated by periodic alerts: as A. J. Secretan (Natal Mounted Police) noted, 'We were lying amongst thousands of dead, both black and white . . . I myself was lying in a pool of blood and a ghastly corpse was just beside me.'[42]

At sunrise the spectacle was even worse. Secretan observed that some British soldiers had died 'formed up in square, where they held their ground till all were slain where they stood'. Like many others, he was appalled by the mutilated corpses and the 'horses and oxen all lying about, stabbed and ripped up'.[43] Several soldiers (Charles Mason, Daniel Sullivan, John James and R. Wilson) as well as Lieutenant Hillier (Lonsdale Horse) claimed that disembowelled band boys hung from butcher's hooks.[44] Whether these stories, like similar tales already documented, were true or were the products of rumour, hearsay and fevered imagination – as has been suggested[45] – they circulated widely, feeding the hatred of the Zulu and the desire, as expressed by Private G. Griffiths (2/24th), for 'revenge on the black heathens'.[46] Such feelings, though, had to fester for some time, as the column had lost its colours, stores, valises, blankets, coats, tents and ammunition. 'The Zulus', wrote Private D. Buckley (2/24th), 'took everything they could carry and what they could not carry they burnt.'[47] As Chelmsford promptly ordered a withdrawal from Isandlwana, and retired on to the defensive in Natal, his soldiers consoled themselves as they awaited reinforcements. Many counted their blessings, as they too had been vulnerable, possessing only seventy rounds of ammunition per man.[48] They extolled the achievements of their fallen comrades: 'The enemy', wrote Private P. Thomas (2/24th), 'had to pay dearly for their day's work', a view echoed by the many who greatly exaggerated the number of Zulu dead.[49] Similarly many were quick to blame Durnford for the debacle – and to identify other scapegoats: 'those d——d volunteers and Native Contingent', claimed Private Thomas Harding (2/24th), 'ran away as soon as they saw the enemy coming'.[50]

British morale, nonetheless, revived after the heroic defence of Rorke's Drift (22–3 January 1879), when some 140 men – 35 of whom were sick – resisted an onslaught from an estimated 4,000 Zulus (the uNdi Corps, a reserve not employed in the attack on Isandlwana). The base at least had warning of the impending attack, enabling Lieutenant Gonville Bromhead (2/24th) and Assisting Acting Commissary James Dalton, a former sergeant in the 85th Foot, to begin organising a perimeter defence while Chard, the officer in command, closed down the pontoon operations. Apart from two wagons, the perimeter consisted of piles of mealie bags and biscuit boxes – 'a broken and imperfect barricade at the best, and nowhere more than two feet high'.[51] Private E. Stephens (B Company, 2/24th) informed his mother that

> a farthing would have bought all our lives. Then we got our guns and ammunition, struck camp, and barricaded the old storehouse as well as we could. Some were posted one place and another, and about an hour elapsed when we could see them coming. They say it was 4,000 altogether. Every man was to his post, and all the 300 natives we got ran away, and there was 146 of us altogether. We kept firing; it began about

three o'clock – kept on for two hours – when they succeeded in setting fire to the little house used as an hospital. It was getting dark then, and we expected help. We thought the General would come to us, but not so. We said we would die brave. We kept it up until daybreak, and, thank God, they ran away, and we went round to bury the dead, and we killed a good number.[52]

From the hospital a Dundonian in the 1/24th, almost certainly Private John William Roy, who was mentioned in despatches, afforded a more garbled account:

> When we heard the rapid firing we fortified the Mission Station as well as we could. The hospital was the missionary's dwellinghouse, and the sick (about 20 of us) manned that, while the company were inside the for-tification. We had only about three-quarters of an hour to secure our-selves as well we could. They came down upon us about three o'clock in the afternoon . . . They very nearly overpowered us. They took the hos-pital and set fire to it, while I and another old soldier were inside at the back window, and we did not know they had taken it at the front. My rifle got disabled, so I fixed my bayonet and charged out of the house . . . There were about 30 Zulus chasing us, but the men inside the fort shot them before they could harm us. There were four men burned alive in the hospital, they being unable to move with the fever. We kept our position until the morning and then the General came to our assistance.[53]

An anonymous account in the *Warwick and Warwickshire Adver-tiser* was more informative. The Zulus initially 'advanced quietly but quickly at a run, taking advantage of every bit of cover. It seemed as if they had expected to surprise the camp. Our men opened fire at 500 yards.' As the advance party broke and scattered to their left, occupy-ing

> the garden and orchard, where there was plenty of cover . . . Others came on in a continuous stream, occupied the hill above, and gradually encir-cled the two houses. All men who had guns were stationed on the hill, and kept up a continuous and rapid fire on the yard . . .. Had they been good marksmen the place was untenable, but they fired wildly and badly for the most part.

Meanwhile parties of 15–20 Zulus 'repeatedly attacked the end room of the hospital. They made these attacks in the most deliberate manner, advancing after the manner of their dancing, with a prancing step and high action; they cared nothing for slaughter'. They were resisted with bullet and bayonet: 'seven or eight times at least, Lieu-tenant Bromhead, collecting a few men together, had to drive them off with a bayonet charge'. The shooting was deliberate and effective: in the morning, outside the window of the hospital defended by Private

Joseph Williams, 'a young Welshman, with under two years' service', there were fourteen dead warriors 'and several more down his line of fire'. After the hospital was vacated, the 'fighting in places became hand to hand over the mealie sacks. The assailants used only their assegais. These they did not throw but used as stabbing weapons.' The fighting continued until 4 a.m. when they gradually withdrew, carrying as many of their dead and wounded as they could. 'The last of them left just before dawn. They left 370 dead on the field. These were counted and buried in heaps.'[54]

On the same day as the battle of Isandlwana, Pearson's column encountered some 6,000 Zulus at the River Nyezane. The column had spent ten days struggling across the river-laced terrain of long grass and bush, gaining a foretaste of how slow and frustrating movement would be in Zululand. The teams of 16 oxen pulling each of the 130 wagons posed difficulties at river crossings where, as Sergeant Josh S. Hooper (2/Buffs) noted, 'we had to drag most of the waggons across as the bullocks instead of pulling have a great inclination to lay down in the water'.[55] The column's length straggled over several miles, compounding its vulnerability, and, at the Nyezane, the advance guard bore the brunt of the Zulu attack. To prevent the Zulus from enveloping the lead units, Pearson ordered the Naval Brigade under Captain H. Fletcher Campbell, Lieutenant Lloyd's artillery and two companies of Buffs to seize the crest of a nearby knoll. This split the enemy's advance and brought into action two 7-pounders, rocket tubes and later a Gatling gun, while the remaining Buffs, the 99th (Duke of Edinburgh's Lanarkshire) and a portion of the Naval Brigade skirmished on the flanks. Within an hour the enemy fled. While the column suffered 10 deaths and 16 wounded, official estimates of the Zulu dead exceeded 300.[56]

Although the participants tended to exaggerate both the length of the battle and the number of Zulu casualties,[57] they recalled key features of the engagement. Once again the native auxiliaries fled (many of their officers and non-commissioned officers could not speak the auxiliaries' language, and some could not even speak English). While Dr Mansell, a surgeon with the column, appreciated that these were poorly armed soldiers (only every tenth man had a rifle), he was appalled that some tried to find shelter in the ambulance wagons. The credit for the victory, he added, belonged to 'about five hundred men comprising a portion of the Buffs and the 99th Regiments'.[58] Yet the gunners, sappers, mounted troops and the Naval Brigade contributed, too, with the sailors firing 300 rounds from the Gatling gun. While Lieutenant Main described the Zulus as 'splendid fighters, but stood no chance against the white man & his Martini rifle, as long as the latter remained steady',[59] Zulu fire-power inflicted relatively few casualties because it was aimed far too high: some sailors were among the first injured because they climbed into trees to get a better line of sight and were inadvertently shot.[60]

The column moved on to a Scandinavian mission at Eshowe, where work began on the construction of a fort. This involved digging a trench some 10–12-feet deep, and 20-feet wide, with stakes planted inside. The earth from the trench was used to create a breastwork, with steps inside, and beyond the trench smaller holes were dug, containing sharpened stakes linked by wire to entangle the legs of any onrushing Zulus.[61] The labour of constructing the trench soon paled by comparison with the boredom of living within its vicinity. Despite some mounted forays, several officers chafed at Pearson's decision to wait for relief lest it demoralise the men.[62] The fort was isolated (until a heliograph link with the Tugela was established) as runners rarely reached Natal (and, ironically, a couple who did get there brought news of the disaster at Isandlwana). Once 'the extent of the loss became known', wrote Mansell, 'the men were much depressed about it'.[63] Morale flagged within the fort: as Lieutenant A. V. Payne observed: 'I have not had a single letter from home yet: we are reading some old papers we found up here 10 years old, principally old Illustrated News.'[64] Even worse, fever and dysentery swept through the ranks as men endured extremes of climate (fierce heat in daytime often followed by heavy rain at night), impure water, cramped conditions each night in a sodden earthwork fort and short daily rations (½lb of mouldy biscuit, 12oz wholemeal, usually in the form of dark and sour bread, 3oz of preserved vegetables and half the allowance of salt and pepper). By 5 March, 'the Church (our hospital)', wrote Sergeant Hooper, 'is full of men, many raving and often too bad and weak to rave'; by 26 March, the sick on 'Convalescent Hill' were 'all very much emaciated . . . not one is able to lift his hand to even drive off the flies which continually worry them . . . the stench in the hospital is beyond my description'.[65]

On 12 March another disaster befell the British forces near the Transvaal border when 800 to 900 Zulus attacked a camp on the banks of the Ntombe (Intombi) River. Their target was a convoy of eighteen wagons carrying stores, ammunition and provisions from Lydenburg to Natal, escorted by 106 soldiers of the 80th under Captain D. B. Moriarty. As the river had been swollen by heavy rain, sixteen wagons were on the northern bank, arranged in a V-shaped laager (a formation criticised by Major Charles Tucker when he visited the camp on the previous day because of the gaps between the wagons and the distance between the 'legs' of the V and the river[66]). With the bulk of the men and the oxen within the laager, thirty-four men were left on the southern bank, initially with Sergeant Anthony Booth in charge and later Lieutenant H. H. Harward. Under the cover of an early morning fog the Zulus crept to about 90 metres of the northern camp, whereupon, at approximately 5 a.m., they opened fire and attacked the camp with assegais. The only effective response came from the southern bank where the men were standing to, following an earlier errant shot. Sergeant Booth wrote: 'I rallied my party by the waggon and poured heavy fire into them as fast as we could . . . I commanded the party on this side as Lieutenant Harward saddled his horse and galloped away leaving us to do the best we could.' Booth's section provided covering fire for some fifteen men, 'all as naked as they were born', who swam the river, and then held off 200–300 Zulus by firing volleys in a phased retreat to a mission station about 3 miles away.[67] Captain Moriarty perished with seventy-eight men in this action, for which Booth earned a VC. Harward, who rode off to alert Major Tucker at Luneburg, later survived a court martial, but his career was ruined.[68]

Wood's No. 4 Column, though expected to march towards Ulundi in support of the Centre Column, had to pacify the territory *en route* to ensure the protection of the border town of Utrecht and the hamlet of Luneburg. Wood's Column included two infantry battalions (1/13th and 90th), an artillery battery less one section, six troops of mounted volunteers (including a Boer contingent under Piet Uys) and two battalions of locally recruited Zulus, known as 'Wood's irregulars'. They were soon skirmishing with larger bodies of Zulus, burning their kraals and capturing thousands of head of cattle, sheep and horses. Morale soared as the enemy repeatedly broke before Wood's fire-power. 'We gave them volley after volley', wrote Private G. Betts (90th), 'which made them run in all directions.'[69] 'We are in good fighting trim', claimed a Crieff veteran, 'we are old warriors (for this is our second war), and are used to fighting darkies.'[70] After receiving news of Isandlwana, Wood abandoned the march on Ulundi and established a camp at Khambula. A medical officer noted:

> On one side of the camp is a precipice and the other side is very steep. In front there is a narrow open stretch of ground, and immediately in rear of our camp, about 250 yards off, perched on a small isolated eminence about 100 feet above us, is a fort with a deep ditch, mounting two guns. The camp consists of two laagers, an outside square one composed of about 90 waggons end to end, and an inner circle of about 50 waggons, where the oxen are kept at night. In addition the camp is intrenched [*sic*].[71]

A trooper of the Frontier Light Horse (FLH) described how mounted outposts were positioned 5 miles from the camp and a mile at night, men had to 'sleep with their boots and clothes on, with their ammunition around them', and the ammunition boxes were 'kept unscrewed and ready for use'.[72]

Wood kept despatching mounted forces under Buller to seize cattle and destroy nearby Zulu homesteads. Some Zulus surrendered, swelling the ranks of Wood's irregulars, but the refractory abaQulusi frequently retreated to a mountainous plateau on Hlobane mountain. On 28 March Wood attacked this stronghold using a pincer movement, involving mounted troops and native levies. Although Buller's force (some 160 FLH and 200 irregulars) reached the summit and began driving off Zulu cattle, supporting units (the Border Horse) became separated in the darkness and the abaQulusi harassed the rear guard. When the other part of the pincer withdrew at the sight of a massive Zulu army approaching along the valley below, Buller's command had to conduct a fighting retreat. An officer of the FLH described how

> We galloped along the top of the mountain, and found the way down was simply a sheer rocky descent . . . The Dutchmen in front rushed to try and get down first, as the Zulus were only 500 yards behind us on top, and the enemy approaching was apparently going to try and cut us off below. Nothing more or less than a terrible panic ensued . . . I and my horse fell a matter of 30 feet . . . On reaching the bottom I found men of all the different corps massed together preparing for a precipitous flight . . . the mass refused to listen to any of the eight officers down there. We beseeched, threatened, and cursed them, calling them cowards, and had actually to fire on them. It was no good, about 20 or 30 stopped, and we waited for what men to come down who could. Most arrived dismounted, and we had to watch helplessly the Zulus assegaing the brave fellows at the top. It was an awful sight. We then picked up what men we could get away, and made our way home.[73]

If few British regulars were involved in this rout – a rare example of a small body of men caught on a mountain top and harried by the Zulu – they were appalled by the spectacle of bedraggled men returning to Khambula. 'It was an extraordinary sight', wrote Lieutenant Fell (90th), 'to see the men return into camp. All the horses deadbeat. Some carrying three men. Many had thrown away boots, coats, trousers, arms, and ammunition, in fact everything which could inconvenience them.'[74] Even worse were the tales of the slaughter, involving the loss of 15 officers and 79 men, mostly colonial irregulars, and at least 100 of Wood's irregulars. During the night most of Wood's remaining irregulars deserted,[75] and the Dutch contingent departed after the death of their leader, Piet Uys. Forewarned of the approach of the Zulu army, some 20,000-strong, the 2,086 officers and men, including 88 sick, awaited the attack on the following day. By mid-morning, wrote Corporal Hutchinson, 'the hills around us were black'[76] as the Zulus advanced in five enormous columns. By despatching his mounted troops as skir-mishers, Wood provoked the right horn into a precipitate attack, whereupon it foundered, as Fell described, before 'a storm of lead from our men in the laager'.[77] Over the next four hours the Zulus mounted a succession of assaults, with their bravery all too obvious: 'no matter how many were killed', Hutchinson recalled, 'still they kept coming on and still they were getting killed'.[78] Although disciplined fire-power disrupted their attacks and kept them from reaching the fort, the rifles became so hot that soldiers could not hold them, whereupon 'one party cooled their arms while the other fired . . .'.[79] A bayonet charge by two companies of the 90th dispersed some Zulus who broke into the cattle laager: 'they did not stand it', wrote Private John Graham (90th), and many were shot retreating down the hill.[80] When the Zulus eventually withdrew, Wood let forth his mounted troops. An officer of the FLH wrote: 'We chased a column of 6,000, only 150 of us, but our blood was up and the enemy in retreat. We were no longer men but demons, screaming the same refrain "Remember yesterday!"'[81] While Buller's troops left a trail of slaughter over 8 miles, a company of the 90th left the fort, shooting and bayoneting the enemy. Fell claimed that this was revenge for Isandlwana, but the battle in which over 2,000 Zulus died (compared with 29 dead and 55 wounded within the camp) had a much greater significance: as Private George Davies (mounted infantry) observed, 'The battle will greatly dishearten them and do us a great deal of good . . .'.[82]

Bolstering morale was certainly necessary, as the remnants of Glyn's column languished in the cramped and unhealthy conditions at Helpmekaar and Rorke's Drift with little to do once they had fortified the depots. In lengthy letters to his father, Lieutenant Charles E. Com-meline, (RE), fully described the two months of tedium awaiting rein-forcements, building earthworks and roads, bringing forward stores, ammunition and equipment, and coping with transport difficulties.[83] Amid the frustrations came criticisms of Chelmsford: 'The Zulus have completely out-generalled us', wrote one of his column, while another feared that they had lived 'in such a fool's paradise, over-estimating our knowledge of the enemy and under-estimating their strength and tac-tics'.[84] As these concerns found reflection in the press, Commeline doubted that Chelmsford 'can remove the unfavourable impression that has been created'.[85]

From mid-March onwards reinforcements began to arrive in Natal. They included five infantry battalions, two cavalry regiments, addi-tional artillery, engineers and other support services, with most of the home-based units brought up to strength with volunteers from other units. Huge crowds had cheered the 'Avenging Army' when it left

Portsmouth and Southampton, while local newspapers, such as the *Ayr Advertiser* and the *Bridge of Allan Reporter*, engaged officers – from the 21st (Royal Scots Fusiliers) and 91st (Argyllshire) Highlanders, respectively – to write regular columns from the front. During the voyage officers and other ranks practised with their weapons, attended lectures on the Zulu, and read about events in Zululand (300 copies of the *Graphic* were sent to the steamship carrying the Argylls).[86] If this could hardly prepare soldiers for the stress of acclimatisation – what Private Charles Godfrey, a volunteer from the 45th to the 58th (Rutlandshire), would describe as 'very hard marches in the burning sun of Africa'[87] – they arrived at the front highly motivated and eager to grapple with the Zulu.[88]

The Anglo-Zulu War: second invasion of Zululand

Chelmsford employed the reinforcements initially to relieve Eshowe. On 29 March Chelmsford's column (3,390 Europeans and 2,280 natives) entered Zululand, moving slowly across the swampy terrain and forming wagon laagers with external entrenchments every night. Travelling without tents, new soldiers, like Private C. Coe (3/60th Rifles), despaired of the torrential rains at night.[89] On the morning of 2 April, when the relief force was still ensconced within its entrenched square laager at Gingindlovu, some 6,000 Zulus attacked. For an hour they swept round the sides of the square, suffering heavy casualties from the disciplined volleys and the Gatling guns at two corners (two naval 9-pounders fired from the other corners). Once again Zulu firepower proved largely ineffective (leaving 15 killed, 49 wounded and 3 severely wounded), but their skirmishing and bravery were highly praised. Captain William Crauford (91st) admired 'very much the way they advanced to the attack, our men can't hold a candle to them . . .'.[90] Whereas Private Coe regarded the fire-fight as 'fine sport whilst we were going at it', a colour-sergeant of the 91st commented: 'Nothing in the world could stand our fire . . . yet very hard to see our fellow-creatures sent to eternity'.[91] As the Zulus withdrew, the mounted infantry and natives pursued them, killing many of the wounded and retreating enemy. Dr A. A. Woods was appalled by the difficulty of treating the wounded with 'very defective' medical stores and appliances; the confinement of wounded Zulu prisoners, left lying in the mud that 'did not by any means redound to our credit as a civilised nation'; and the behaviour of the native auxiliaries: 'Cowards naturally, they fear a Zulu as one would a mad dog. Dirty, lazy, and gluttonous beyond all conception, these are the *allies* who are helping to fight the Zulus, and whom their own officers utterly despise and treat as beasts.'[92]

Gingindlovu, nonetheless, was another decisive victory with over 700 Zulus killed and the relief of Eshowe accomplished on the following day.

Thereafter Chelmsford spent nearly two months accumulating forces, stores and transport for another two-pronged invasion of Zululand. Major-General E. Newdigate's Second Division (5,000 men) was to strike across from Blood River, joining with Wood's renamed 'Flying Column' (3,200 men) and later with Major-General H. H. Crealock's First Division (7,500 men), once it had pacified the coastal region, in a joint thrust towards Ulundi. Only one day into the invasion (1 June) Prince Louis Napoleon, who had volunteered to join the reinforcements, was killed while sketching, but five of his eight-strong escort, including Lieutenant J. B. Carey, escaped without him. On 2 June Lancers, some of whom had recently completed a burial detail at Isandlwana, recovered the body of the Prince Imperial, naked save for a thin gold chain and scarred with seventeen assegai wounds. Captain R. Wolrige-Gordon (attached to the 94th) was not alone in regarding Carey as a 'coward', who 'ought to be shot', and a sergeant in the 1st King's Dragoon Guards correctly anticipated that the death would cause 'a great sensation in England and on the Continent . . .'.[93]

The Second Division pressed slowly onwards, forming entrenched laagers at night, periodically stopping to construct fortified depots, and suffering several night-time alerts in which some soldiers were shot by nervous pickets.[94] Officers and men seemed eager to confront the enemy; they praised the rejection of Cetshwayo's peace envoys, and consoled companies left behind to garrison Fort Newdigate and Fort Marshall.[95] As mounted patrols skirmished with Zulus and burnt kraals, some of the Flying Column bemoaned the slowness of the advance, attributing it to the 'vacillation which has characterised the Commander-in-Chief's actions ever since the fatal day of Isandala [sic]'.[96] Notwithstanding Chelmsford's caution, the delays derived chiefly from the difficulties of moving 700 ox-driven wagons (when the Second Division joined with the Flying Column) over roadless, undulating terrain. Crealock's Division moved even slower, with fewer oxen and many of them emaciated, struggling across rivers and marshy ground. It never made the assault on Ulundi. 'A British army', observed a Royal Scots Fusilier, 'is a terribly cumbrous machine, and quite incapable of rapid movement.'[97]

On 30 June after waiting in vain for Crealock, and knowing that Wolseley had been sent to supersede him, Chelmsford ordered the final advance on Ulundi. With 15 miles to go, the columns screened by the mounted troops, descended 'into a great bushy valley'. Engineers and pioneers led the way, 'axe in hand, felling timber all the way', to the

White Mfolozi River. As the wagons had to move three or four abreast, an engineer recalled: 'We were knocked up and expected an attack at every minute.'[98] Having laagered near the river, they suffered another false alarm on the night of 1 July, whereupon the native pickets and a company of the 24th stampeded into the laager: Wolrige-Gordon noted: 'A sergeant, private, and drummer of the 24th are to be tried for it.'[99] Two days later the regulars watched anxiously as the mounted horse crossed the river, with Baker's Horse dispersing 30 Zulu snipers and then acting as a covering party for Buller's 500 horsemen as they undertook a reconnaissance mission and narrowly avoided a Zulu ambush. Meeting 4,000 Zulus, Buller conducted a skilful retreat, with only 3 dead and 4 wounded.[100]

Before dawn on the following day Chelmsford launched his final advance, with 4,166 white and 958 black soldiers, 12 pieces of artillery and 2 Gatling guns. Once across the river, they advanced in square formation, 'four deep, the ammunition and tool carts in the centre, the cavalry out all around us', a difficult formation in which to manoeuvre over 'rough and bushy' ground, especially with wagons and carts.[101] By 8.30 a.m. the square, having set one kraal on fire, reached the area reconnoitred by Buller on the plain of Ulundi. An army of 15,000–20,000 Zulus advanced towards the square: 'We saw them', wrote one engineer, 'on our right, then front, then left, then they worked their swarms to our rear face . . .'.[102] Mounted troops, including the Basuto scouts, fired on the Zulus, bringing them within range before retreating in orderly manner into the square.[103] Soldiers marvelled at the manoeuvring of the Zulus: James Lambert (veterinary surgeon, 17th Lancers) described how they took 'advantage of every bit of cover afforded by the inequalities of the ground and a very few bushes, and only showing their heads above the long grass'.[104] Once the artillery and Gatlings opened fire (before the latter jammed), volley-firing followed, with the rear two ranks standing and the front two kneeling, pausing periodically to let the smoke clear. This firepower kept the enemy, as a corporal of the 90th claimed, at 'a respectful distance', but the artillery had to fire case as well as shrapnel and rockets, and at some points the Zulus got within 30 yards of the line.[105] The Zulus appeared less determined than previously: as Corporal Roe (58th) observed, it only took about half an hour before they began to withdraw from the 'dreadful fire of our rifle and canon', and some Fusiliers complained that they had not even fired ten rounds of ammunition (the average consumption was only 6.4 rounds per man).[106] Lancers and Dragoons harried the retreating enemy over 3 miles, crossing a deep donga and riding through high grass and over pot-holed ground. The Dragoons, as one of their number described, 'galloped as hard as we could, but the Zulus ran very nearly as fast as we, so instead of losing time in dismounting we, with one consent, halted and fired.'[107] Yet the Lancers, despite losing a few men and many horses, claimed at least 150 victims, and returned with all their lances red with blood.[108] When the Zulus reached the nearby hills and began to mass out of reach of the cavalry, the 9-pounders were moved out and began firing: 'Oh! how they bolted', wrote Mr France, a wagon master in the square, 'But to little purpose, for shell after shell followed them and told most effectively on them.'[109] Buller's Horse completed the Zulu humiliation by burning the king's kraal and all the nearby kraals.

Having buried their 12 dead (another would soon die), the square collected their 69 wounded men and withdrew. As Wolrige-Gordon recalled: 'We passed several dead Zulus, all of whom having their stomachs ripped open; this was done by our natives, who, as soon as the battle was over, began to get plucky, and went about killing the wounded without mercy.'[110] Soldiers, though, realised the magnitude of their achievement. They had defeated the Zulu army in the open, exactly in the area between the Nodwengu and Ulundi kraals where Cetshwayo had wanted to fight. 'We evidently astonished them', wrote a Bristolian with the Flying Column, 'by marching close to their kraal . . . and fighting them sans protection of earthwork of any sort'.[111] The young short-service soldiers, despite the false alarms, had proved steady in battle (and apparently steadier than some of their comrades when Lieutenant-Colonel Francis Northey fell mortally wounded at Gingindlovu): 'a British force', argued a Fusilier officer, 'properly handled can easily defeat four times its numbers'.[112] Lord Chelmsford, who planned the battle and remained mounted throughout it, impressed many observers: in the opinion of Sergeant O'Callaghan (58th), he had 'proved himself an able general, and a cool, brave, and determined leader'.[113] At home, however, such comments failed to assuage criticism of Chelmsford's command or of his costly and cumbersome transport arrangements.[114] Nevertheless, Chelmsford had routed the Zulu army, killing some 1,500 warriors and undermining the authority of Cetshwayo (who would be caught on 28 August 1879 by a squadron of dragoons). 'The battle of Ulundi', asserted Lambert, had 're-established the prestige of the white man over the black, and probably decided the fate of southern Africa for many generations.'[115]

Notes

1 Emery, *Red Soldier*, pp. 258–62; and *Marching Over Africa*, pp. 185–6.
2 S. Clark (ed.), *Invasion of Zululand 1879: Anglo-Zulu War Experiences of Arthur Harness; John Jervis, 4th Viscount St Vincent; and Sir Henry Bulwer* (Johannesburg:

Brenthurst Press, 1979); and S. Clarke, *Zululand at War: The Conduct of the Anglo-Zulu War* (Johannesburg: Brenthurst Press, 1984).

3 D. Child (ed.), *The Zulu War Journal of Colonel Henry Harford, CB* (Pietermar-itzburg: Shuter & Shooter, 1978).

4 *The Curling Letters*, ed. Greaves and Best.

5 A. Preston (ed.), *Sir Garnet Wolseley's South African Journal, 1879–1880* (Cape Town: A. A. Balkema, 1973); and J. P. C. Laband (ed.), *Lord Chelmsford's Zululand Campaign 1878–1879* (Stroud, Gloucestershire: Alan Sutton for the Army Records Society, 1994).

6 PP, *Further Correspondence Respecting the Affairs in South Africa* (hereafter, *Further Correspondence, SA*), C 2260 (1878–79), LIII, pp. 80–5, 98–102; PRO, WO 33/34, pp. 257–8, 278–80, 291, 321–4; C. L. Norris-Newman, *In Zululand with the British throughout the War of 1879* (London: W. H. Allen, 1880), Appendix H, pp. 301–12.

7 F. W. D. Jackson, *Isandhlwana 1879: The Sources Re-Examined* (The Barracks, Brecon: South Wales Borderers, 1999), pp. 9, 13, 17, 25–7, 31–2, 35; I. Knight (ed.), *'By Orders of the Great White Queen': Campaigning in Zululand through the Eyes of the British Soldier, 1879* (London: Greenhill Books, 1992); *The Sun Turned Black: Isandlwana and Rorke's Drift – 1879* (Rivonia: William Waterman, 1995), and *The National Army Museum Book of the Zulu War* (London: Sidgwick & Jackson, 2003); D. R. Morris, *The Washing of the Spears* (London: Jonathan Cape, 1966), p. 420.

8 M. Lieven, 'The British Soldiery and the Ideology of Empire: Letters from Zululand', *JSAHR*, 80 (2002), 128–43.

9 'Letters from Welsh Soldiers', *North Wales Express*, 11 April 1879, p. 6; Royal Regiment of Wales Museum (RRWM), ZC/2/1, no. 10, Pte (Private) G. Morris to father, 20 March 1878; 'Letter from an Usk Man at Rorke's Drift', *South Wales Weekly Telegram*, 25 April 1879, p. 4; 'The Light Horse and the Zulus', *Tamworth Herald*, 3 May 1879, p. 8; Pte W. G. Wilson, *Totnes Times*, 29 March 1879, p. 3.

10 Maj. G. Tylden, 'The British Army and the Transvaal, 1875 to 1885', *JSAHR*, 30 (1952), 159–71; Lord Grenfell, *Memoirs of Field-Marshal Lord Grenfell* (London: Hodder & Stoughton, n.d.), p. 36.

11 Royal Engineers Library (REL), Acc. 11315, 'Recollections of Lt. Thomas Ryder Main', n.d., pp. 108, 110; see also General Sir Arthur Thurlow Cunynghame, GCB, *My Command in South Africa, 1874–1878* (London: Macmillan, 1879), pp. 372–3.

12 'The Sekukuni Campaign', *Natal Mercury*, 14 December 1878, p. 5; Clarke, *Zululand at War*, p. 44.

13 Somerset Light Infantry Archive (SLIA), ARCH/332, 'Impressions of Zululand, 1875 to 1879, by Lieutenant-Colonel J. M. E. Waddy of the Somerset Light Infantry'.

14 'The Kaffir War', *Somerset County Gazette*, 23 February 1878, p. 7; *Curling Letters*, pp. 34, 36, 40.

15 'The Kaffir War', *Uttoxeter New Era*, 20 February 1878, p. 3.

16 'The Caffre Outbreak', *Hereford Times*, 2 March 1878, p. 15.

17 'Volunteers and Regulars', *Natal Mercury*, 2 December 1878, p. 3; *Invasion of Zululand 1879*, p. 40; but there are more appreciative comments in Lieutenant-Colonel I. H. W. Bennett, *Eyewitness in Zululand: The Campaign Reminiscences of Colonel W. A. Dunne, CB, South Africa, 1877–1881* (London: Greenhill Books, 1989), p. 76.

18 REL, Acc. 11315, 'Recollections of Main', p. 111; Clarke (ed.), *Invasion of Zululand*, p. 35; Emery, *Red Soldier*, pp. 39–40.

19 RRWM, Z C/2/2, Pte G. B. Morris to his mother, 5 November 1878; 'Letter from a Slain Private in Zululand to his Father in Pontyminster', *South Wales Weekly Telegram*, 11 April 1879, p. 5.

20 War Office (Intelligence Branch), *Narrative of the Field Operations Connected with the Zulu War of 1879* (London: Greenhill Books; 1989 reprint of 1881 volume), pp. 145–6.

21 'A Sheffield Soldier's Letter from the Cape', *Sheffield Daily Telegraph*, 10 March 1879, p. 3; see also 'Letter from an Abergavenny Man', *South Wales Weekly*

Telegram, 28 March 1879, p. 3; 'Letter from a Liverpool Volunteer in Zululand', *Liverpool Mercury*, 22 March 1879, p. 6.

22 'A Voice from the Dead', *Western Daily Mercury*, 27 March 1879, p. 5.

23 R. W. F. Droogleever, *The Road to ISANDHLWANA: Colonel Anthony Durnford in Natal and Zululand 1873–1879* (London: Greenhill Books, 1992), pp. 188–93; Laband (ed.), *Lord Chelmsford's Zululand Campaign*, p. 73.

24 Jackson, *Isandhlwana*; Knight, *The Sun Turned Black*, chs 5–9; Droogleever, *The Road to ISANDHLWANA*, pp. 200–31; P. S. Thompson, *The Natal Native Contingent in the Anglo-Zulu War 1879* (Pietermaritzburg: University of Natal, 1997), pp. 103–70.

25 RRWM, 6/A/4, Capt. W. Penn Symons, 'Report on Isandhlwana', 1879, p. 63.

26 Compare 'The War at the Cape', *Daily News*, 24 February 1879, p. 5, with 'Mr H. C. Young and Isandhlwana', *Natal Mercury*, 16 May 1879, p. 3; Knight, *The Sun Turned Black*, pp. 141–2.

27 Jackson, *Isandhlwana*, pp. 37–40; and 'The First Battalion, Twenty-Fourth Regiment, Marches to Isandhlwana', in I. Knight (ed.), *There Will Be an Awful Row at Home About This*, special publication no. 2 (Victorian Military Society, 1979), pp. 3–16; see also Clarke, *Invasion of Zululand*, pp. 72, 75.

28 'The Responsibility for Isandula', *Bristol Times and Mirror*, 6 June 1879, p. 3.

29 'Letters of an 'Eye-Witness'', *Evening Standard*, 15 March 1879, p. 5; and letter of Mr Muirhead, *Staffordshire Advertiser*, 22 March 1879, p. 6. See also PRO, WO 33/34, pp. 257–8, 291 and Droogleever, *Road to ISANDHLWANA*, p. 205.

30 'The Zulu War', *The Times*, 2 April 1879, p. 11; Colonel G. Paton *et al.* (eds), *Historical Records of the 24th Regiment, from its Formation, in 1689* (London: Simpkin, Marshall, 1892), p. 230; Jackson, *Isandhlwana*, pp. 10–12; Morris, *Washing of the Spears*, pp. 333–4.

31 Emery, *Red Soldier*, pp. 136–8.

32 'The Battle of Isandula', *Montgomeryshire Express*, 1 April 1879, p. 3.

33 'The Zulu War', *Newcastle Courant*, 14 March 1879, p. 3.

34 'Heroic Conduct of Army Medical Officers', *Fleetwood Chronicle*, 14 March 1879, p. 3.

35 'Narrative of a Survivor at Isandula', *Bristol Times and Mirror*, 13 March 1879, p. 3.

36 'Battle of Isandula', p. 3.

37 'Strange Statement by an Officer', *Western Morning News*, 7 April 1879, p. 3.

38 'A Manchester Soldier's Experiences in Zululand', *Yorkshire Post*, 3 April 1879, p. 3; Pte J. Powell in 'Letters from Welsh Soldiers in Zululand', *Carmarthen Journal*, 28 March 1879, p. 6.

39 'Letter from an Abergavenny Man', *Abergavenny Chronicle*, 29 March 1879, p. 3.

40 Pte T. Harding, Bandsman R. Wilson, Ptes E. Herbert and C. Lewis in 'Letters from Merthyr Men', *Western Mail*, 25 March 1879, p. 3; 'Letters from Warwickshire Men', *Birmingham Daily Post*, 24 March 1879, p. 8; 'Interesting Letters from Local Soldiers' and 'Letters from Local Men', *South Wales Daily News*, 24 March 1879, p. 3.

41 Ptes F. Ward and R. Taylor in *South Wales Daily News*, 9 April 1879, p. 3; and 'Letter from a Briton Ferry Man at Rorke's Drift', *Western Mail*, 4 April 1879, p. 3.

42 'The Zulu War', *Folkestone Chronicle*, 29 March 1879, p. 7, see also Pte J. James, 'Letters from Monmouthshire Men', *South Wales Weekly Telegram*, 4 April 1879, p. 7.

43 *Folkestone Chronicle*, 29 March 1879, p. 7; Capt. Church and Ptes W. McNulty, W. Rees and A. Kelly in 'Echoes from the Front', *Evening Standard*, 14 April 1879, p. 2; *North Wales Guardian*, 5 April 1879, p. 8; 'Letter from Another "Missing" Soldier', *Western Mail*, 9 April 1879, p. 3.

44 NAM, Acc. 8401/62/2, Pte Mason to Cary *et al.*, 8 February 1879; *South Wales Daily News*, 27 March 1879, p. 3; 'Letter from a Blaenavon Man', *Abergavenny Chronicle*, 12 April 1879, p. 4; 'Letters from Warwickshire Men', p. 8; 'The Massacre at Isandula', *Somerset County Herald*, 5 April 1879, p. 2.

45 Emery, *Red Soldier*, pp. 95, 140; Knight, *The Sun Turned Black*, pp. 162–3.

[55]

46 *South Wales Daily News*, 28 March 1879, p. 3; see also Sgt Pilcher and J. James in *Western Daily Mercury*, 19 March 1879, p. 3; and 'Letters from Merthyr Soldiers at Rorke's Drift', *Western Mail*, 24 March 1879, p. 3.

47 'Letter from a Plymouth Soldier', *Western Daily Mercury*, 25 March 1879, p. 3; see also Ptes T. Davies and W. Thomas, *South Wales Daily News*, 27 March 1879, p. 3.

48 Ptes J. A. Hancock, G. Holly and J. French in *South Wales Daily News*, 27 March 1879, p. 3; 'Letters from Monmouthshire Men', p. 7; and 'The Battle of Isandula', *Western Mail*, 29 March 1879, p. 3.

49 'Letter from an Abercarn Man in the 24th Regiment', *Western Mail*, 11 March 1879, p. 3; for claims as high as 5,000–8,000 dead, see Pte J. Williams, 'Letter from T. Williams of the 2–24th Regt', *South Wales Daily News*, 8 March 1879, p. 3, and Ptes L. Cummings and T. Harding, 'Letters from Merthyr Men', *Western Mail*, 25 March 1879, p. 3; whereas recent estimates indicate about 1,000 dead and many more wounded: Knight, *The Sun Turned Black*, p. 156.

50 'Letters from Merthyr Men', p. 3; see also Pte W. Light, 'Bristolians in Zululand', *Bristol Observer*, 5 April 1879, p. 4; 'A Letter from Private Parry, a Merthyr Man', *South Wales Daily Telegram*, 16 April 1879, p. 3; Sgt E. Daly, 'Letters from the Front', *Dover Express*, 28 March 1879, p. 3.

51 'The Fight at Rorke's Drift', *Warwick and Warwickshire Advertiser*, 5 April 1879, p. 3. In places the contours of the ground made this a more formidable obstacle, but the defensive arrangements had weaknesses: Knight, *The Sun Turned Black*, pp. 167–70; Bennett, *Eyewitness in Zululand*, pp. 95–6; PRO, WO 32/7737, Lt J. Chard to Col. Glyn, 25 January 1879.

52 'Letters from Local Men', *South Wales Daily News*, 25 March 1879, p. 3.This is almost certainly the 'Private Thomas Stevens' listed by Holme in *The Noble 24th*, p. 362: the spelling of 'Stephens' is the same as on the 'Chard Roll' and the letter was sent to his parents at the same address – Robin Hood Inn, Dowlais.

53 'The Disaster at Rorke's Drift', *Weekly News* (Dundee), 8 March 1879, p. 5; see also Holme, *The Noble 24th*, p. 315.

54 'Fight at Rorke's Drift', p. 3.

55 NAM, Acc. No. 2001/03/73, Sgt J. S. Hooper, typescript (TS) diary, 20 January 1879; see also Capt. H. G. MacGregor to Col. Home, 14 February 1879 in Clarke, *Zululand at War*, p. 145.

56 PP, *Further Correspondence, SA*, C 2260, pp. 4–5; see also 'Letter from One of the Naval Brigade', *Salisbury Journal*, 8 March 1879, p. 2; REL, Acc. 11315, 'Recollections of Main', 125.

57 NAM, Acc. No. 2001/03/73, Hooper, diary, 22 January 1879; Emery, *Red Soldier*, pp. 185–6; S. Iggulden (Royal Marines), 'Letter from One of the Besieged Garrison at Ekowe', *South Wales Weekly Telegram*, 23 May 1879, p. 3.

58 'The Zulu War', *Bradford Daily Telegraph*, 28 April 1879, p. 3; PP, *Further Correspondence, SA*, C 2260, p. 5.

59 REL, Acc. 11315, 'Recollections of Main', 127–8; see also Emery, *Red Soldier*, p. 185; PP, *Further Correspondence, SA*, C 2260, p. 10; and 'Letter from One of the Naval Brigade', p. 2.

60 NAM, Acc. No. 2001/03/73, Hooper, diary, 22 January 1879.

61 H. O'Cleary, 'Facing the Zulus', in Small (ed.), *Told from the Ranks*, p. 168.

62 REL, Acc. 11315, 'Recollections of Main', 132–33; Clarke, *Zululand at War*, p. 141.

63 *Bradford Daily Telegraph*, 28 April 1879, p. 3; see also NAM, Acc. No. 2001/03/73, Hooper, diary, 3 February 1879; Clarke, *Zululand at War*, p. 145.

64 'Letter from Lieut. A. V. Payne', *Citizen*, 21 April 1879, p. 4.

65 NAM, Acc. No. 2001/03/73, Hooper, diary, 5 and 26 March 1879: on food, see Hooper's diary entries for 3, 8 and 12 February 1879; water, *Bradford Daily Telegraph*, 28 April 1879, p. 3; and the effects of fever, 'Letter from Lieut A. V. Payne', p. 4.

66 PRO, WO 33/34, p. 323; Morris, *Washing of the Spears*, p. 473.

67 Sgt A. Booth to his wife, 14 March 1879, in R. Hope, *The Zulu War and the 80th Regiment of Foot* (Leek: Churnet Valley Books, 1997), pp. 94–7; Emery, *Marching*

Over Africa, pp. 72–4; see also 'Interesting Account of the Intombi Disaster', *Manchester Courier*, 24 April 1879, p. 8.

68 Hope, *The Zulu War*, pp. 74, 77–8, 94.

69 'A Sheffield Soldier with Colonel Wood's Column', *Sheffield Daily Telegraph*, 26 March 1879, p. 3; see also 'Soldiers' Letters from the Front', *Liverpool Mercury*, 1 March 1879, p. 7; and 'Letters from a Beverley Gentleman with Colonel Wood's Column', *Yorkshire Post*, 24 April 1879, p. 6.

70 'Letter from a Soldier (A Native of Crieff) Serving in Colonel Wood's Column', *Strathearn Herald*, 5 April 1879, p. 2.

71 'The Zulu War', *Manchester Guardian*, 2 May 1879, p. 8.

72 'With Colonel Wood', *Bristol Times and Mirror*, 9 April 1879, p. 3; 'A Sheffield Soldier in Zululand', *Sheffield Daily Telegraph*, 22 April 1879, p. 3; 'With Colonel Wood in Zululand', *Liverpool Mercury*, 5 April 1879, p. 6.

73 'A Combatant's Account of the Fighting at Zhlobane [sic] and Kambula', *Tiverton Times*, 20 May 1879, p. 8.

74 'The Battle of Kambula', *Lancaster Guardian*, 31 May 1879, p. 3; see also I. Knight, *Great Zulu Battles 1838–1906* (London: Arms & Armour Press, 1998), p. 146.

75 'A Manchester Soldier's Account of Col. Wood's Victory', *Manchester Courier*, 14 May 1879, p. 6.

76 'The Fight at Kambula', *Liverpool Mercury*, 22 May 1879, p. 7.

77 'Battle of Kambula', p. 3.

78 'Fight at Kambula', p. 7; see also 'Battle of Kambula', p. 3.

79 'Battle of Kambula', p. 3.

80 'Letter from Zululand', *Ayr Advertiser*, 26 June 1879, p. 5.

81 'A Combatant's Account of the Fighting at Zhlobane and Kambula', p. 8.

82 'Battle of Kambula', p. 3 and 'Letters from an Abergavenny Man', *Abergavenny Chronicle*, 10 May 1879, p. 3.

83 Emery quotes from two letters of Commeline in *Red Soldier*, pp. 56–60, and another three in 'At War with the Zulus 1879', *REJ*, 96 (1982), 33–9; but a more extensive set of correspondence can be found in the *Citizen* (Gloucester), 3, 22, 25 March, 19 and 22 April, 19 and 24 May, 14 and 26 June, 15 and 25 July, 1879.

84 'Letter from a Plymouth Man', *Western Daily Mercury*, 26 March 1879, p. 4; 'The Disaster at Isandula', *Morning Advertiser*, 11 April 1879, p. 6; see also Clarke, *Zululand at War*, pp. 120–9; Emery, *Red Soldier*, pp. 223–4.

85 'Letter from Lieutenant Commeline', *Citizen*, 24 May 1879, p. 4.

86 'Reinforcements for the Cape' and 'The 91st Highlanders at the Cape', *Bridge of Allan Reporter*, 8 March 1879, p. 2, and 19 April 1879, p 3; Northamptonshire Regimental Museum Collection (NRMC), 397, Cpl W. Roe, TS diary, para. 10.

87 'A Clay Cross Soldier in Zululand', *Sheffield Daily Telegraph*, 21 June 1879, p. 3.

88 'Letter from a Sheffield Soldier' in *ibid.*; 'Sheffield Soldiers in Zululand', *Sheffield Daily Telegraph*, 17 May 1879, p. 3.

89 'A Sheffield Soldier in Zululand', 17 June 1879, p. 3; see also 'With the 91st at the Cape', *Bridge of Allan Reporter*, 5 July 1879, p. 3.

90 Argyll and Sutherland Highlanders Museum (ASHM), N-C91.1, Capt. W. R. H. Crauford to father, 4 April 1879; see also 'Letter to a Fleetwood Gentleman', *Fleetwood Chronicle*, 30 May 1879, p. 6; *Irish Times*, 23 May 1879, p. 5; *Bridge of Allan Reporter*, 10 May 1879, p. 3, and 24 May 1879, p. 3.

91 'A Sheffield Soldier in Zululand', p. 3; *Bridge of Allan Reporter*, 10 May 1879, p. 3.

92 'Letter to a Fleetwood Gentleman', p. 6; see also Pte., 60th Rifles, in *Lancaster Guardian*, 28 June 1879, p. 7.

93 ASHM, N-C91.GOR.W, R. Wolrige-Gordon, diary, 2 and 4 June 1879; 'A Visit to Isandhana [sic]', *Chichester Express*, 22 July 1879, p. 3; see also 'The Late Prince Imperial', *Manchester Guardian*, 17 July 1879, p. 6; Sgt J. F. Bolshaw in *Northampton Mercury*, 26 July 1879, p. 3; and Morris, *Washing of the Spears*, pp. 530–1.

94 'A Thrilling Incident in the Zulu War', *Sheffield Daily Telegraph*, 24 July 1879, p. 3; ASHM, N-C91.GOR.W, Wolrige-Gordon, diary, 6, 21 June and 1 July 1879.

95 *Ayr Advertiser*, 24 July 1879, p. 4, 14 August 1879, p. 5, and 11 September 1879, p. 5.

96 'The Expedition to Ulundi', *Eastern Province Herald*, 18 July 1879, p. 5.
97 *Ayr Advertiser*, 14 August 1879, p. 5; see also ASHM, N-C91.1, Crauford to father, 21 May 1879, and to Carry, 28 June 1879.
98 'A Soldier's Description of the Battle of Ulundi', *Manchester Weekly Times*, 23 August 1879, p. 8; 'The Battle of Ulundi', *Manchester Courier*, 10 September 1879, p. 3.
99 ASHM, N-C91.GOR.W, Wolrige-Gordon, diary, 1 July 1879.
100 'The Battle of Ulundi', p. 3; see also J. Laband, *The Battle of Ulundi* (Pietermaritzburg: Shuter & Shooter, 1988), pp. 16–18.
101 Laband, *Battle of Ulundi*, p. 21; 'A Soldier's Description of the Battle of Ulundi', p. 8; 'The Battle of Ulundi', *Manchester Guardian*, 6 September 1879, p. 7.
102 'A Soldier's Description of the Battle of Ulundi', p. 8.
103 'Before and After Ulundi', *Chichester Express*, 16 September 1879, p. 3.
104 *Manchester Guardian*, 6 September 1879, p. 7; 'The 21st Royal Scots Fusiliers at the Battle of Ulundi', *Ayr Advertiser*, 28 August 1879, p. 4.
105 *Manchester Courier*, 10 September 1879, p. 3; *Manchester Guardian*, 6 September 1879, p. 7; PP, *Further Correspondence, SA*, C 2482 (1880), L, p. 67.
106 *Ibid.*, p. 65; NRMC, 397, Roe, diary, paras 67–8; 'The Victory, Capture and Burning of Ulundi', *Ayr Advertiser*, 11 September 1879, p. 5.
107 'Before and After Ulundi', p. 3.
108 *Ayr Advertiser*, 28 August 1879, p. 4; *Manchester Guardian*, 6 September 1879, p. 7; ASHM, N-C91. GOR.W, Wolrige-Gordon, diary, 4 July 1879.
109 'The Battle of Ulundi', *Yorkshire Post*, 9 September 1879, p. 8.
110 ASHM, N-C91.GOR.W, Wolrige-Gordon, diary, 4 July 1879.
111 'A Letter from Zululand', *Bristol Times and Mirror*, 1 September 1879, p. 3; 'Statements of Prisoners Captured at Ulundi', *Brecon County Times*, 23 August 1879, p. 6.
112 *Ayr Advertiser*, 11 September 1879, p. 5; Col. G. Hamilton-Browne, *A Lost Legionary in South Africa* (London: T. Werner Laurie, 1912), pp. 207 and 213.
113 'What the Soldiers Think of Lord Chelmsford', *Sheffield Daily Telegraph*, 23 August 1879, p. 2; see also *Ayr Advertiser*, 28 August 1879, p. 4, and Lt-Col. A. Harness, 'The Zulu Campaign from a Military Perspective', *Fraser's Magazine*, 101 (1880), 477–88.
114 Laband (ed.), *Lord Chelmsford's Zululand Campaign*, pp. xvii–xix, xxxii and xlv–xlvi.
115 *Manchester Guardian*, 6 September 1879, p. 7; Laband, *Battle of Ulundi*, pp. 45–8; Major R. Marter, *The Capture of Cetywayo* (Wokingham: R. J. Wyatt, n.d.).

CHAPTER THREE

Battling the Boers

In superseding Chelmsford as GOC, South Africa, Sir Garnet Wolseley assumed wide-ranging powers as both high commissioner in south-eastern Africa and governor of Natal and the Transvaal. He sought to impose a settlement upon both Zululand and the neighbouring Trans-vaal (the former South African Republic that Britain had annexed in 1877). Setting aside the confederation plans of Sir Bartle Frere, he resolved that Zululand (other than the disputed territory left in Boer hands) should be ruled by thirteen minor chiefs.[1] He then moved into the Transvaal to restore British prestige by overthrowing Sekhukhune, whom the Boers had failed to defeat in 1876. The strategy had only short-term impact and, after barely a year, 4,000 Boers at their national convention voted to restore the South African Republic, by force of arms, if necessary. In the ensuing conflict, the First Anglo-Boer War (1880–81), soldiers had their first encounter with a well-armed African foe, who was mobile, adept at skirmishing and capable of conducting siege warfare. Some 1,800 soldiers served in the Transvaal and all were besieged in isolated garrisons throughout the war, with few managing to send letters beyond their beleaguered posts. Even the relief force from Natal struggled to maintain its line of communications, and few war correspondents reached the front (none covered the first two bat-tles and only three observed the final battle at Majuba). As the war lasted little more than two months, contained a series of unrelieved disasters, and divided British opinion about its propriety, it aroused scant enthusiasm at home. Indeed the newspapers, at least latterly, were preoccupied with the assassination of the Tsar and the death of Benjamin Disraeli.[2]

To attack Sekhukhune, Wolseley assembled a formidable composite force, comprising the 2/21st and the 94th (2/Connaught Rangers), with two companies of the 80th, four guns, a party of Royal Engineers with explosives, a troop of mounted volunteers under Commandant Fereira,

another mounted troop of volunteers and natives under Major Carrington, and about 8,000 Swazis. As the force advanced into the eastern Transvaal, it endured extreme heat and had to move through thick
bush. The sappers, wrote Commeline, were 'employed from dawn till
dark', cutting pathways, preparing drifts for ox-driven wagons, and
organising the construction of forts: by comparison, he added,'the Zulu
war was a joke'.[3] On 28 November Lieutenant-Colonel Baker Russell
launched a two-phased assault on Sekhukhune's stronghold, employing the Carrington Horse to attack the town from the north and the
Fereira Horse to attack the kraal from the south, while the Swazis
seized the flat-topped mountain above. Once those objectives were
secured, British regulars attacked Sekhukhuni's 'Fighting Kop', a separate rocky salient some 200 feet high that overlooked the town and
kraal. As the kopje was honeycombed with caves and crannies, some
of which were protected by stone walls, artillery proved relatively inef-
fectual, forcing the infantry to storm the kopje and take terrace after
terrace in fierce hand-to-hand fighting.[4] Even so, many of the Pedi
would not yield, prompting the sappers to spend an hour-and-a-half
placing charges of gun cotton into as many of the caves as possible.
Commeline ruefully reflected that 'they did not kill very many . . . yet
wounded many and from the dust and smoke produced terrible thirst,
and reduced the garrison to a most pitiable condition'. The attacking
force had suffered, too:

> We had been fighting for seven hours and our casualties are very heavy,
> probably 200 is under the mark as the Swazis lost a great number . . .
> Almost all the wounds have been inflicted at close quarters, they are as
> a rule serious and probably the death toll will yet be considerably
> swelled. As a battle Ulundi could not be compared to this one where we
> were the attackers.[5]

Lieutenant-Colonel Philip R. Anstruther, (94th), who commanded the
fight in the valley, recalled that the Pedi ensured that 'I had a very
rough time of it the whole night. As the beggars kept trying to bolt out
of the caves . . . we were firing hard the whole night through'. He also
reckoned that the Swazis were responsible for much of the carnage –
they were 'grand fellows and most picturesque' (wearing 'leopard skins
and huge bunches of black feathers'), but fearful demons ('they don't
spare any living thing, man, woman, child'): 'I don't know what we
could have done without them. You see a British soldier is all very
well, but he is no match in moving about hills – for these naked savages.'[6] Once the Pedi surrendered on the following day, the British had
to protect them from 'the fury of the Swazis'.[7] Three days later
Sekhukhune was captured.

Wolseley hoped that the parading of Sekhukhune through the streets of Pretoria would overawe the Boers, whom he disparaged as 'in some respects far inferior to the Zulu, and . . . certainly the most ignorant & bigotted [sic] & small-minded of white men'.[8] Anstruther agreed; he thought that the victory would have 'an immense effect' on the Boers, whom he regarded as 'nasty, cowardly brutes'.[9] Corporal William Roe (58th) observed how 'thousands of people' came out to see Sekhukhune as he was escorted through Pretoria on 9 December 1879, and noted that many cheered Wolseley when he later addressed the townsfolk. Roe thought that this display of force, followed by a field day, the award of a VC to Lieutenant Darcy of the Light Horse and the arrest of two Boer spokesmen would settle the 'Dutch question'. Given the relatively large number of experienced soldiers still in the Transvaal, Roe maintained that if the Boers 'had started to fight, we should show them no mercy at all'.[10]

Within four months Wolseley returned to England, claiming: 'The quiet and settled aspect of the Transvaal is even to me a matter of surprise: I attribute it greatly to the arrests I made, and to the show of force.'[11] He was replaced in July 1880 by another Asante veteran, Sir George Pomeroy Colley. Meanwhile the Boers' hopes of independence had been raised by the election of a Liberal Government under William E. Gladstone in April 1880, only to be dashed by the inability of the cabinet, split between Whigs and Radicals, to devise an agreed policy. Thereafter Boer grievances mounted over the revenue-raising activities of Sir W. Owen Lanyon, the administrator of the Transvaal, and the behaviour of the British soldiery. The British forces in the Transvaal were reduced when Wolseley departed, and were cut again under Colley until he had only 1,800 men, with no cavalry and only four guns. The soldiers were also widely dispersed in six isolated posts.[12] As the men endured a dreary and monotonous existence under canvas in all seasons, bereft of a varied diet, many found solace in drink and some sought the charms of Boer women. Desertions reached unprecedented numbers as soldiers were tempted by the propinquity of the diamond fields and mining interests in the Orange Free State. A Royal Scots Fusilier explained: 'Life here is provocative of every vice, not for vice's sake, but by way of protest against the aggressive morality not only of the Boers, but also of the British who are only different from them in name and birthplace. They have all the narrowness of Scottish elders without their good qualities.'[13]

The rebellion was triggered by local events, namely the attempt of the authorities to recover 'legal costs' by selling the wagon of Piet Beziudenhout at Potchefstroom after a dispute about his tax arrears. When local Boers blocked the public auction (11 November), Lanyon despatched a field force with two 9-pounder guns to aid the civil power at Potchefstroom, without anticipating 'any serious trouble'.[14] The Boers, however, brought forward their national convention from January to December, and, on 13 December, demanded a restoration of the republic. They established a provisional capital at Heidelberg, where a 'Triumvirate' – Paul Kruger, Piet Joubert and Marthinus Pretorius – was to organise a government. With about 7,000 Boers liable for active service, the first shots were fired at the garrison at Potchefstroom and, three days later, shots were exchanged near Pretoria.[15]

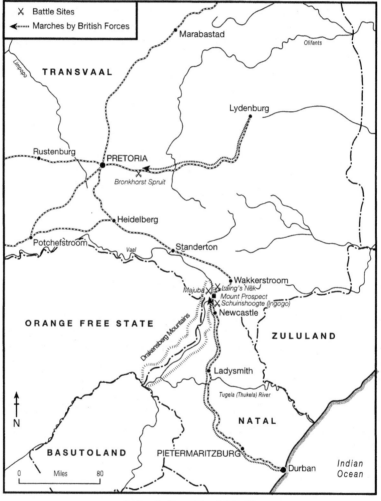

3 Anglo-Boer War, 1880–81

The first engagement of the war occurred at about 12.30 p.m. on 20 December 1880 nearly two miles from Bronkhorst Spruit, where a column of the 94th, marching to Pretoria, was intercepted by a Boer commando led by Commandant Frans Joubert. The column, under the command of Anstruther, included a convoy of thirty-four wagons stretching out over a mile on the road, accompanied by 268 men of all ranks, 3 women and 2 children. En route since 5 December, the column marched with little sense of apprehension – only 2 mounted scouts preceded it, the regimental band about 40-strong and unarmed was playing at its head, and a rearguard of twenty men was about 200–300 yards behind the last of the wagons. Conductor Ralph Egerton (Army Service Corps), who was one of the more lucid commentators, had ridden ahead with the colonel and his adjutant, Lieutenant H. A. C. Harrison, to select a camping ground. When the band ceased playing, they turned around to see 150 armed, mounted Boers, spaced about ten paces apart, along a ridge on the left-hand side of the road. Egerton rode to meet a Boer horseman under a flag of truce, and took a sealed despatch from him to the colonel, who had dismounted. The despatch stated that the Transvaal had been declared a republic, and that any advance by the column beyond the spruit would be interpreted as a declaration of war. Given two minutes in which to reply, Anstruther insisted that he must follow orders and proceed towards Pretoria. The two parties returned to their respective forces, but the Boers, who had filtered through thorn bushes to about 200 yards from the column, opened fire before Anstruther rejoined his column. 'The fire of the Boers', wrote Egerton, 'was directed on the officers, oxen, and ammunition wagons, the latter being denoted by a red flag.'[16]

The opening volleys caught the column before it could deploy, hitting soldiers lolling on the tops of three wagons as well as the unarmed cooks, grooms, bandsmen and prisoners seeking ammunition, and all but three of the rear guard.[17] After a fire-fight of only fifteen minutes in which fifty-seven officers and men were killed and another 100, including a woman, were wounded, the column surrendered. Many, like the colonel, had suffered severe and multiple gunshot wounds – an average of five wounds per man – as calculated by Dr Harvey Crow, who came out from Pretoria to tend the wounded. Another twenty men would die of their wounds, including Anstruther after his leg was amputated.[18] In the immediate aftermath few of the survivors could explain the debacle other than by claiming that the Boers had carefully planned the ambush (which seemed plausible), and that they had an overwhelming advantage in numbers (which was less likely).[19] One of the survivors recalled that the Boers took advantage of any available cover – 'a sort of "little bush", and an incline in their favour', and that they 'told us afterwards they had everything arranged beforehand, the distance having been ascertained exactly'.[20] Although the 94th, as Private Thomas Crann recalled, had tried to follow the colonel's injunction and kept firing, they soon found their ammunition running low (as they were carrying only thirty and not seventy rounds of ammunition per man).[21] Egerton recognised, too, that their firing was relatively ineffective, and a corporal explained that the soldiers 'in their hurry sighted their rifles at 650 yards'.[22] E. H. Brett, a wagon master, almost certainly exaggerated when he claimed that the Boers had suffered significant casualties – twenty-seven dead and 'a large number of wounded' – Egerton saw one dead and five wounded, while Crow counted only ten dead horses 'close to the camp' (the Boers claimed that two commandos died and five were wounded).[23]

If the British were appalled at the spectacle of the Boers riffling through the pockets of the dead, they appreciated the permission granted them to pitch their tents, care for the wounded and bury their dead. Egerton and Sergeant Bradley were also allowed to seek further medical assistance from Pretoria (enabling Egerton to smuggle out the regimental colours, to the immense relief of the dying Anstruther).[24] The survivors realised that the Boers had not only prevented a concentration of soldiers at Pretoria but had captured valuable arms, ammunition and wagons. All soldiers, other than the thirty left to tend the injured, were taken prisoner and others were removed to Heidelberg when they recovered from their wounds. Dr Crow, who spent three months tending the wounded, expressed admiration for the calm and courageous way that Anstruther met his death, for the many acts of kindness by local Boers and for the unremitting efforts of Dr Ward, the regimental surgeon, and Mrs Smith on behalf of the wounded. However severe the loss to the 94th and to British 'prestige', Crowe could not blame 'our men', who 'had no cover at all – nor time to get under cover, but had to lie on a wide level road . . .'.[25] Their uniforms, as Lieutenant J. J. F. Hume later conceded, had compounded this vulnerability, namely 'scarlet jackets, white helmets, white pipe-clayed belts and equipment straps, pouches, etc.'.[26]

Colley recognised that the disaster of the 94th had 'changed the whole aspect of affairs. The loss of 250 men out of our small garrison was no trifling one, and the moral effect, of course, much greater.'[27] He feared lest the conflict would precipitate a wider war between the two white races in South Africa, and that the Transvaal Boers would attract support from the Orange Free State and the Dutch populations of Cape Colony and Natal. Hence, in planning to relieve the British garrisons, he resolved to assemble a field force without enrolling volunteers from Natal and Kimberley but insisted upon the inclusion of cavalry (in case a guerrilla war ensued) and artillery to exploit the 'moral effect which guns have on the Boers generally'.[28] Having chosen Newcastle, a small town in northern Natal as a place of assembly, he brought together 1,474 of all ranks, including a strong body of infantry (five companies of the 58th, five of the 3/60th Rifles and a draft of the 2/21st), a mounted squadron (and some mounted Natal Police), a Naval Brigade (with two Gatling guns and three 24-pounder rocket tubes), and six guns (four 9-pounders and two 7-pounders).[29]

Delays in procuring transport and in moving soldiers across rain-sodden terrain prevented the Natal field force from assembling fully before 19 January. A Rifleman recalled that the march was a 'a hard dragging' ordeal, with the men pulling 'mules and wagons along by sheer force'.[30] Spirits improved when they arrived at Newcastle: soldiers cheered Colley's speech after a parade of the field force, while Lieutenant Percy Scrope Marling (3/60th Rifles) wrote that the Government should not 'show any misplaced weakness as regards the Boers, they have committed the most cruel & cold blooded murders & ought to be punished accordingly. They have treated the Kaffirs also in the most brutal manner'.[31] Even when the field force began its advance towards the Natal–Transvaal border on 24 January, it could move only a few miles each day, struggling across drifts and up a rocky hill known as Schuinshoogte before reaching Mount Prospect on 26 January. Piet Joubert had anticipated this incursion, moving his forces inside Natal as early as 1 January and, when he learned of Colley's advance from Newcastle, moving forward to occupy the heights above the key pass of Laing's Nek along the road from Mount Prospect.

'Torrents of rain', as described by Lance-Sergeant W. J. Morris (58th),[32] prevented any advance on 27 January, but, on the following day, Colley ordered an advance with four companies of Rifles, five of the 58th, the mounted squadron, most of the Naval Brigade, some supporting troops and about fifty mounted police (the remainder guarded the camp). At 9.30 a.m. he ordered the shelling of the Boer positions with rockets and the 9-pounders firing shrapnel. Although Joubert admitted that the Boers 'suffered heavily' from the bombardments, their losses were many fewer than some British infantry anticipated.[33] Accordingly, when the mounted squadron of 100 men, led by Major William Brownlow and Troop Sergeant-Major Lunny (King's Dragoon Guards), charged up Table Hill – on the left of the Boer position – the leading troopers encountered volleys of rifle fire. All observers praised the 'splendid' charge with Brownlow and Lunny (the latter was killed in the attack), exhorting their men onwards, but the squadron soon retreated (with 17 killed, wounded or missing, and 32 horses lost).[34] The charge had foundered, in the opinion of Sergeant Jeremiah Madden

(King's Dragoon Guards), because the squadron was a mixed body 'made up of K.D.G.'s and transport train' (and some mounted infantry), the climb was very steep ('the true summit ... was invisible to us'), and the Boers opened fire while they were 'wheeling'. So,

> before the left troop had completed its movement to bring us again in line, the order to charge was heard. In a moment we were face to face with the Boers, who fired sharp at us. The Sergeant-Major, with his revolver, got right in amongst the men, and shot one dead, wounding another with his pistol, when he fell – horse and man shot down together.[35]

The 58th, led by Colonel Deane, struggled up the steep open spur of the hill and came under fire from front and right (where Commandant Bassa's picket provided enfilade fire after thwarting the mounted troops). The letter written by Morris, much of which was reproduced by Emery, exaggerated the odds against the 58th who, he said, were 'outnumbered by five to one' and made claims about a final charge that were at variance with Colley's official report ('when the men got near the top they were too fatigued and breathless for a charge').[36] Private M. M. Tuck, 58th, confirmed that an order to charge was made but as the men were 'so much exhausted it could not be done to any good advantage'.[37] Nevertheless, Morris endorsed the official report by lauding the gallantry of Colonel Deane before he fell mortally wounded and by praising the resolve of the Boers, who charged the British soldiers at short range and harried them in their retreat. He noted that the Boers were 'dead nuts' in targeting officers and non-commissioned officers, and identified Sergeant Bridgestock as the soldier who saved the colours.[38]

Private Joseph Venables, (58th), who was captured after the attack, gave another perspective:

> Our path was through the grass, and the march very exhausting. (The incline was 1 in 15) ... The advance was steadily continued, but the men were teaming from perspiration, which ran into their eyes. We got flank fire from a hollow, and half a company was thrown back to check it, but was at once shot away, but one man standing when I saw it. Then we met the enemy almost muzzle to muzzle, with some of the guns all but crossed ... I reckon the force opposed to us at 80 men. The extended companies fought very well, but the exhaustion of the men, and the deadly accurate fire, forced them down. An immense number fell, and I was all but alone when the artillery re-opened, hurting many of our wounded in the attempt to check the Boers now charging and shooting down the retreating companies.[39]

Riflemen looked askance at the 58th being 'literally slaughtered' and the 'regular butchery' as they reached the summit and then retreated.[40]

Although Sergeant Henry Coombs (Army Hospital Corps) was reason-ably accurate in his estimate – 'We lost 70 men killed, seven officers killed, and 119 men wounded' (some of these men later died of their wounds) – he thought that the Boers might have suffered 'between 400 and 500 casualties' (whereas Joubert reported losses of only 'twenty-four of our best men').[41]

In official correspondence Colley remained resolutely confident that the 'political effect' of Laing's Nek would not be great: the Boers, he affirmed, would soon tire of the war, and the arrival of large reinforce-ments from India and England would protect Natal. Privately, he con-ceded that the repulse 'had a bad effect, both in prolonging the investment of our garrisons and in giving further encouragement to the Boers'.[42] The vulnerability of Colley's camp at Mount Prospect was soon exposed by a Boer attempt on 7 February 1881 to intercept the mail along his line of communications to Newcastle. On the following day, Colley led a small column of five companies of the 60th Rifles, a detachment of 38 mounted men, 2 field and 2 mountain guns with some medical support to patrol the road for part of the way. After 5 miles the column reached the Ingogo River where Colley detached one company and the two 7-pounder guns to guard his retreat, while the remainder crossed the river. Within another 3 miles, scouts encoun-tered a large body of Boers which Colley decided to engage from the bolder-strewn plateau at Schuinshoogte. An officer of the Rifles recog-nised that the 'position was much too large for our numbers, which were only 290 all told . . .'. Outnumbered (by possibly 300 Boers, later reinforced to between 800 and 1,000) and almost surrounded, he added: 'Half an hour after the fight began everyone considered the fight as hopeless . . .' because the Boers

are the perfection of skirmishers, taking advantage of every atom of cover, and shooting with the greatest accuracy and precision. Before the first five minutes were over the guns were firing case. This will give you an idea how rapidly the Boers advanced . . . They directed their fire prin-cipally at the guns, and very soon they had killed every man but one at one of the guns, including poor Captain Greer . . .

The action commenced at twelve and went on until eight p.m. We were exposed not only to frontal fire but also to enfilade and reverse – in fact, there was a perfect hail of bullets coming over us from all four sides for eight hours . . . The whole of our men behaved like heroes. They were as cool and well disciplined as if they had been at a review, never throw-ing a shot away for we had no reserve ammunition.[43]

Once the Boers withdrew, soldiers gathered the wounded together (about 50 per cent of the fighting strength), with many, like Lieutenant Haworth, suffering from multiple gunshot wounds. 'We had been 12 hours without food', wrote Coombs, 'and were quite tired and worn out',[44] but, as only a withdrawal could avert the prospect of a surrender, Colley ordered a retreat at about 10 p.m., leaving the wounded behind. As an officer of the Rifles admitted, this seemed a 'dreadful' decision: it was, however, 'imperative' as the column lacked either ambulances or a water cart and had only one doctor. The officer was nearly drowned crossing the swollen Ingogo (an officer and seven men drowned either in the retreat or in returning to assist the wounded); and he encountered further difficulties: 'I was in command of the advanced guard, and it was very hard work finding the road, for there was a tremendous storm, and the night was as dark as pitch. This was a good thing, as it concealed our movements from the Boers.'[45] Retrieving the guns became a desperate ordeal, 'as there were only twelve horses left, and two of them were wounded. One gun came in with four horses, one of which was shot through the knee. Going up the hill the horses were taken out, and our fellows pulled them up the three-mile hill with drag-ropes.' After twenty-one hours the Rifles returned to camp, having fought for eight hours and marched for 18 miles, half of that distance at night, without any food and only a canteen of water apiece: 'Our getting back to camp was one of the luckiest things on record. Our men behaved quite magnificently.'[46]

As five officers and sixty-one men had been killed at Schuinshoogte, and another four officers and sixty-eight men wounded, confidence in Colley began to ebb. After Laing's Nek one veteran officer doubted that Colley should be trusted with a corporal's guard on active service, and, in his diary of 10 February, Marling wrote: 'The General telegraphed home the fight at Ingogo was a success – we certainly did pass the mails through to Newcastle and remained on the field of battle, but one or two more Pyrrhic victories like that and we shan't have any army left at all.'[47] Colley seemed oblivious of these concerns: he lauded the men after each reverse, commending 'the conduct of the young soldiers of the 60th at the Ingogo' and claiming that the 'health and spirit of the troops remain excellent'.[48] He was correct inasmuch as the mood within the camp fluctuated rapidly: even the Riflemen whom Colley ordered on 12 February to exhume the bodies of officers at Schuinshoogte for re-burial at Mount Prospect (a thoroughly nauseating task in rain-soaked conditions) were enjoying athletics and cricket in the camp three days later.[49] Spirits rose on 23 February when the first reinforcements from India arrived, including the 15th Hussars, 2/60th Rifles and the 92nd (Gordon) Highlanders (all veterans of the Second Afghan War), a Naval Brigade from HMS *Dido* and HMS *Boadicea*, and some drafts for units already based at Mount Prospect. As Colley pondered a riposte to the reported Boer fortifications of the Nek (by seizing 'some ground which has hitherto been practically unoccupied by either party'), he affirmed: 'These fine Indian regiments will make a most valuable addition to my force; but I doubt if even they, fine soldiers as they are, can fight better than my young soldiers have done on the two late occasions.'[50]

So the seeds were sown for the fateful decision to occupy the summit of Majuba, a mountain 2,000 feet above Laing's Nek, on the night of 26 February, with a mixed force (two companies of the 58th, two of 3/60th, three of the 92nd, a company-strength Naval Brigade and smaller supporting units). As Major T. Fraser, RE, recalled, each man was ordered to carry seventy rounds of ammunition, a blanket, greatcoat, water bottle and three days' rations, with six picks and four shovels per company. In great secrecy (only Colley, Fraser and Lieutenant-Colonel Herbert Stewart, Colley's replacement military secretary, knew the destination), the march began at 10.30 p.m. Two companies of Rifles and, further on, a company of Highlanders were detached to guard the line of march as the force scrambled up the mountain, enabling Colley with his staff and some 350 infantry to occupy the summit between 3.40 a.m. and 5.40 a.m. Fraser had 'never had such a climb . . . the men were very done and the General too'.[51] Colley had the men dig two wells but reportedly considered them too tired to make entrenchments or fortified positions. He and his staff seemed to regard the summit as unassailable,[52] but some soldiers constructed small stone walls as they were dispersed at intervals of about fifteen paces around a perimeter of three-quarters of a mile (other than an unformed mixed reserve of about 110 men). More significantly, as Fraser testified, discipline slipped when some men opened fire, without orders, on the Boer patrols below, thereby revealing their position and prompting a Boer counter-attack (once it was clear that the British lacked any guns on the summit).[53]

Utilising long-range covering fire to pin down soldiers and sailors on the perimeter (mortally wounding Commander Romilly, RN, in the process), the Boers exploited the 'dead ground' and natural cover to scale the northern slopes. They then extended unseen around a grassy terrace below the outer knoll held by five or six Highlanders and began to mass in vastly superior numbers. Fraser confirmed that Lieutenant Ian Hamilton, who commanded the Gordons on the forward knoll, repeatedly requested reinforcements; but Colley, who slept for part of the time, was unperturbed. In any case, detecting the Boers or establishing a good field of fire remained problematic, even after the first Boer fusillade had overwhelmed the Gordons on the forward knoll and driven back the few survivors. Although Colley belatedly deployed his reserves, another series of rapid Boer volleys drove them back to a central ridge. Here Colley still held the Highlanders in check, refusing to let them mount a bayonet charge (which may or may not have worked, but was the one riposte that the Boers actually feared).[54] From the central ridge, admitted Fraser, 'we had but little command of the ground, which rolled from the crest up to it in rounded form', and so when the Boers launched their next attack, firing on the British positions from three sides, 'with extraordinary rapidity . . . We could see nothing but rifle-muzzles and smoke; I told my men to fire at the grass; they did so for a few moments and then, without any order to retire . . . they began to fall back'.[55] In the ensuing rout Colley was killed, and morale collapsed save for about twenty men, mostly of the 58th, who stood at a kopje with Second Lieutenant Hector Macdonald, (92nd), until all but two were dead or wounded. In only thirty minutes the British were swept from the summit, with the numbers killed, wounded or taken prisoner representing 78 per cent of the officers engaged and 58 per cent of the other ranks. They had suffered latterly from indiscriminate fire as experienced by Lance-Corporal Farmer, AHC, who earned a VC when he waved a white bandage as a flag of truce over some wounded men and was promptly shot, first in the right wrist and then the left elbow. He reckoned that 'even a "savage" foe would have respected such a signal'.[56]

Morale plummeted in the camp: 'Our men', wrote Private Tuck, 'are getting in low spirits through these defeats.'[57] Hampered by rain-sodden conditions, and fatigued by alerts lest the Boers attack the camp, soldiers had the arduous task of bringing down the wounded and burying the dead. As some of the wounded languished on Majuba for twenty-four hours, they were in a pitiful state, 'soaked through and through with the rain and mud'.[58] What exacerbated the anguish of the burial parties was their inability to find any Boer wounded or dead, giving credence to Piet Joubert's claim that the Boers had suffered only a single fatality and five wounded.[59] In these circumstances resentments mounted: Colley may have died gallantly, prompting Fraser to describe him as a 'Homeric hero', but death, argued Marling, may have been 'most fortunate' for this 'much liked man'. 'After Ingogo', wrote Marling, Colley 'hardly slept at all', and many officers felt that he 'was determined to get Laing's Nek before some other General came up to supersede him'.[60] There were regimental recriminations, too. After Fraser specifically praised the 92nd in his official report ('The conduct of the 92nd was excellent throughout'), Colonel W. D. Bond took every opportunity to defend the reputation of the 58th.[61] Many blamed Colley for employing a mixed force. Captain Charles W. H. Douglas, (92nd), who was not present at the battle but who interviewed several survivors, reckoned that some of the 92nd 'should have behaved better,

& not have been carried away by the 58th . . . I think the ninety twas [*sic*] might have made a better fight of it & undoubtedly they c[oul]d have had the whole Reg[iment] been up Majuba instead of a mixed force'.[62]

If they had not done so before, most soldiers now recognised that they had greatly underrated the Boer as a fighting man. 'There is no doubt', wrote Douglas, 'the Boers are magnificent skirmishers, and A1 shots, and as plucky as possible'; they also possessed, in the opinion of a staff officer, Major Fitzroy Hart, the 'best' of rifles (predominantly the Westley Richards) and benefited from 'a life spent in the stalking of game, the judgment of distance, and the practice of aiming . . .'.[63] Such recognition only made British soldiery even more determined to prevail in battle and avenge fallen comrades. The British believed that reinforcements under Sir Frederick Roberts would bring superior numbers, artillery and cavalry to turn the tide against the Boers.[64] Hence they felt deeply affronted when the armistice talks between Piet Joubert and Sir Evelyn Wood, the acting-governor of Natal and high commissioner of the Transvaal, evolved into peace negotiations at the behest of Gladstone's Government (and after a conciliatory letter from Paul Kruger). When an agreement was signed, on 23 March 1881, Marling claimed: 'Everyone is cursing Gladstone and the Radical Government . . . A more disgraceful peace was never made.' Douglas agreed that it was a 'disgraceful peace', and Fitzroy Hart wrote that he felt 'inclined to weep with vexation . . . the vexation of not being allowed to fight it out to the end'.[65]

As controversy raged over the peace, Wood's role in producing a settlement and, within military circles, the failure to award a campaign medal,[66] there was little interest in the post-war accounts of the beleaguered garrisons in the Transvaal. Apart from official despatches and testimony before courts of enquiry, only a few letters were published in contemporary British and colonial newspapers, and a couple of longer accounts in periodicals.[67] The Reverend C. M. Spratt, the military chaplain at Standerton, was disappointed that he had not been able to emulate the achievements of the Reverend George Smith, who had distinguished himself at Rorke's Drift. The well-provisioned and fortified garrison had provided refuge for some 60–70 civilians and, apart from an engagement with the Boers during a sortie on 29 December, had not encountered any 'fighting of importance'. As the Boers were too 'cowardly' to attack and settled for long-range firing,

> Our Commandant has contented himself with holding his own and constructing outworks to keep the enemy at a distance while he has attended to the Commissariat with a view to feeding the whole town and garrison equally until the Relief Column under Sir George Colley arrives.[68]

[71]

At Wakkerstroom two companies of the 58th provided the garrison for the camp and town, where they protected thirty-three civilians. Once again, as described by Sergeant M. O. O'Callaghan, it was largely a passive defence in the face of long-range fire, much of which 'was quite harmless and caused us a deal of amusement'. As the garrison awaited reinforcements, O'Callaghan's motivations ran the gamut from patriotism ('all our hard work is for the glory of Old England') to contempt for the 'most cowardly race of men on the face of the earth', and, following news of the Bronkhorst Spruit massacre and the killing of Captain Lambert, 'many a vow of retributive vengeance has been registered against them'. He repeatedly thanked 'our heavenly Father' as bullets whistled harmlessly by, and remained 'proud of the uniform I wear and the gallant regiment I am serving in. I am proud of the officers too. No better gentlemen are in our Army.'[69]

Despite the debacle at Bronkhorst Spruit, Pretoria remained the largest, best-supplied and best-equipped garrison in the Transvaal, with the aid of about 170 mounted volunteers and 150 foot volunteers. It was able to protect some 3,700 men, women and children either in the military camp or the fortified laager that bounded the gaol and convent. Sappers, as Commeline recalled, had 'an immense amount of work', constructing shelters, cattle kraals and blockhouses on hills overlooking the camp. Each of the blockhouses were manned by 25–30 men and held Krupp 4-pounder guns (liberated from the arsenal of the former republic) to keep the Boers at bay. Commeline, who regarded the Boers as a 'foe worth fighting', spent his time in command of a blockhouse, strengthening his position, watching the movements of the enemy and signalling to the camp below (by flags during the day and lanterns at night). He also monitored several sorties from the camp, which were feasible from the Pretoria garrison by virtue of its relatively large proportion of mounted men. Even so, by 6 February, he feared that the Boers would never attack Pretoria 'because their loss would be so great as to cripple them for any future resistance'.[70]

Another anonymous letter, dated 7 April 1881, concluded that the Pretoria defence was 'most successful. The Boers never came within six miles. Five successful sorties were made. Provisions were plentiful, and the laagers strong enough to defy any possible attack.' By contrast it reported that the Potchefstroom garrison 'suffered severely from their daily exposure to the enemy's fire and the scarcity of food'.[71] At Potchefstroom, where the only surrender occurred, Lieutenant-Colonel R. W. C. Winsloe (21st/Royal Scots Fusiliers), commanded 213 soldiers, including 45 officers and men of N battery, operating two 9-pounder guns, 26 mounted infantry, 2 companies of the 21st and supporting units. Outnumbered from the start of the siege, they were also ill-positioned and poorly provisioned. They had tried to hold a small fort – partially built at the outset and only 25 yards square when completed – as well as the office of the Landrost (magistrate) and the gaol. Under heavy fire from close quarters, the Landrost garrison soon surrendered and the garrison withdrew from the gaol to the fort after suffering several casualties from Boer bullets that penetrated the loopholes in the lower walls and passed through upper walls which were only one brick thick.[72] Thereafter the small fort, bereft of adequate supplies, accommodated some 200 soldiers, 48 refugees and 61 native drivers and leaders. Although the garrison found an adequate supply of water, Winsloe admitted: 'For food we were badly off the whole time.'[73] By 5 March 1881, as casualties from wounds and disease mounted, Second Lieutenant James R. M. Dalrymple-Hay recorded that 'enteric, dysentery and scurvy are rife amongst us'.[74] Although a majority of the refugees and natives left the fort, thirty-three remained to the end, sharing the meagre supplies of mealies and corn (all damaged after three months on the parapets), with the sick receiving preserved meat and rice. By 20 March the garrison held only 24lbs of preserved meat and 16lbs of rice for the sick; and, as General Piet Cronjé was unwilling to honour the terms of the armistice by letting eight days' supply of provisions and firewood through to the garrison,[75] Winsloe surrendered on 23 March. However galling the fate, Winsloe took comfort from his ability to modify the Boer terms, so surrendering his guns and rifles (but not any ammunition), and leaving with full military honours and not as prisoners of war. The '"battle of words"', he reckoned, had ended 'much to our advantage'.[76]

So 23 March involved both a surrender and a peace settlement, an ironic twist of timing that compounded the sense of frustration felt by the British military. Wood negotiated the settlement but affirmed that the British 'should have undoubtedly taken the nek about the end of March; and I think, such a victory would have been a gain to all – English, Dutch, Kaffirs, and to humanity generally'.[76] Although the surrender was later rescinded by the 'triumvirate', and the two guns and most of the rifles returned, resentment persisted. It reflected a lingering contempt for the Boers and a feeling that tactical errors by Colley had thwarted the British soldiery just as much as, if not more than, the Boers' proficiency in skirmishing and short-range marksmanship. Wood felt that the tactical errors made it difficult to draw lessons from the war, other than a need to improve standards of shooting. He believed, too, that the presence of long- and short-service soldiers on Majuba rendered it 'useless to argue on short or long service from this illustration'.[77]

Notes

1 This was an unstable arrangement that fuelled tribal battles when Cetshwayo returned in 1883 and a clash with the Boers in 1886: J. Guy, *The Destruction of the Zulu Kingdom* (London: Longman, 1979), ch. 5; I. Knight, *Great Zulu Battles 1838–1906* (London: Arms & Armour Press, 1998), pp. 165–92.

2 Emery, *Marching Over Africa*, pp. 100–2; Lady Bellairs (ed.), *The Transvaal War* (Edinburgh: Blackwood, 1985), pp. 27–8.

3 Gloucestershire Record Office (GRO), D 1233/45/26, Lt C. Commeline to his father, 23 November 1879; see also Major G. Tylden, 'The Sekukuni Campaign of November–December 1879', *JSAHR*, 29 (1951), 128–36.

4 *The Memoirs of Major-General Sir Hugh McCalmont KCB, CVO* ed. Sir C. E. Callwell (London: Hutchinson, 1924), p. 174.

5 GRO, D 1233/45/26, Commeline to his father, 29 November 1879.

6 NAM, Acc. No. 5705/22, Lt-Col. P. R. Anstruther, letters of 30 November and 7 December 1879.

7 GRO, D 1233/45/26, Commeline to his father, 29 November 1879.

8 Preston, *Wolseley's South African Journal*, pp. 134, 138–9, 179, 186–7.

9 NAM, Acc. No. 5705/22, Anstruther, letter of 30 November 1879.

10 NRMC, 397, Roe, TS diary, paras 123–6.

11 Preston, *Wolseley's South African Journal*, p. 264.

12 Pretoria, Rustenburg, Lydenburg, Marabastad, Wakkerstroom and Standerton. When tensions mounted in November 1880, the British also established a garrison at Potchefstroom.

13 Quoted in D. Blackburn and Captain W. Waithman Caddell, *Secret Service in South Africa* (London: Cassell & Co., 1911), p. 108; see also Bellairs, *Transvaal War*, pp. 32–42.

14 PP, *Further Correspondence, SA*, C 2740 (1881), LXVI, No. 61, Sir W. O. Lanyon to the Earl of Kimberley, 14 November 1880, p. 109.

15 I. Bennett, *A Rain of Lead: The Siege and Surrender of the British at Potchefstroom* (London: Greenhill Books, 2001), pp. 43–59; J. Lehmann, *The First Boer War* (London: Jonathan Cape, 1972), ch. 3; Tylden, 'British Army and the Transvaal', 164.

16 'The Disaster to the 94th Foot', *Broad Arrow*, 29 January 1881, p. 149; see also PP, *Further Correspondence, SA*, C 2866 (1881), LXVII, pp. 47–8.

17 PP, *Further Correspondence, SA*, C 2866 (1881), LXVII, pp. 47–8; 'What a 94th Corporal Said'; and Sergt. Hook in 'Bronker's Spruit', *Natal Mercury*, 14 January 1881, p. 3, and 4 March 1881, p. 3; Bellairs, *Transvaal War*, p. 86.

18 'With the Wounded at Bronkhorstspruit', *Transvaal Argus*, 16 April 1881, p. 3; Brigadier General J. J. F. Hume, 'A Narrative of the 94th Regiment in the Boer War, 1880–81', *The Ranger*, 4:8 (1925), 163–77.

19 While the military authorities came to believe that 1,000 or more Boers were involved, Egerton reckoned that no more than 300 attacked the head of the column – an estimate only marginally larger than the Boer claims. Compare PP, *Further Correspondence, SA*, C 2866, p. 48, with evidence of Pte. D. Campbell, PP, C 2866, p. 56; Bellairs, *Transvaal War*, p. 82; and 'The Transvaal Insurrection', *The Times*, 8 February 1881, p. 4.

20 'Transvaal Insurrection', p. 4; see also 'What a 94th Corporal Said', p. 3.

21 'Narrative of the Disaster', *Natal Witness*, 11 January 1881, p. 3; 'The Transvaal Insurrection', p. 4; Bellairs, *Transvaal War*, p. 82.

22 'Disaster to the 94th Foot', p. 149; 'What a 94th Corporal Said', p. 3.

23 'A True Statement of the Bronker's Spruit Massacre', *The Times of Natal*, 28 February 1881, p. 6; 'Disaster to the 94th Foot', p. 149; 'With the Wounded at Bronkhorstspruit', p. 3; Lehmann, *The First Boer War*, p. 118.

24 'With the Wounded at Bronkhorstspruit', p. 3.

25 *Ibid.*; see also 'True Statement of the Bronker's Spruit Massacre', p. 6; and evidence of Pte King, PP, *Further Correspondence, SA*, C 2866, p. 57.

26 Hume, 'Narrative of the 94th Regiment', 177.

27 The extract from his letter of 7 February was published in the *Sheffield Daily Telegraph*, 5 April 1881, p. 3.
28 PP, *Further Correspondence, SA*, C 2866, Colley to the Earl of Kimberley, 25 January 1881, pp. 15–16.
29 *Ibid.*, Colley to H. C. E. Childers, 1 February 1881, pp. 89–94.
30 'The Boer Rebellion', *The Times of Natal*, 16 February 1881, p. 3.
31 NAM, Acc. No. 7005/21, Private M. M. Tuck diary, 23 January 1881, p. 54; GRO, D 873/C110, Lt P. S. Marling to his grandmother, 22 January 1881.
32 Emery identified the author of this long but not entirely accurate letter, entitled 'The Disaster at Laing's Nek, Northamptonshire Man's Account of the Fight', *Supplement to the Northampton Mercury*, 19 March 1881, p. 1; see also Emery, *Marching Over Africa*, pp. 103–4.
33 Compare 'The Boer Version of Laing's Nek Fight', *Liverpool Mercury*, 4 March 1881, p. 5, with 'Disaster at Laing's Nek', p. 1 and 'Boer Rebellion', p. 3.
34 Lehmann, *The Boer War*, p. 152.
35 'Interesting Letter from Lange's [sic] Nek', *Natal Witness*, 31 March 1881, p. 3; see also 'The Boer Rebellion', p. 3 and PP, *Further Correspondence, SA*, C 2866, p. 91.
36 Compare 'Disaster at Laing's Nek', p. 1, with PP, *Further Correspondence, SA*, C 2866, p. 91.
37 NAM, Acc. No. 7005/21, Tuck diary, 28 January 1881, p. 59.
38 PP, *Further Correspondence, SA*, C 2866, pp. 91–2, 94; 'The Disaster at Laing's Nek', p. 1.
39 'Interesting Letter from Lange's Nek', p. 3.
40 'The Battle of Laing's Nek. Descriptive Letter from a Gloucestershire Officer', *Citizen*, 19 March 1881, p. 3; 'The Boer Rebellion', p. 3.
41 Colley reported that 7 officers and 76 other ranks died, 111 were wounded and two were taken prisoner; see Lehmann, *The Boer War*, p. 155; 'The Transvaal War. Letter from a Sheffield Soldier', *Sheffield Daily Telegraph*, 5 April 1881, p. 2; 'Boer Version of Laing's Nek Fight', p. 5.
42 Compare his letter of 7 February in the *Sheffield Daily Telegraph*, 5 April 1881, p. 3, with PP, *Further Correspondence, SA*, C 2866, Colley to the Earl of Kimberley, 1 February 1881, p. 88.
43 'The Rifles in South Africa', *Hampshire Chronicle*, 9 April 1881, p. 5; on Boer numbers, see PP, *Further Correspondence, SA*, C 2866, Colley to Childers, 12 February 1881, p. 183.
44 'Transvaal War', p. 2.
45 'Rifles in South Africa', p. 5.
46 *Ibid*. Those dragging the guns took another five hours to reach camp: 'Transvaal War', p. 2.
47 P. S. Marling, *Rifleman and Hussar* (London: John Murray, 1931), pp. 41 and 51; see also Bellairs, *The Transvaal War*, p. 378.
48 Colley to Childers, 16 February 1881 in Lt-Col. Spencer Childers, *The Life and Correspondence of the Right Hon. Hugh C. E. Childers 1827–1896*, 2 vols (London: John Murray, 1901), vol. 2, pp. 21–2.
49 Marling, *Rifleman and Hussar*, pp. 49–52; NAM, Acc. No. 7005/21, Tuck diary, 15 February 1881, p. 64.
50 Colley to Childers, 23 February 1881 in Childers, *Life and Correspondence*, vol. 2, p. 24.
51 Maj. T. Fraser, 'Majuba', *REJ*, 11 (1 June 1881), 114–17.
52 T. F. Carter, *A Narrative of the Boer War: Its Causes and Results* (London: John MacQueen, 1900), pp. 264–5; Maj. T. Fraser, 'The Battle of Majuba Hill', *Army and Navy Gazette*, 7 May 1881, p. 353; and for a contrary view on the tiredness of the men, see General Sir Ian Hamilton, *Listening for the Drums* (London: Faber & Faber, 1944), p. 133.
53 PRO, WO 33/38, 'Correspondence Relative to Military Affairs in Natal and the Transvaal', Maj. J. C. Hay, 2 March 1881, p. 221; Fraser, 'Majuba', 115.
54 British Library Asia Pacific and Africa Collections (hereafter APA), MSS Eur

F108/91, White MSS., Capt. C. W. H. Douglas to Sir G. White, 5 April 1881; Major G. Tylden (translation), 'Majuba, 27th February, 1881: A Contemporary Boer Account', *JSAHR*, 17 (1938), 9–12.

55 Fraser, 'Majuba', 115; see also PP, *Further Correspondence, SA*, C 2950 (1881), LXVII, p. 79.

56 'The Only Man Who Won a V.C. at Majuba', *Cheltenham Chronicle*, 6 January 1901, p. 1; PRO, WO 33/38, 'Correspondence . . . in Natal and Transvaal', 2nd Lt H. A. Macdonald, 13 April 1881, p. 221; I. Castle, *Majuba 1881: The Hill of Destiny* (London: Osprey, 1996), pp. 78–83.

57 NAM, Acc. No. 7005/21, Tuck diary, 28 February 1881, p. 70; Marling, *Rifleman and Hussar*, pp. 54–5.

58 A Rifleman in 'The Battle of Amajuba', *Transvaal Argus*, 13 April 1881, p. 3; see also NAM, Acc. No. 7005/21, Tuck diary, 27 February 1881, p. 69; S. G. P. Ward (ed.), 'The Diary of Colonel W. D. Bond, 58th Regiment', *JSAHR*, 53 (1975), 87–97.

59 'The Transvaal War', *Kentish Gazette*, 8 March 1881, p. 3; 'Joubert's Report of the Engagement on Majuba Hill', *Ilkley Gazette*, 7 April 1881, p. 2.

60 Marling, *Rifleman and Hussar*, p. 55; Fraser, 'Majuba', 117.

61 PP, *Further Correspondence, SA*, C 2950, Fraser to General Officer Commanding, Natal, 5 March 1881, p. 79; Ward, 'Diary of Colonel Bond', 93, 97.

62 APA, MSS Eur F108/91, White MSS., Douglas to White, 5 April 1881; see also Hamilton, *Listening for the Drums*, p. 139; Marling, *Rifleman and Hussar*, p. 55.

63 APA, MSS Eur F108/91, White MSS., Douglas to White, 5 April 1881; Maj. Fitzroy Hart to May, 30 March 1881 in, *Letters of Major-General Fitzroy Hart-Synnot* ed. B. M. Hart-Synnot (London: E. Arnold, 1912), p. 187.

64 *Letters of Major-General Fitzroy Hart-Synnot*, pp. 187–88; Marling, *Rifleman and Hussar*, p. 55.

65 Marling, *Rifleman and Hussar*, p. 56; APA, MSS Eur F108/91, White MSS, Douglas to White, 5 April 1881; Fitzroy Hart to May, 30 March 1881, in *Letters of Major-General Fitzroy Hart-Synnot*, p. 188; see also *Memoirs of Sir Hugh McCalmont*, p. 196.

66 On the general controversy, see Lehmann, *The First Boer War*, pp. 280–4, 289–92; Wood to Childers, 31 May 1881 in Childers, *Life and Correspondence*, vol. 2, pp. 27–8; Bennett, *A Rain of Lead*, p. 239.

67 PRO, 33/38, 'Correspondence . . . in Natal and Transvaal', Appendix, pp. 269–61; W. E. Montague, 'Besieged in the Transvaal: The Defence of Standerton', *Blackwood's Magazine*, 130 (1881), 1–20; R. W. C. Winsloe, 'The Siege of Potchefstroom', *Macmillan's Magazine*, 47 (1883), 443–63.

68 'The Siege at Standerton', *Natal Witness*, 6 April 1881, p. 3.

69 'The Boers' Treachery', *Sheffield Daily Telegraph*, 29 March 1881, p. 2.

70 'The Transvaal War. Letter from Lieut. Commeline, R.E.', *Citizen*, 11 May 1881, p. 3; see also PP, *Further Correspondence, SA*, C 2950, p. 46; 'The Transvaal: The Story of the Siege of Pretoria', *Natal Witness*, 22 April 1881, p. 3.

71 'The Transvaal: A Letter from Pretoria', *Western Morning News*, 18 April 1881, p. 3.

72 Winsloe, 'Siege of Potchefstroom', 446; 'The Defence of Potchefstroom. December, 1880–March 1881. Leaves from the Diary of 2/Lieut James R. M. Dalrymple-Hay, 21st Foot', *Journal of the Royal Scots Fusiliers* (henceforth, *JRSF*), 2 (1929), 106–11; Bennett, *Eyewitness in Zululand*, p. 145.

73 Winsloe, 'Siege of Potchefstroom', 455.

74 'The Defence of Potchefstroom', *JRSF*, 3 (1930), 30–4.

75 On Cronjé's strategy, see Bennett, *Rain of Lead*, ch. 17.

76 Winsloe, 'Siege of Potchefstroom', 456–8; 'Defence of Potchefstroom', 34.

77 Wood to Childers, 31 May 1881 in Childers, *Life and Correspondence*, vol. 2, p. 27.

78 Wood to Childers, 14 July 1881 in Childers, *Life and Correspondence*, vol. 2, pp. 29–30.

CHAPTER FOUR

Intervention in Egypt

Intervention in Egypt contrasted dramatically with recent campaigns in Africa and Afghanistan. It involved the largest expeditionary force despatched by Britain since the Crimean War and achieved a decisive outcome in less than two months, that is, from the passing of a vote of credit by the House of Commons for an expeditionary force (27 July 1882) to the crushing victory at Tel-el-Kebir (13 September) and Wolseley's entry into Cairo (15 September 1882). The campaign avoided any embarrassing reverses like Isandlwana, Maiwand (27 July 1880) or Majuba, and reflected impressive co-operation between the armed services (with the navy assisting in the transportation of 35,000 men to the Egyptian theatre, deploying Marines and a 565-strong Naval Brigade as direct support, seizing the Suez Canal, transporting supplies along the Sweetwater Canal, and providing fire support from Gatling machine-guns, artillery and an armoured train).[1] Many soldiers used the new Army Post Office Corps to send letters home, describing their 'baptisms of fire', the rigours of campaigning in Egypt, the battle of Tel-el-Kebir, and the reporting of their achievements. When such letters were passed on to newspapers, they often embellished reports from special correspondents which were censored for the first time. Although Emery quoted from nineteen letters in his account of the campaign, there were many more (and at least that number from the Black Watch alone).[2] This chapter relies primarily, if not exclusively, upon previously unused correspondence.

The intervention was a response to the growth of the nationalist movement in Egypt under the military leadership of Arabi Pasha, the Egyptian minister of war, and its burgeoning hostility towards European control over Khedive Tewfik's Government and its finances. This hostility reached a crescendo when riots erupted in Alexandria (11 June 1882), involving the so-called 'massacre of Christians' and the flight of many Europeans. As these activities seemed to vindicate the alarmist reports of Sir Edward Malet, the British consul-general in Cairo, and Sir Auckland Colvin, who along with his French colleague was responsible for Egypt's 'financial credit', Gladstone's cabinet authorised military intervention to restore order in Egypt.[3] Several weeks of planning ensued. A naval bombardment of Arabi's fortresses at Alexandria on 12 July confirmed that military resistance was likely and that a substantial force under Wolseley would have to be sent ashore.[4] Meanwhile the reluctance of the Porte or France to support intervention ensured that this would be an exclusively British affair. The entire First Class Army Reserve (11,600 men) was called out (contrary to Cardwell's expectation that it would be employed only in a national emergency) and forces were despatched from England, the Mediterranean garrisons and India. As early as 3 July Wolseley intimated that he planned to advance on Cairo along the Sweetwater Canal from Ismailia, a route 45 miles shorter than that from Alexandria. He hoped to deceive Arabi by ini-

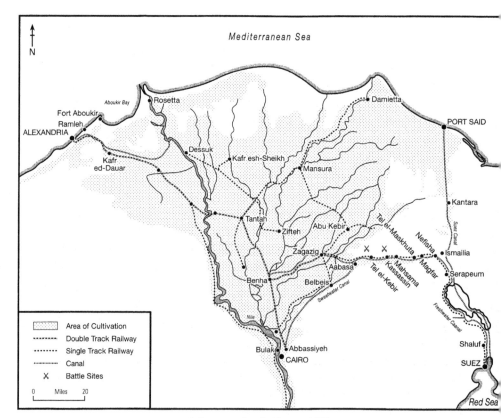

4 Intervention in Egypt, 1882

tially deploying forces near Alexandria and by conducting active operations in that vicinity.[5]

Egypt was a convenient theatre for British forces – only a twelve-day sail from Britain and a much shorter one from Gibraltar or Aden. Advanced units under Sir Archibald Alison arrived in Alexandria on 17 July and others soon followed. Forces based in Britain left to rapturous send-offs: when the 1/Black Watch, as Bandsman A. V. Barwood recalled, travelled by train from Edinburgh to London, 'people, knowing we were going to war, turned out in great numbers at every station to cheer us'.[6] Even larger crowds gathered in London for the departure of the Guards, thronging the route from their barracks to the point of embarkation (Westminster Bridge Pier), whereupon 'the cheering was deafening', wrote Private Macaulay (1/Scots Guards), 'as we passed down the river'.[7] While the Seaforths endured 'a very rough sail' from Aden, the Black Watch, in Private Lauchlan McLean's opinion, enjoyed a 'delightful' voyage, with reasonable liberty, books, papers and evening concerts, 'more like an excursion party than anything else'.[8] However rough or long the voyage, soldiers had to adapt rapidly to Egyptian conditions, a more daunting experience for soldiers coming directly from Britain. 'In passing through Alexandria', added McLean, 'the heat was something fearful, the sand about six inches deep, and the dust so thick that we could not see three paces in front of us'.[9]

Soldiers were observant, nonetheless, as they moved through Alexandria and camped near Ramleh. Private George Snape, having seen Alexandria prior to the naval bombardment, now described how the 'forts, houses, shops, and public buildings in some parts were a mass of ruins – something dreadful to look at'.[10] Macaulay, like others, could distinguish between collateral damage from the naval bombardment and the pillaging of houses at Ramleh by Arabi's followers. Private W. Bond (1/South Staffordshires) was appalled by the way Arabi and his army 'had plundered and ravished all he came across', while McLean added: 'Arabi's vermin destroyed everything they could not take away.'[11] After several minor engagements near Ramleh, British soldiers formed a very low opinion of the enemy's military capacity. 'Arabi Pacha [sic]', noted Snape, 'has plenty of men, but they are not up to much;' while another Marine observed: 'The Arabs are very poor marksmen, or else they could have killed every man in my company, for it advanced across a plain as open as any man could be exposed, and there was not one single man wounded all through the fight.'[12]

Private S. Smith (1/South Staffordshires) described some of the early fighting near Ramleh:

> There are only two regiments here, us and the 60th Rifles, and we have our work cut out, I can tell you. We are on some duty from morning till

night, and every third night all night doing outlying picket and outpost duty, which is very hazardous work, as we are being fired upon continually. My company . . . have had a regular battle with the enemy's outposts, but none of our side were injured; besides which we had one pitched battle with the main body, which lasted about two hours and a half. We were outnumbered fearfully, but eventually succeeded in driving them off. Their bullets . . . were all too high, otherwise the slaughter must have been terrible indeed. As it was we had four killed and twenty-seven wounded, some of whom have since died.

He added perceptively: 'Arabi Pasha is not our only enemy out here. We have another formidable enemy in the shape of the heat, which is cruel, especially when you have to go out trench digging with arms and 70 rounds of ball cartridge.'[13]

Alison's mission was to convince Arabi that the troops in and around Alexandria were preparing to attack his entrenchments at Kafr ed-Dauar and then move on to Cairo. Hence he periodically launched forays along the railway line and its adjacent canal, utilising the armoured train with skirmishing columns in support. On 5 August the mounted infantry advanced, as recounted by one of its number, Private Bond, with the infantry in the rear and the Naval Brigade on the right:

When near his stronghold, his cavalry met us and the battle commenced. We were only thirty-seven strong, but not a flinch. We exchanged a few shots, then the Infantry joined us . . . We continued fighting until, with his heavy losses and his entrenchments taken, he retired . . . out of our small band of 37, we had lost one officer killed, one private killed, and three wounded. The Naval Brigade lost a few, also the Marines.[14]

For many soldiers, these minor engagements constituted their baptism of fire. Sergeant John Philip (2/Duke of Cornwall's Light Infantry) subsequently recalled their feeling of 'trepidation' as the DCLI advanced through the Egyptian shellfire: men had 'quivering lips and firm-set teeth' and uttered the occasional 'forced' laugh as shells flew harmlessly overhead. The 'Dukes' were relieved when the Naval Brigade returned 'the compliment from their guns on the train' and even more so when they themselves opened fire: in the place of 'nervousness . . . came a fierce desire to push on, and close with the enemy'.[15] The 1/Gordon Highlanders had similar experiences on 20 August when engaged in late afternoon skirmishes. Lieutenant Henry W. D. Denne, writing about his 'baptism', described the men as 'perfectly steady', but Lieutenant Heywood W. Seton-Karr observed their relief whenever the artillery retaliated, 'as it proved demoralizing to be shelled without firing a shot in return'. He also thought that his men entertained 'a great dread of cavalry even when they are only Bedouins'.[16]

The Gordons had followed the advanced party from Malta, finding the heat no worse than at Malta, with the agreeable sea breeze and opportunities to bathe regularly at Ramleh. However Denne was by no means alone in regarding the 'glare very bad indeed'; he referred also to the discomfort occasioned by 'insects you can't imagine' – '½ doz. fleas is a moderate bag when you take off your clothes, the flies settle on you all day long & bite . . . They don't settle one at a time but in hundreds. The mosquitos very bad at night.'[17] Soldiers soon found distractions in the nearby towns: 3 Gordons were found drunk on guard from Alexandria and 12 Riflemen were seen lying 'dead drunk' in Ramleh railway station. Deprived of the lash, which had been abolished on active service in 1881, military authorities struggled to respond, the colonel of the Gordons having been initially in favour of shooting the offenders, though he was later content to fine and imprison them with hard labour.[18]

When Wolseley ordered the re-embarking of units at Alexandria, he tried to deceive Arabi that the objective was Aboukir, though he planned to sail through the Suez Canal to Ismailia. As he sought to maintain the utmost secrecy by informing only his chief of staff, Sir John Adye, Denne was certainly perceptive in observing: 'The Guards, 60th & 46th embarked on Thursday last for Ismailia, it is said.'[19] Secrecy was more apparent on the transports, and as soon as the convoy passed Aboukir, conjecture became rife: 'Fifty different places', recalled a Dundonian Marine, 'were named, supported by as many theories.'[20] Yet the journey through the canal was uneventful, apart from the grounding of the transports, *Catalonia* and *Batavia*, after the French authorities refused to provide pilots. The navy soon had control of the waterway, with two small gunboats specially rigged with 'Gatlings ready for action in their tops' and torpedo boats cruising up and down.[21]

Wolseley knew that occupying the Suez Canal was only a temporary expedient, conveniently linking the forces from Britain and the Mediterranean with those of the Indian contingent, and that it was potentially hazardous. As soon as Arabi learnt of the deception, he could cut the supplies of fresh water to Ismailia and Suez, and block the rail link alongside the Sweetwater Canal.[22] Consequently while the navy was securing the Suez Canal, HMS *Seagull* and HMS *Mosquito* carried 200 Seaforth Highlanders from Suez to Shaluf, where some 600 Egyptian infantry guarded the lock gates. In a brief encounter the Egyptians were easily routed and the lock gates closed (as were the gates at Serapeum on the following day). Inevitably a Seaforth Highlander regarded this engagement as not simply a means of ensuring the flow of drinking water to Suez, but an occasion to test 'what kind of stuff they (the enemy) were made of'.[23]

After the landing at Ismailia on 21 August, Wolseley ordered the seizure of the nearby railway junction at Nifshia by a detachment under Major-General Gerald Graham, VC. As sappers and fatigue parties laboured to expand the dock facilities at Ismailia, unloading stores, horses and ammunition, and repairing rail and telegraph connections, water levels in the Sweetwater Canal began to fall. Local intelligence confirmed that dams had been constructed at Magfar, about 10 miles from Ismailia, and then further inland at Tel el-Maskhuta, where the enemy forces were entrenched in force. Wolseley sent reinforcements to Graham and ordered a westwards advance along the railway line to Magfar. 'It was fearful heavy marching', recalled a corporal with the Army Hospital Corps (AHC), 'it was ankle deep in sand.'[24]

Having quickly dispersed the skirmishers at Magfar, Wolseley sought to engage the enemy at Tel el-Maskhuta but the protracted artillery duel, involving two guns of the Royal Horse Artillery (later supported by two Gatling guns), deterred the enemy and prompted a withdrawal. 'For once', wrote a Marine, 'we had nothing more serious to do than watch our artillery shell Arabi's forces out of the village of Tel-el-Mahuta.'[25] As the Egyptian guns fell silent, three squadrons of Household Cavalry, the 4th and 7th Dragoon Guards, and some mounted infantry followed. A cavalry charge into the large camp at Mahsama was repulsed by heavy fire from artillery and well-entrenched infantry: 'I never expected to come out of that alive', claimed Private Robert Gamble (7th Dragoon Guards), 'the shells were dropping all around us, there was a lot of horses shot, but there was only two men killed.'[26] An artillery bombardment and fire from the mounted infantry prepared the way for a second charge. Trooper T. Gittins (1/Life Guards) described the advance from a walk to a trot and then a gallop: 'The sight was too much for the Egyptian warriors, for they bolted, leaving us in entire possession of the camp baggage, hundreds of arms, and tons of ammunition, seven breech-loading Krupp guns (beautiful weapons) and last, but not least, a train load of stores, etc. (about 80 trucks).'[27] Although another train escaped, a detachment of 4th Dragoons moved ahead to seize Kassassin Lock on 26 August, enabling Graham's Brigade to occupy the Lock area on the same day. His forces were now within striking distance (some 7 miles) of the main Egyptian entrenchments at Tel-el-Kebir.

Soldiers realised the risks that Wolseley had taken by advancing so rapidly ahead of his transport and supplies. The Guards and the DCLI, who followed as reinforcements in the heat of the day (24 August), suffered acutely. Many men fell out on the line of march, water-carts broke down and the guardsmen could not be prevented from drinking polluted water. 'All day', bemoaned a Scots Guardsman, 'we toiled through the burning sand, our tongues parched with heat and thirst.'[28] The 'Dukes' at least found a field of melons and so were able to slake their thirst, while the sick toll among the Scots Guards grew alarmingly 'after drinking bad water from the swamp after the march . . .'.[29]

Lieutenant Charles Balfour (1/Scots Guards) deplored the 'disgraceful' lack of medical stores as the Guards had 'no provision for the wounded'. Admittedly the Foot Guards with a royal duke, the Duke of Connaught, in command, were not exposed in the front line (and so grumbled about the lack of action);[30] but those in range of the Egyptian gunnery regarded it as highly accurate. As shells with percussion fuses burrowed into the sand on impact, casualties were kept to a minimum, but when a direct hit shattered the leg of a Life Guardsman, the bearer recounted: 'We had to carry him about five miles back to camp, and we were all parched with thirst, and could not get a drop of water . . . I fell down twice, and could scarcely get up again. I passed dozens of men lying down exhausted from thirst, crying for water. And then we got nothing to eat for two days.'[31]

Throughout the early advance from Ismailia, medical support remained problematic. Working in single-lined tents Dr Alex S. Rose struggled in the intense heat and the recurrent sandstorms and with the all-pervading flies, as wearing veils was 'not always convenient when we had our medical duties to perform'. He despaired of the water from the canal, the smell and taste of which was 'more easily . . . imagined than described', and of the bread which was 'anything but good'. Even worse, he could not find any horses to carry the hospital stores: 'Unfortunately, the transport service had broken down, the result being that we were much hampered in all our movements, and sometimes were left quite helpless.'[32]

At least those who reached the Egyptian camps at Tel-el-Maskhuta and Mahsama found provisions, clothing and tents in abundance. At the former, a Dundonian Marine regarded the 'biscuits and tents left by Arabi's troops' as 'very acceptable, the heat being overpowering'. In Mahsama, the Marine wrote, 'we got a fresh supply of camels, all their tents, and plenty of rice, flour, onions, beans, biscuits, and tinned soup . . . without Arabi's stores we should have been absolutely starving'.[33] The men needed all their energy as they had to dredge numerous corpses (both men and animals) from the canal, breach both dams across the canal (particularly arduous tasks), and remove a major blockage from the railway. Further forward, soldiers constructed entrenchments to protect their exposed position at Kassassin.[34]

On 28 August Arabi Pasha challenged Graham's weak brigade at Kassassin which comprised Marine Artillery, small detachments of mounted infantry and the 4th Dragoon Guards, the DCLI and the York and Lancaster Battalions, a troop of 7th Dragoon Guards and two 13-pounders (another two were soon sent forward). After a preliminary cavalry charge failed, the Egyptians launched a major infantry assault in three lines, with massive reserves and sixteen cannon. Sergeant Philip, who was in the firing line of the 'Dukes', remembered opening fire 'with a vengeance' from within 900 yards and, after several hours of continual firing, suffering a severely bruised shoulder from the recoil of his rifle. Like others he lauded the achievements of the Marine Artillery, who had mounted one of the captured Krupp guns on a couple of trucks and continued firing long after the horse artillery.[35]

Although Graham's force held its position, brought up reinforcements and saw the enemy retire, the 'moonlight charge' by the Household Cavalry from the right flank turned the repulse into a rout. The cavalry, as Trooper Gittins recalled, had already been called out 'in the heat of the day' to wait for hours in support before returning to camp.[36] When summoned again, they marched for 5–6 miles until they encountered the enemy's fire. Thereupon, as Lieutenant-Colonel the Hon. Reginald Talbot (1/Life Guards) recorded,

> General [Drury] Lowe shortly ordered our guns to unlimber and reply, and the 7th Dragoon Guards to clear the front of our guns, which they did by retiring, making us the first line. The Household Cavalry continued to advance at a walk, when in a moment became visible a white line of infantry in our immediate front, which opened a tremendous fire upon us. Not a moment was to be lost: 'Form front in two lines!' 'Draw swords!' 'Charge!' and we were upon them . . . We rode them down in solid rank; but, as they dispersed, we opened up and pursued. They fell like ninepins.[37]

Troopers appreciated that the proximity of the initial encounter had served them well: 'They opened a terrific fire on us at a very short distance', wrote Gittins, 'and lucky for us it was a short one, for they invariably fire high.'[38] Life Guardsmen recounted vicious hand-to-hand fighting, with Trooper Browning claiming that he had decapitated two of the enemy before he himself fell unconscious.[49] Some found the aftermath an appalling spectacle: 'It was a ghastly sight', recalled Private H. Tripper (7th Dragoon Guards), 'to see the enemy's dead lying about in the moonlight', while Private Richard Williams (AHC) observed 'some fearful sights among the wounded'.[40] None of the cavalrymen mentioned charging the enemy's guns, so vindicating the official historian's review of the battle as distinct from contemporary mythology.[41]

On the following day four companies of Marines and a cavalry escort toured the battlefield, finding large quantities of ammunition and several mutilated corpses of cavalrymen. These findings only added to their sense of enmity and the desire to attack Arabi, a prospect made more feasible by the arrival of the first train bringing supplies to Tel-el-Maskhuta on 28 August.[42] The railway company under Major Wallace, RE, had had to repair 230 yards of track from Ismailia to Magfar and bring engines from Suez to Ismailia (as they could not be unloaded at Ismailia) before they could send even one engine along the line. By 31 August they sent a train to Kassassin, and increased the number of trains to 2 per day from 1 September, increasing to 4 per day from 7 September. The engineers also established telegraphic connections between Ismailia and Tel-el-Maskhuta by 31 August and between Ismailia and Kassassin on the following day. As supply boats began to operate beyond Magfar on 2 September, stores accumulated rapidly and more units were pressed forward.[43]

By 8 August a Marine recorded that the Kassassin camp now included 'the Royal Irish (18th); Duke of Cornwall's (46th); York and Lancaster (84th); 3rd Battalion King's Own Rifles (60th); West Kent (50th); Marine Artillery; Marine Light Infantry; and about 2000 cavalry'. In a nearby camp, he added, the Bengal Lancers appeared and 'it was a grand sight to see them, with gay pennons on their lances . . .'.[44] Stores were now plentiful but the numbers suffering from dysentery, diarrhoea and fever rapidly grew, including medical staff such as Dr Rose. Fortunately many of these illnesses proved transitory, but soldiers 'were getting sick of this place' and wanted to take the offensive, especially as an armoured train had now appeared.[45]

Early on the morning of 9 September Arabi launched another assault on Kassassin, with some 8,000 men, supported by twenty-four guns. Outpost patrols of the 13th Bengal Lancers detected the advance and raised the alarm at about 6.45 a.m. While the Indian Cavalry Brigade sought to delay the Egyptians, Graham prepared a counter-offensive with his Marines and Riflemen along the line of the canal and railway. He had the DCLI and Royal Irish in support, with the Yorks and Lancs ready to counter any move from the northern sandhills, and cavalry on the right to thwart any flanking movements. The infantry pressed forward, as Marling recounted, 'by short rushes of from 50 to 100 yards' and maintained 'a tremendous musketry fire on them',[46] but the artillery duel was once again decisive. Initially the Egyptian gunners sustained a heavy and accurate bombardment: 'shells were flying about like hailstones', recalled a corporal of the Engineers,[47] and twice the engineer sections at the extreme front had to vacate their positions. Direct hits, as seen by Sapper Powell, could be devastating – one Rifleman lost both legs – but many shells buried themselves in the sand: as Lieutenant-Colonel Kendal Coghill (19th Hussars) observed, 'Their artillery fire is very good, but bursting of shells bad.'[48] Once the British gunners limbered up and advanced, they wrecked the range-calculations of their Egyptian counterparts and opened up an effective counter-battery fire. By 9 a.m. the infantry began to advance and within an hour-and-a-half the combined British force had driven the Egyptians from the field, capturing 40,000 rounds of ammunition and three guns. They pursued the enemy to within 5,000 yards of the entrenchments at Tel-el-Kebir.[49] As many soldiers had rushed into battle without breakfast and even with unfilled water-bottles, the Marines and Riflemen had many exhausted men, with several cases of sunstroke, when they returned to camp.[50]

Wolseley had halted the pursuit, preferring to assemble his full army for a pre-dawn assault on Tel-el-Kebir (to minimise casualties and so ensure that he could follow up via Belbeis and Zagazig to seize Cairo). He now brought forward the Guards Brigade, the remaining artillery and cavalry, and the four battalions of the Highland Brigade that had languished on ships off Ismailia since 1 September. They had disembarked only to undertake fatigues, and on the 4th the Camerons had received a welcome draft of reservists (3 officers, 12 non-commissioned officers, 3 drummers and 150 privates); but these reservists, contrary to official claims, came from different regiments. Captain and Adjutant Kenneth S. Baynes recorded: 'Amongst them were a few old 79th men, but the majority were from the 93rd, 91st, and other regiments.'[51] On the 9 September the brigade began its march at 3.30 p.m. – 'the hottest part of the day', as bitterly remembered by a Yorkshireman in the Black Watch.[52] With cavalry on one flank and artillery on the other, the Gordons led the march, followed by the Camerons, Highland Light Infantry (HLI) and then the Black Watch. During the first day men sank to their ankles, sometimes their knees, in soft sand,[53] struggling through the dust to cover 6 miles by sunset. The camp site, as recalled by the Camerons' Quartermaster John Ainslie, had 'nothing to be seen to the front, right or left but a sea of sand. Behind us the tall masts of the transports rose like a forest out of gathering gloom.'[54] Many never appreciated the view as they had fallen out along the line of march and had to catch up by morning. Some officers of the Black Watch were less than candid in claiming that 'very few' or 'some twenty or thirty of our men fell out', whereas private soldiers reckoned that 'about 100 of ours' succumbed. Lieutenant-Colonel Duncan Macpherson later conceded that 'the men were as game as possible, but one day 150 fell out from exhaustion, and one died'.[55] The brigade continued to suffer from the lack of food and shelter during the next two days. Lieutenant Henry H. L. Malcolm (Camerons) claimed that 'another 200 men fell out' on the second day, 'principally from the 75th', before reaching Mahsama where the 'stink was excessive' from the rotting Egyptian corpses.[56] Seton-Karr admitted that sixty-five Gordons had fallen out on 10 September, and that everyone was relieved to reach Kassassin on the following day, where tents had been brought up by train and the men could eat, rest and recuperate.[57]

By 12 September 17,401 British and Indian officers and men, with 61 guns and 6 naval Gatlings, were ready for the assault. After several days' reconnaissance and gathering evidence from spies, Wolseley and his staff had studied the enemy's defences, manned by 20,000 soldiers and seventy-five guns, and observed the laxity of their pre-dawn watch. His plan of maximising surprise by a silent evening march over the 7 miles to Tel-el-Kebir, with unloaded rifles, had an immediate appeal for Highlanders such as Drummer Bogle (1/Black Watch). The Highland Brigade would lead the charge (flanked by Graham's Brigade to the right and the Indian contingent to the left) and it would 'be done in the old Scotch style – by the bayonet', with no firing until inside the entrenchments.[58] The men were to carry 100 rounds of ammunition, one day's rations (not two as often claimed) and water bottles filled with tea.[59] With each battalion marching slowly in two lines, in half-battalion columns of double companies, they bivouacked for an hour-and-a-half at Ninth Hill, where a rum ration was issued to widespread approval.[60]

At 1.30 a.m. the march resumed, utilising telegraph poles laid out over 1,000 yards from the hill, and with Lieutenant Rawson, RN, directing the Highlanders by the stars. Private George Bedson (Black Watch) recalled the 'grand sight to see the two lines advancing in the night; they looked like walls moving'.[61] Apart from a drunken private of the HLI, who was quickly suppressed, the sound of the march was also memorable: 'the monotonous tramp', wrote Captain Baynes, 'the sombre lines, the dimly discerned sea of desert, faintly lighted by the stars, were at once ghastly and impressive'.[62] So deep was the silence that when Quartermaster Ainslie with his water carts and pack mule fell behind, he could detect the sound only by listening, ear to the ground, and so hearing 'a murmur like the sea breaking on the shore to my right'.[63] When clouds concealed the stars, the two wings of the Highland Brigade turned inwards and virtually faced each other, but the alignment was restored and just before dawn the brigade found itself about 200 yards from the Egyptian lines. One shot from the enemy was followed by others 'until the whole horizon' seemed to a Black Watch bandsman 'one mass of flame'.[64] The Highlanders, who were 600 yards ahead of Graham's Brigade, were so close that most of the fusillade passed harmlessly overhead. 'As soon as they opened fire', added Sergeant Charles Riley (Camerons), 'we fixed bayonets, and with a good ringing British cheer we charged the trenches'.[65]

An Egyptian officer admitted that the surprise was complete, and that their guns had been sighted for a range of 2,000 yards:

> Instead of 2,000 yards, they must have been 200 off. We fired, but most of our shots must have gone over their heads. Almost at the same moment . . . they were scrambling over us, first over our right [where the Highlanders attacked] and then rolling down the line like a wave. We never expected a war like this. Our soldiers stood fire at a distance very well . . . but these men came close up to us and the only way to save life was to run away.[66]

Soldiers' memories of the battle, which lasted barely an hour, were perforce limited. As for the Highlanders, who were unsupported for the first 10–15 minutes, they had the experience of plunging into the 5-foot-deep ditch with perpendicular sides and then scrambling up a parapet on the other side. Private Donald Cameron (Cameron Highlanders) was the first man up and the second killed as the Camerons and Gordons were the first into the enemy's trenches. 'We were mixed up', recorded Seton-Karr in his diary, '75th and 79th in inextricable confusion, but keep advancing after the flying masses, while those in the rear drive their bayonets through those the front men have shot down.'[67] On the right of the line, where the Black Watch had to cut steps with their bayonets in the 14-foot-high embankment, Private Donald Campbell (Black Watch) characterised 'our men' as 'half-mad to see their comrades falling before they were able to strike a blow; and whenever they got within reach of the enemy they fought like lions'.[68] On the left the 2/HLI attacked a five-gun battery protected by a formidable ditch and suffered the heaviest casualties of any Highland battalion. 'There were cross fires in all directions', wrote Lieutenant-Colonel Abel Straghan, and the artillery fire had a 'demoralising' effect until his men worked round to an easier ditch on the left and climbed into the redoubt.[69]

Soldiers of every rank described their near escapes, or, in some cases, their multiple injuries. They praised the achievements of fallen comrades, such as Sergeant-Major John McNeill (Black Watch), who led his men over the parapet before being shot in the thigh, stomach and groin.[70] They acknowledged the havoc caused by cross-fire from the shelter trenches in the rear, with the Camerons having to turn a Krupp gun on the enemy, but they persevered with their bayoneting. As Bandsman George Paterson (Black Watch) observed: 'You should have seen the faces the poor wretches put on as the bayonet was driven into them. It is a sight I shall never forget all my life.'[71] They were grateful, too, when the horse artillery appeared and the infantry helped to lift the guns over the parapet. Viscount Fielding (RA, N/2 battery) then galloped down 'one side of a long line of entrenchment', periodically stopping to enfilade the enemy while the Black Watch ran along the other side of the trenches: 'We went on like this down the whole of the line, nearly two miles', sometimes firing case at only 200 yards.[72] While N/2 went on to shell Arabi's train, the following battery had, according to one of its gunners, 'great practice; but it was cruel butchery. A shell from my left gun took a man's head clean off, and then went on, burst, and killed five more. After four or five rounds from each gun, we limbered up, and advanced to Arabi's camp'.[73]

Graham's Brigade made rapid progress in its sector. Although the Marines and the infantry had to cross a longer fire zone, most of the Egyptian fire was aimed too high. The Yorks and Lancs company of Sergeant McChesney

> took no notice of being a support, what we wanted was to be up in the front . . . we took no notice of any orders, but fixed our bayonets, and off we went like wild men, charging and shouting till we were hoarse again. The scene was awful when we got up to the trenches, as it was every man for himself. However, it did not last long, it was all over in about half an hour.[74]

The Royal Irish Fusiliers advanced in short rushes, and, unlike the Royal Marines, fired several volleys before charging the entrenchments, where Sergeant R. D. Healey found large numbers of Arabs either killed or wounded:

> We bayoneted all who came in our way. You should have heard the yells of the beggars as we 'let daylight into them'. It was something terrible. The majority retreated to another ridge, where they again opened fire, but a few shots, a cheer, and charge, had the effect of making them move at a pace unusual with their habits. Then their retreat became more general . . . We followed them for a couple of miles, halting ultimately to let the Artillery and Cavalry perform their part of 'not a bad day's work'.[75]

South of the canal the Indian contingent and the Naval Brigade moved against the well-fortified right flank, where the Seaforths advanced towards trenches filled with Egyptians and four 7-pounder guns. A non-commissioned officer described how the Seaforths responded in kind to the Egyptian volleys and made 'great gaps in the rebel ranks. For over half-an-hour this work continued, the enemy gradually retiring and we occupying their trenches. One gallant comrade near me fell dead, being shot through his Afghan medal.' Following Brigadier-General Oriel V. Tanner and a young subaltern, they charged the enemy's guns, precipitating a wholesale retreat: 'All ran but the gunners, who, to their credit be it said, remained to the last and were cut down.'[76] Another Seaforth veteran reckoned: 'It was about the shortest fight that ever I had, and as cheap a medal that ever an army got.'[77]

The cavalry poured through on both sides of the canal, albeit at different rates. While a squadron of the 6th Bengal Cavalry tried to cut off fugitives from the southern side of the canal, the main Indian Brigade advanced from the north ahead of the Heavy Cavalry Brigade which, as Coghill asserted, 'had not calculated on such a sharp & decisive business so crept slowly round the enemy's right'. Meanwhile Coghill's squadron of the 19th Hussars galloped through the centre, making straight for the railway where he claimed to have blocked the departure of three trains by 'dropping a camel' across the tracks. Although there were competing claims for the disruption of the rail network, Coghill is correct in maintaining that the rapidity and depth of the cavalry pursuit, with the hussars chasing for about 12 miles, 'completely routed and demoralised' the enemy,[78] and secured both Belbeis with its telegraph office and Zagazig later in the day.

For the Foot Guards and other units coming up in reserve, the brevity of the engagement was an intense frustration. As Balfour reflected, 'we never did anything during the fifty minutes the action lasted', claiming that 'the Egyptians made such a poor showing no support was required by the first line'.[79] Most soldiers agreed, one Black Watch officer even asserting: 'How they can run, those Arabs, and what a capital 'fox' they would make for a paper chase at home!';[80] but they exempted the Egyptian gunners, who died at their posts, and the black Sudanese soldiers. As Major Robert Coveny (Black Watch) acknowledged: 'The Soudan warriors, thick-lipped negro-typed creatures in light blue tunics, died very game, their bodies lying perfectly thick in the trenches.'[81]

Many were appalled by the aftermath of the battle in which a total of perhaps 2,000 Egyptians died as well as 57 British soldiers (with another 382 wounded and 30 missing). Private James Judson, another Yorkshireman in the Black Watch, found the scene 'heartrending', that is 'the sight of the dead and dying, who lay all around us – an old man here, a young man there, or a riderless horse galloping madly on in the confusion'.[82] One of his comrades described the canal as 'full of dead and dying horses, camels, and men. Confusion reigned everywhere, our cavalry firing and mowing them down, the artillery stretching dozens at a time. We captured about 50 tons of ammunition at the station, and stores of every description, including horses and camels – in fact, all his camp equipage.'[83] The wounded were in a desperate state: many cried

out for water and some buried their heads in the sand to cool themselves. A Crieff soldier, in trying to help, filled his water bottle from
the canal 'with water that you would not wash the door-step with, as
it was thick with blood and mud'.[84] Several chronicled the dangers of
moving over the battlefield, when some Egyptians either feigned injury
or turned on those who gave them water, and, as soon as they passed,
shot them in the back.[85] None of these incidents deterred soldiers from
the wholesale looting of Arabi's camp: 'Lots of our fellows', admitted
Quartermaster Ainslie, 'picked up valuable articles . . . and near the
station were immense stores of all sorts, and they all fell into our
hands, along with a great number of baggage animals and cavalry
horses'.[86]

The AHC, as Private Richard Williams recalled, struggled to cope:
'We could see some of the firing, but, after a time, our work commenced. The wounded began to be carried in and oh! to see some of the
poor fellows smothered in blood and arms and legs blown to pieces, and
they were groaning and crying for water, which was something dreadful to hear.' After treating the British wounded, he confirmed that the
AHC spent several days assisting the Egyptian wounded, whose numbers overwhelmed their services. Within a few days they had 300 Arabs
under treatment and were losing 'five or six a day', with the flies and
mosquitoes tormenting all concerned.[87] On 17 September an AHC corporal led a party of eleven men and six carts across the battlefield,
where some dead lay unburied and the 'stench was fearful'. They collected another thirty-six Arabs, whose 'wounds were in a fearful
state'.[88]

Wolseley's priority had been to complete the dispersal of Arabi's
army and reach Cairo as quickly as possible. Accordingly the Indian
contingent marched on to Zagazig (15 miles from Tel-el-Kebir) by the
afternoon of the battle, while the mounted infantry and 4th Dragoon
Guards rode ahead to Belbeis. After a short rest they proceeded to
Cairo, arriving at the Citadel at 5 p.m. on 14 September, where Arabi
and 8,000 soldiers surrendered to 120 men from the mounted infantry
and dragoons. The Foot Guards arrived by train on the following day:
as Private Geddes (Scots Guards) informed his parents, 'We marched
triumphantly into this city . . . amidst the cheers of the Europeans and
all the native Christians, who were intoxicated with delight at our success'.[89] Many Egyptian soldiers were keen to ingratiate themselves,
with Sapper Powell finding them to 'take a great interest in trying to
catch and repeat different English words, and . . . very anxious to show
their good feeling, bringing us oranges, dates, sugar, cigarettes, etc.'.[90]
Arabi's several hundred prisoners were particularly glad to see the
Guardsmen and recount their tales of torture and food deprivation: the

Guards fed the prisoners and put 'the officer (a Bey) who carried out Arabi's orders . . . in irons'.[91]

Although soldiers were restricted in their movements, they were impressed by Cairo and the nearby pyramids. 'Without doubt', wrote Bandsman Paterson, 'Cairo is as pretty a city as ever I saw. The streets are lined with tall, shady trees on each side, while the houses (in the principal part of the city) are magnificent.'[92] Soldiers were not so impressed by the quarters that they had to inhabit. Both the Citadel and the Kasr-el-Nil barracks were found utterly squalid and verminous. Sergeant Charles Spraggs (Scots Guards) recorded how a great many men preferred to sleep at night on the parade ground to avoid 'the large number of Bugs and insects'.[93] Several palaces were found to be in similar condition – 'dusty and filthy in the extreme' to quote Dr Rose [94] – so that many units remained in encampments on the outskirts of Cairo or near Zagazig and Belbeis before quarters were established on the island of Bulak. Conditions were grim: the Black Watch spent eight days outside Belbeis with no tents, sleeping in their kilts and consuming nothing but hard biscuits, preserved meat and muddy water.[95] The number of those sick rapidly mounted, with the Gordons, after twelve days at Tantah, forced to send off 5 officers and 140 men for medical treatment.[96] Once again the medical authorities struggled initially: Dr Rose found himself 'very much overworked' and had only 4 orderlies to treat 245 patients sent in on a single day.[97] Patients suffered from fever, ophthalmia and diarrhoea, with Sergeant Spraggs finding the medical remedies for severe diarrhoea somewhat drastic, namely 'some Castor oil and oppium [sic] to see if that will do me any good'.[98]

Soldiers wrote many of their letters as they languished in encampments after Tel-el-Kebir, and some moved beyond descriptive narratives to praise the tactical planning of Wolseley, especially the night march prior to battle. A Scots Guards private called it 'a splendidly-planned attack', while a corporal of the Royal Engineers regarded Sir Garnet 'as a fine General; his Generalship was unsurpassable'.[99] Yet Wolseley's reports on the battle proved profoundly contentious. As the telegraph unit, with 10 miles of cable, had followed the infantry across Tel-el-Kebir to establish a telegraph office at the railway station, Wolseley was 'greatly pleased' to send news of the victory with unprecedented rapidity.[100] Rumours quickly circulated that his despatch had heaped praise on the Guards under their royal duke (so appeasing the Queen), on the achievements and discipline of the young soldiers (so endorsing the Government's army reforms) and on the efficiency of the support services (so concealing the main shortcomings of the campaign). Privately, Wolseley, who expected (and received) a peerage and a pension for his services, insisted: 'The government owe me a great deal . . .. The battle of Tel el Kebir has been worth millions to Gladstone's administration', while the Queen's 'only sympathies & solicitude are for Her own selfish self and Her family'.[101]

The Marines and Highlanders were incensed. Whereas the former, who suffered the heaviest casualties of any unit at Tel-el-Kebir, regarded themselves as 'second to none', the latter considered that they did 'the whole of the work'. Both deplored plaudits for the supporting units; 'The Guards, etc.', wrote a Black Watch sergeant, 'were – I don't know where; anyhow they did nothing' and the 3/60th, in the rear of the Gordons, were in Denne's words 'not so swift to the front that they trod our heels off'.[102] Aggrieved soldiers believed that Wolseley had exploited his powers of censorship: 'the correspondents', asserted a Black Watch private, 'are not allowed to send home any news but what is approved of by Sir Garnet Wolseley'.[103] Soldiers had mixed feelings towards the war correspondents: they had enjoyed their company socially but criticised the risks they took in battle, which could bring down fire on themselves, and deprecated some of their reporting. If Lieutenant Walter S. Churchward, RA, exaggerated in claiming that 'newspaper men are all liars & wrote absurd accounts in the papers especially The Times and Standard', soldiers complained in their letters about the failure of the transport and commissariat, aware that the press could not do so.[104] By 15 October, Denne readily observed: 'The correspondents, now supervision has ceased, are showing up the comm[issaria]t & hospital defects, all they say & more is true.'[105]

On the issue of whether the campaign vindicated army reforms, as claimed by Wolseley and Childers,[106] opinions divided. While Sergeant Healey agreed that the young soldiers had proved themselves in Egypt, Denne reckoned that the 72nd (1/Seaforths) were 'a fine regt. of old soldiers & the smartest I have ever seen'.[107] In fact, there was not a sharp gulf between the home- and India-based battalions. Many of home-based units had left behind all soldiers under 20 years of age and most had a nucleus of older or long-service men.[108] Even more impressive, argued Sergeant-Major Greig, RA, were 'our native Indian troops, strong muscular fellows, and like greyhounds on the leash eager to be at the foe'.[109] The achievements of all these soldiers were magnified by the incapacity of the Egyptians: as Denne remarked, 'Sir F. Roberts had much greater difficulties to contend with [in the Second Afghan War] & did much more than Wolseley'.[110]

Most soldiers, though, emerged from the campaign with their sense of self-esteem enhanced. They had overcome natural obstacles and numerical odds, and believed that they had done so in a righteous cause. The chorus of Drummer Bogle's poem 'The Highland Brigade' extolled

The success to the few, the gallant few,
   Of that famous Scottish band,
Who are ready to fight in the cause of the right,
   And the honour of their native land.[111]

Soldiers appreciated the profusion of medals and promotions awarded (not only a campaign medal with a clasp for those at Tel-el-Kebir but the Khedive's bronze star and 165 Orders of the Osmanieh and the Medjidieh from the Sultan of Turkey). They relished, too, the parade in review order before the Khedive on 30 September. As the culminating spectacle of the campaign, Sergeant Philip maintained that the purpose 'was to overawe and instil into the dull native mind the overpowering strength of the nation they had been opposing . . . [and] to give the ruler and his subordinates a sight of the army that beat and sent their countrymen flying from the trenches at Tel-el-Kebir in such a short time on that eventful morning'.[112]

Notes

1 Brooks, *Long Arm of Empire*, pp. 171–80.
2 Emery, *Marching Over Africa*, pp. 187–8. The profusion of letters from the Black Watch may reflect its prominence in the assault on Tel-el-Kebir and the fact that it was the only unit in the Highland Brigade that had joined the expedition directly from Britain, and so had the more immediate ties with family and friends at home.
3 H. C. G. Matthew, *Gladstone, 1875–1898* (Oxford: Clarendon Press, 1995), pp. 130–7; A. Schölch, 'The "Men on the Spot" and the English Occupation of Egypt in 1882', *Historical Journal*, 19:3 (1976), 773–85.
4 Duke of Cambridge to Childers, 13 July 1882 in Childers, *Life and Correspondence*, vol. 2, pp. 91–2; see also M. J. Williams, 'The Egyptian Campaign of 1882', in Bond (ed.), *Victorian Military Campaigns*, pp. 243–78.
5 Colonel J. F. Maurice, *Military History of the Campaign of 1882 in Egypt* (London: HMSO, 1887), pp. 6–9; Wolseley to Childers, 29 July 1882, in Childers, *Life and Correspondence*, vol. 2, pp. 99–100.
6 BWA, 0203/1, A. V. Barwood, diary, 1 December 1882, p. 1.
7 Private Macaulay, 'With the Guards in Egypt', in Small (ed.), *Told from the Ranks*, pp. 44–60; see also Ward, 'The Scots Guards in Egypt', 80–1.
8 'The Battle of Tel-el-Kebir: Letter from Another Crieff Soldier', *Strathearn Herald*, 21 October 1882, p. 2, and 'Letter from an Invergordon Young Man in Egypt', *Invergordon Times*, 13 September 1882, p. 3.
9 'Letter from an Invergordon Young Man', p. 3.
10 'Letter from a Northampton Private', *Northampton Mercury*, 9 September 1882, p. 6.
11 Macaulay, 'With the Guards in Egypt', p. 46; 'Death of a Lichfield Man', *Lichfield Mercury*, 8 September 1882, p. 8; 'Letter from an Invergordon Young Man', p. 3.
12 'Letter from a Northampton Private', p. 6; 'The War in Egypt. Letter from a Son of the Rock', *Stirling Observer*, 28 September 1882, p. 4.
13 'Letter from a Wolverhampton Man in Egypt', *Midland Counties Express*, 26 August 1882, p. 7.
14 'Death of a Lichfield Man', p. 8; see also Col. W. L. Vale, *History of the South Staffordshire Regiment* (Aldershot: Gale & Polden, 1969), p. 187.
15 J. Philip, *Reminiscences of Gibraltar, Egypt, and the Egyptian War, 1882* (Aberdeen: D. Wyllie & Son, 1893), pp. 41–2.

16 GHM, PB64/1, Maj. H. W. Denne to his father, 22 August 1882 and PB228, Lt H. W. Seton-Karr, diary, 20 and 21 August 1882.
17 GHM, PB64/1, Denne to his father, 22 August 1882, and PB228, Seton-Karr, diary, 19, 20 and 29 August 1882; see also BWA, 0203/1, Barwood, diary, 1 December 1882, p. 6.
18 GHM, PB64/1, Denne to his father, 22 August 1882, and PB228, Seton-Karr, diary, 19, 20 and 29 August 1882.
19 GHM, PB64/1, Denne to his father, 22 August 1882; see also Williams, 'The Egyptian Campaign of 1882', p. 259.
20 'A Dundee Soldier's Description of the Recent Fighting', *Weekly News*, 23 September 1882, p. 7.
21 *Ibid.*; see also Ward, 'Scots Guards in Egypt', 87.
22 Wolseley to Childers, 29 July 1882, in Childers, *Life and Correspondence*, vol. 2, pp. 99–100.
23 'Battle for Tel-el-Kebir: Letter from Another Crieff Soldier', p. 2.
24 'A Maidstone Soldier at the Seat of War', *Kentish Gazette*, 24 October 1882, p. 3.
25 'A Dundee Soldier's Description of the Recent Fighting', p. 7.
26 'Letters from Ludlow Men Serving in Egypt', *Hereford Journal*, 7 October 1882, p. 3.
27 'Letter from a Staffordshire Soldier', *Staffordshire Advertiser*, 16 September 1882, p. 2.
28 'A Dundee Soldier at Tel-el-Kebir', *Weekly News*, 7 October 1882, p. 7.
29 Philip, *Reminiscences*, p. 55; Ward, 'The Scots Guards in Egypt', 91.
30 Ward, 'Scots Guards in Egypt', 91 and 93.
31 'A Maidstone Soldier at the War', p. 3.
32 'Letter from a Townsman in Egypt', *Brechin Advertiser*, 10 October 1882, p. 3.
33 'A Dundee Soldier's Description of the Recent Fighting', p. 7.
34 *Ibid.*; 'A Dundee Soldier at Tel-el-Kebir', p. 7; Macaulay, 'With the Guards in Egypt', pp. 48–9.
35 Philip, *Reminiscences*, pp. 69, 72; 'Letter from a Staffordshire Soldier', p. 2.
36 'Letter from a Staffordshire Soldier', p. 2; see also *Memoirs of Sir Hugh McCalmont*, p. 215.
37 'Letter from a Local Officer of the Guards in Egypt', *Midland Counties Express*, 30 September 1882, p. 7.
38 'Letter from a Staffordshire Soldier', p. 2.
39 *Ibid.*, and 'A Guardsman's Recollection of the Great Cavalry Charge', *Lancaster Guardian*, 9 September 1882, p. 4.
40 'A Stafford Trooper's Experiences in Egypt', *Lichfield Mercury*, 13 October 1882, p. 7.
41 Maurice, *Military History of the Campaign of 1882*, p. 64; D. Featherstone, *Tel El-Kebir 1882: Wolseley's Conquest of Egypt* (London: Osprey, 1993), pp. 56, 61.
42 'A Dundee Soldier's Description of the Recent Fighting', p. 7.
43 Maj. A. W. Mackworth, 'The Field Telegraph Corps in Egypt', and Capt. S. Smith, 'Diary of Work Performed by the 8th Company, R.E., in Egypt', *REJ*, 12 (1 December 1882), 269–72, and 13 (1 January 1883), 4–8; see also Williams, 'The Egyptian Campaign of 1882', pp. 267–70.
44 'A Dundee Soldier's Description of the Recent Fighting', p. 7.
45 *Ibid.*; 'Letter from a Townsman in Egypt', p. 3; Ward, 'The Scots Guards in Egypt', 94.
46 GRO, D 873/C110, Marling to his father, 10 September 1882.
47 'Letters by a Soldier to his Crieff Friends', *Strathearn Herald*, 14 October 1882, p. 2.
48 NAM, Acc. No. 7112/39/4, Coghill MSS, Lt-Col. K. Coghill to Flo, 10 September 1884; see also 'An Oxonian in Egypt', *Abingdon and Reading Herald*, 28 October 1882, p. 6, and 'Letter from the Hon. Rupert Leigh', *Coventry Herald and Free Press*, 6 October 1882, p. 4.
49 Philip, *Reminiscences*, pp. 80–2.
50 GRO, D873/C110, Marling to his father, 10 September 1882, and 'The Marines at

Tel-el-Kebir', *Weekly News*, 14 October 1882, p. 7.

51 Queen's Own Highlanders Collection (QOHC), Capt. K. S. Baynes, *Narrative of the Part Taken by the 79th Queen's Own Cameron Highlanders in the Egyptian Campaign, 1882* (private, 1883), p. 12.

52 'A Yorkshireman's Account of the Capture of Tel-el-Kebir', *(Batley) Reporter*, 7 October 1882, p. 3.

53 *Ibid.*; 'Letter from the Black Watch', *Bridge of Allan Reporter*, 21 October 1882, p. 2.

54 'Soldiers' Letters', *Scotsman*, 6 October 1882, p. 5.

55 Compare 'Royal Highlanders (42ND)', *Broad Arrow*, 7 October 1882, p. 502, with 'The Highland Brigade', *Scotsman*, 11 October 1882, p. 7; 'March of the Highland Brigade from Ismailia to the Front', *Nairnshire Telegraph*, 4 October 1882, p. 4; 'A Dundee Highlander at Tel-el-Kebir', *Weekly News*, 14 October 1882, p. 7; 'A Yorkshireman's Account of the Capture of Tel-el-Kebir', p. 3.

56 'Extracts from the Diary of Lieut. H. H. L. Malcolm, 79th, Q. O. Cameron Highlanders, during the Egyptian War, 1882', *79th News*, 202 (April 1933), 150–5.

57 GHM, PB 228, Seton-Karr, diary, 31 August 1882.

58 'The Black Watch at Tel-el-Kebir', *Stirling Observer*, 12 October 1882, p. 2; see also Featherstone, *Tel El-Kebir*, p. 72.

59 'Highland Brigade', p. 7; 'The Storming of Tel-el-Kebir', *Strathearn Herald*, 7 October 1882, p. 2; 'A 42D Man at Tel-El-Kebir', *Kinross-shire Advertiser*, 28 October 1882, p. 3.

60 GHM, PB 64/2, Denne to his father, 20 September 1882; BWA 0204, Lt-Col. Coveny, 'Letters from Egypt and the Sudan', 28 September 1882, p. 7; 'A 42D Man at Tel-El-Kebir', p. 3.

61 'A Private Soldier's Description of the Battle of Tel-el-Kebir', *Staffordshire Advertiser*, 30 September 1882, p. 6.

62 QOHC, Baynes, *Narrative of the Part taken by the 79th*, p. 19; see also Lt-Col. L. B. Oatts, *Proud Heritage: The Story of the Highland Light Infantry*, 4 vols. (London: Thomas Nelson, 1959), vol. 2, p. 363.

63 'Soldiers' Letters', p. 5.

64 'A Dundee Highlander at Tel-El-Kebir', p. 7.

65 'Hairbreadth Escapes of a Cameronian [*sic*] Highlander', *Sheffield Daily Telegraph*, 5 October 1882, p. 3.

66 'A Native Account of the Battle of Tel-el-Kebir', *Staffordshire Advertiser*, 7 October 1882, p. 6.

67 GHM, PB 228, Seton-Karr, diary, p. 7; see also 'A Perthshire Hero at Tel-el-Kebir', *Kinross-shire Advertiser*, 7 October 1882, p. 3.

68 'A Rothesay Man at the Charge at Tel-el-Kebir', *Rothesay Express*, 18 October 1882, p. 3; see also 'The Battle of Tel-el-Kebir (By a 42D Highlander)', *(Edinburgh) Daily Review*, 5 October 1882, p. 5.

69 'More About Tel-el-Kebir: Interesting Letter to Herefordshire People', *Hereford Times*, 21 October 1882, p. 2; see also 'A Glasgow Highlander's Description of Tel-el-Kebir', *Glasgow News*, 10 October 1882, p. 5, and Oatts, *Proud Heritage*, vol. 2, pp. 363–6.

70 'Battle of Tel-el-Kebir (By a 42D Highlander)', p. 5; 'Black Watch at Tel-el-Kebir', p. 2; 'Extracts from the Diary of Lieut. H. H. L. Malcolm', 153–4; 'Royal Highlanders', p. 502; 'A Soldier's Letter', *Scotsman*, 13 October 1885, p. 5.

71 'The Late Lieutenant G. Stirling', *Strathearn Herald*, 21 October 1882, p. 2; QOHC, Baynes, *Narrative*, p. 21.

72 'The Royal Artillery at Tel-el-Kebir', *Bradford Observer*, 10 October 1882, p. 6.

73 'A Private Letter from Egypt', *Hastings and St Leonards News*, 6 October 1882, p. 3

74 'Letter from a Derbyshire Man', *Derbyshire Times*, 7 October 1882, p. 5.

75 'The Battle of Tel-el-Kebir – Letter from a Blackburn Soldier', *Blackburn Times*, 7 October 1882, p. 6; 'The Services of the Royal Marines in Egypt', *Western Morning News*, 29 September 1882, p. 3.

76 'A Soldier's Experiences at Tel-el-Kebir', *Banffshire Journal*, 10 October 1882, p. 3.

77 'Battle of Tel-el-Kebir: Letter from Another Crieff Soldier', p. 2.
78 NAM, Acc. No.. 7706/14, Coghill MSS, Coghill to Flo, 14 September 1882; see also The Marquess of Anglesey, *A History of the British Cavalry 1816 to 1919*, 8 vols (London: Leo Cooper, 1973–97), vol. 3, pp. 301–2.
79 Ward, 'The Scots Guards in Egypt', 99.
80 'Highland Brigade', p. 7.
81 BWA, 0204, Coveny, 'Letters from Egypt and the Sudan', p. 8; see also 'The Battle of Tel-el-Kebir. Letter from an Invergordon Young Man', *Invergordon Times*, 11 October 1882, p. 2; 'Black Watch at Tel-el-Kebir', p. 2; 'Storming of Tel-el-Kebir', p. 2.
82 'A Soldier's Account of Tel-el-Kebir', (*York*) *Evening Press*, 16 October 1882, p. 3; see also Williams, 'Egyptian Campaign of 1882', p. 274.
83 'Battle of Tel-el-Kebir (By a 42D Highlander)', p. 5.
84 'Storming of Tel-el-Kebir', p. 2.
85 'Soldiers' Letters', p. 6; 'At Tel-el-Kebir', *Kentish Chronicle*, 4 November 1882, p. 2; 'Battle of Tel-el-Kebir – Letter from a Blackburn Soldier', p. 6; 'Conduct of Our Soldiers at Tel-el-Kebir', *Colchester Chronicle*, 21 October 1882, p. 3.
86 'Soldiers' Letters', p. 6; see also 'Highland Brigade', p. 7.
87 'Letters from Ludlow Men Serving in Egypt', p. 3.
88 'A Maidstone Corporal at the Seat of War', p. 3.
89 'The War in Egypt', *Bridge of Allan Reporter*, 14 October 1882, p. 2.
90 'An Oxonian in Egypt', p. 6.
91 'The Torturing of Prisoners in the Citadel', *Scotsman*, 7 October 1882, p. 7; Ward, 'Scots Guards in Egypt', 101.
92 'Late Lieutenant G. Stirling', p. 2; see also 'Letter from Another Crieff Soldier', p. 2.
93 NAM, Acc. No. 7706/14, Sergeant C. Spraggs, diary, 17 September 1882.
94 'Letter from a Townsman in Egypt', p. 3; see also NAM, Acc. No. 7003/25, Churchward MSS, Lt W. S. Churchward to Annie, 25 September 1882; 'The Naval Brigade in Egypt', *Hampshire Telegraph and Sussex Chronicle*, 21 October 1882, p. 8.
95 'A 42D Man at Tel-el-Kebir', p. 3.
96 GHM, PB 64/3, Denne to his father, 15 October 1882.
97 'Letter from a Townsman in Egypt', p. 3.
98 NAM, Acc. No. 7706/14, Spraggs, diary, 6 October 1882; see also 'Letter from a Knighton Man', *Hereford Times*, 21 October 1882, p. 2.
99 'The Duke of Connaught's Pluck', *Strathearn Herald*, 21 October 1882, p. 2, and 'Letters by a Soldier to His Crieff Friends', p. 2; see also Philip, *Reminiscences*, p. 98; 'Services of the Royal Marines in Egypt', p. 3.
100 'Letters by a Soldier to His Crieff Friends', p. 2 and Mackworth, 'The Field Telegraph Corps in Egypt', 271.
101 'Battle of Tel-el-Kebir: Written Despatch from Sir Garnet Wolseley', *Derby Mercury*, 11 October 1882, p. 3; RPLM, Wolseley MSS, W/P.11, Wolseley to Lady Wolseley, 21 and 28 September 1882, ff. 21 and 23.
102 'Slight to the Marines', *Weekly News*, 21 October 1882, p. 7; 'Letter from a Crieff Soldier in Egypt', *Strathearn Herald*, 28 October 1882, p. 2; 'Battle of Tel-el-Kebir (By a 42D Highlander)', p. 5; GHM, PB 64/2, Denne to his father, 20 September 1882.
103 'Letter from a Crieff Soldier in Egypt', p. 2; see also 'Slight to the Marines', p. 7.
104 NAM, Acc. No. 7003/25, Churchward to Annie, 25 September 1882; see also *Evening Standard*, 6 October 1882, p. 8; Ward, 'Scots Guards in Egypt', 92; 'Battle of Tel-el-Kebir: Letter from an Invergordon Man', p. 2; Philip, *Reminiscences*, pp. 56–7.
105 GHM, PB 64/3, Denne to his father, 15 October 1882.
106 'Mr Childers and the Army', *Cornubian and Redruth Times*, 27 October 1882, p. 3.
107 'Battle of Tel-el-Kebir – Letter from a Blackburn Soldier', p. 6; GHM, PB 64/3, Denne to his father, 15 October 1882.
108 The Black Watch had 300 men of over 6 years' service; the Gordons, 370 over 24 years; the Camerons, 460 over 24 years; and the men of the HLI had an average of about 8 years' service: 'The "Young Soldiers" at Tel-el-Kebir', *Manchester Guardian*, 12 October 1882, p. 8.

109 'Letter from Egypt', *East of Fife Record*, 22 September 1882, p. 3; see also 'A Dundee Soldier's Description of the Recent Fighting', p. 7.
110 GHM, PB 64/4, Denne to his father, 1 May 1883.
111 'Black Watch at Tel-el-Kebir', p. 2.
112 Philip, *Reminiscences*, p. 103; on medals, see GHM, PB 64/3, Denne to his father, 15 October 1882;'A Dundee Highlander at Tel-el-Kebir', p. 7 and Featherstone, *Tel El-Kebir*, p. 91.

CHAPTER FIVE

Engaging the Mahdists

Gladstone's Government consolidated victory at Tel-el-Kebir by establishing a *temporary* military occupation of Egypt (both to protect the Suez Canal and to preserve internal order in Egypt). Given the minimal size of the army of occupation, the arrangement worked conveniently within Egypt but difficulties soon arose when Egypt, on behalf of the Porte, sought to crush the rebellion launched by Mohammad Ahmed – the Mahdi, or 'Expected One', in the Sudan. Egypt employed a retired British officer, Lieutenant-General William Hicks, to lead an army of 11,000 men against the Mahdists, an offensive that ended in spectacular failure on the plain of Shaykan, near El Obeid (5 November 1883), where his army was annihilated with only a few hundred survivors. As the rebels threatened further towns, including Khartoum, Gladstone's cabinet wanted to evacuate the remaining Egyptian garrisons from the Sudan. Confronting a popular outcry fanned by the influential *Pall Mall Gazette*, it responded by sending Major-General Charles 'Chinese' Gordon (18 January 1884) up the Nile to 'consider and report' on the situation.[1] In eastern Sudan, however, where the British wished to retain the Red Sea ports round Suakin (both for their commercial value and to prevent them becoming outlets for the slave trade), the Beja tribes (including the Hadendowa, Amarar, Bisharin and others) under Osman Digna commanded the trade route to Berber and besieged the garrisons of Sinkat and Tokar. The Mahdists destroyed another Egyptian relief force under Major-General Valentine Baker at El Teb (4 February 1884) and overwhelmed the garrison of Sinkat four days later as it tried to march to the coast. The slaughter of Egyptian soldiers and civilians from Sinkat, with the capture of their women and children, aroused fervent demands for intervention, not least from Queen Victoria. Gladstone, according to his private secretary, reluctantly agreed to send a British relief force to Tokar; 'It is', added Edward Hamilton, 'in a small way a response to the unreasonable cries of public feeling.'[2]

The ensuing campaign was extremely brief, but represented the first encounter of British forces with the Mahdists and their first experience of campaigning in the eastern Sudan. Some 4,000 men, drawn from the garrisons in Egypt, Aden and India, served under Sir Gerald Graham, VC; they comprised two brigades of infantry, including a body of Royal Marine Light Infantry, a cavalry brigade under Colonel Herbert Stewart, and a naval detachment operating three Gatling and three Gardner machine-guns.[3] Of this small force, composed of soldiers already serving overseas, relatively few wrote letters to family and friends in Britain. Newspapers were also less dependent on them, as several war correspondents had accompanied the ill-fated relief force under Baker Pasha and were ready to report on the next campaign. Given the experience and rivalry of these 'specials', including Francis Scudamore (*Daily News*), John Cameron (*Standard*), James Mellor Paulton (*Manchester Examiner*), Frederic Villiers (*Graphic*), Bennet Burleigh (*Daily Telegraph*), Alex MacDonald (*Western Morning News*) and Melton Prior (*Illustrated London News*), this brief campaign was fully reported.[4] Burleigh gained prominence by 'scooping' his rivals in reporting on the second battle of El Teb (29 February 1884) and by fighting the Hadendowa in the broken square at Tamai (13 March 1884).[5]

Soldiers who had been based in Egypt were delighted to leave a country where cholera had claimed all too many victims and to see action.[6] They also grasped the sense of urgency that characterised the campaign. On 14 February the 1/Black Watch was issued with a new grey field kit and told that it would leave for the Sudan on the following morning, which was 'not much notice', Bandsman Barwood reflected: 'All night most of us sat up drinking and singing, but dozed off towards morning.' He consoled a disconsolate friend who had to remain behind, then left on the train for Suez between 6 and 7 a.m. At Tel-el-Kebir the train stopped, allowing the Black Watch to visit the cemetery where several soldiers took feathers out of their red hackles 'and stuck them in our comrades graves'.[7] After this poignant scene, the train pressed on to Suez where men and horses were crammed into troopships for the 6-day voyage to Trinkitat. The *Orontes* carried 44 officers and 1,169 men, but its lack of horse fittings meant that the mounted infantry, as Marling recalled, had to tie 'the horses up to the ship's rail, where they fought and bit one another worse than ever'.[8]

Whether the voyages were enjoyed, as Captain A. O. Green, RE, later claimed, paying numerous tributes to the entertainment by the Black Watch band on board the *Orontes*, or were 'very miserable', as remembered by Private Peter McRae (1/Gordon Highlanders) on board the *Thibet*, moments of anxiety recurred.[9] These included immediate con-

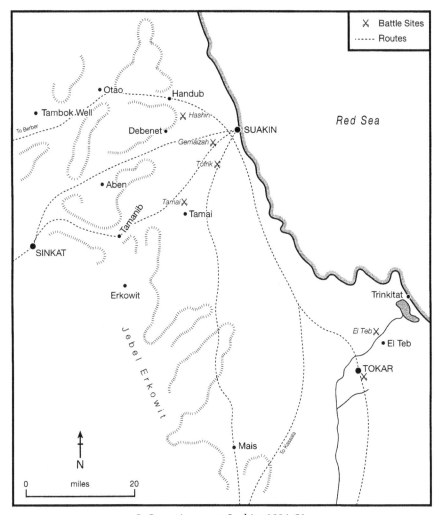

5 Operations near Suakin, 1884–91

cerns as the ships travelled slowly, often stopping, in the shallow
coastal waters south of Suakin (the *Neera* foundered); longer term fears
that Tokar could fall before the troops landed; and the practical difficulty of disembarking troops, horses and stores over the coral reefs at
Trinkitat. Green and his sappers had to erect a suitable pier and then
construct troughs and tanks to hold the 13,000 gallons of water, condensed from the Red Sea, which soldiers and animals required on a
daily basis. Marling saw the water coming into 'the canvas horse

troughs so hot that although the horses were almost mad with thirst we had to take them away for ten minutes to let it cool'.[10]

As the soldiers began to disembark on 21 February, the first news of Tokar's surrender came via an exhausted Egyptian soldier. He was debriefed by Green for the intelligence department and was then 'examined and cross-examined' as he was rowed out to the *Orontes*. Confirmation of the garrison's fall was passed on to London by 23 February when Graham had the bulk of his army ashore.[11] Sir Evelyn Baring (later the Earl of Cromer), who was the British agent and consul-general in Cairo, now found himself pressed by senior military officers to continue the campaign. Although he doubted that further action (beyond leaving a secure garrison round Suakin) would serve any purpose, the Government could not contemplate the political costs of a precipitate withdrawal. As Lord Granville, the foreign secretary, deliberated whether a march to El Teb might be feasible to protect the fugitives and bury the European dead or, if Suakin was threatened, to mount an offensive from Trinkitat or Suakin, it soon became too late to prevent an advance by Graham.[12]

Soldiers were none too impressed by their first few days in the Sudan. They had to work from morning until night unloading vessels and had 'nothing here to cover us', as McRae noted, 'but the sky and a blanket', a combination that had to withstand tropical downpours every night for a week.[13] If strictly rationed to one bottle of water per day, they could at least bathe in the sea each morning and were spared the extremes of heat – Green confirmed that over 'four days the signallers have not been able to utilise the heliograph from absence of sun . . .'.[14] On 25 February the Gordons marched ahead with the Irish Fusiliers, an artillery detachment, a squadron of the 19th Hussars and mounted infantry to establish a forward base at Fort Baker, some 3 miles distant. McRae described how they 'had to march up to the knees in mud and then through prickly bushes which scratch our knees terrible'; the fort built by Baker's Egyptian troops was, however, impressive: as Private John Morrison (Black Watch) commented, 'it is a very strongly fortified place indeed'.[15]

As ever in colonial warfare, the first priorities were base security and logistical supply. Once the engineers had erected a wire entanglement, soldiers were able to bivouac in and around the earthwork, whereupon they laboured to bring stores, artillery and, above all, supplies of fresh water across the marsh. 'Everyone had been crying out for everything simultaneously', wrote Green, but packing casks, tanks and miscellaneous water containers onto camels and then sending them to Fort Baker was his priority; by 27 February he had some 8,000 gallons stored at Fort Baker. Graham completed his base defences by leaving a company of Riflemen, 'all sick and weakly men' and the departmental details at Trinkitat, and another three companies of Riflemen with a Krupp gun and two bronze guns at Fort Baker.[16]

On 28 February the relief force congregated at Fort Baker, with the 1/Yorks and Lancs, who were the last to arrive from Aden, crossing the bog at night. Graham and his staff then deployed his force in a 'rectangular parallelogram of 400 x 250 feet', leaving the men in full kit through another night of rain (albeit fortified by tots of rum).[17] By 8.15 a.m. on the following day, the relief force was ready to assume the offensive, and a sailor claimed: 'The 750 mounted troops looked splendid, and . . . [the] pipers of the 75th and 42nd Highlanders played some of their old stirring war-marches as the force moved over the rough ground'.[18] The rain-sodden ground, 'thickly dotted with scrub . . . about 2½ ft. high',[19] ensured that the first 2 miles were very arduous, particularly for the gunners and sailors dragging their guns by hand. As the fierce sun compounded the fatigue (even if it eased their marching over firmer ground for the final 2 miles), there were frequent halts en route. Near El Teb cavalry scouts crossed the battlefield where Baker Pasha's forces had foundered: 'It was a frightful sight', recalled Private C. Stream (19th Hussars), 'nothing but dead bodies . . . They had been lying there for over a month. The stench was something frightful.'[20]

By about 10 a.m. those scouts found their enemy counterparts and reconnoitred the Mahdists' position, including shallow earthworks, rifle pits and fortified buildings in front of the village and wells of El Teb. Graham, who estimated that the enemy numbered 6,000, marched his formation to the right in the hope of turning the enemy's left but, by 11.20 a.m., his forces came under fire from the rifle pits and two Krupp guns captured from Baker Pasha's expedition. To Private Morrison's relief, the infantry were ordered to lie down while the artillery and naval machine-guns returned fire and 'soon silenced the enemy, upsetting their guns. We continued to move steadily up to them, fighting our way, and succeeded in capturing their guns, and our artillery turning upon them soon made sad havoc.'[21]

Effectively the left face of the Yorks and Lancs, supported by Royal Marines, composed the firing line, with the Gordons and Black Watch on either flank. Private W. G. Martin, a Welsh Gordon Highlander, described how they

> started at a very slow rate. We halted in front of the first fort, where they came down upon us in thousands, but we kept them at bay. The rebels are a lot of brave men. They would come right up to the point of the bayonet when we were firing a storm of bullets into them, and they would not retire, so they all fell by bayonet or shot.[22]

In the ferocious combat, a young Dingwallian was mightily impressed by the example of the senior officers: Baker Pasha was shot in the face but required a 'great deal of persuasion' before he dismounted to get the wound treated; Colonel Fred Burnaby was wounded in the arm but killed 10 men with 20 shots; and Captain A. K. Wilson of the *Hecla*, who would earn a VC, saved several lives and made 'some dreadful havoc' among several Arabs with the hilt of his broken sword before suffering a scalp wound.[23]

Close-range fire-power proved decisive as the soldiers and sailors worked their way through the defensive position. Lieutenant Denne (Gordons) testified to the 'great stand' made at a brick house and huge iron boiler: 'the niggars lay in heaps round it', and, once inside the village, 'our infantry opened on them at close range & so did the Naval Brigade guns'. Then the Mahdists 'threw away their rifles' and charged with their spears: 'Nothing stopped them till the hail of bullets & machine guns floored them mostly at the feet of the front rank of the square, one black hit thro' the body came on & stabbed one of our men in the face before being finally shot down.'[24] Marling regarded the Mahdists as 'the pluckiest fellows I've ever seen'; Sergeant William Danby (10th Hussars) agreed that 'these Arabs are the most fierce, brave, daring & unmerciful men in the world[,] they fear nothing, give & expect no quarter . . .'.[25] Having lost their gun emplacements, and with the Krupp guns turned against them, Osman Digna's forces gradually withdrew.

Unlike what had been experienced at Tel-el-Kebir, a Mahdist withdrawal was not a retreat, as the 10th and 19th Hussars soon discovered. Denne watched the spectacle unfold as 'amid loud cheering the cavalry came round our right flank & charged'.[26] He saw how the thick scrub broke up the close-order formation, while the enemy crouched in the bushes beneath the range of cavalry sabres and then used spears and knives like billhooks to hamstring the horses before stabbing any fallen troopers. 'The cavalry lost very heavily', he noted, a view confirmed by Trooper Stream:

> We had a pretty hard fight at Teb with the blacks. We had a charge, both regiments that are here. The ground was very bad; we could not see where we were going to properly. When we got into their village, they were down in holes, and we could not reach them with our swords. As we went over them they cut the horses down and there was no chance for anyone whose horse fell.[27]

Major Percy H. S. Barrow (19th Hussars), who was severely wounded by a spear, nevertheless wrote about his 'glorious luck': after Lieutenant-Colonel A. G. Webster's wing had become separated, and his own wing became the first line, 'and still better came upon a large mass of the enemy. The leader of the 1st line was not long in communicating his views to the Brigadier [who] you may be sure [was] not long in preparing for attack. There was no hurry or confusion. When we did go the men rode straight and well and deserve all the credit that they have received.'[28]

In several charges the cavalry lost 20 killed and 48 wounded (out of a total of 30 killed and 142 wounded). Danby's twelve-man section followed a 'mad order' to gallop back amidst 'an enemy 400 strong' and recover 6 fallen troopers (2 of whom died and another 2 required amputations). The sight of mutilated corpses inflamed passions further, notably the stripped corpse of Major M. M. Slade (10th Hussars) with 'about 30 wounds from spears . . . & all his fingers broken to get his rings off'.[29] Thereafter, explained Marling, 'We shot or bayonetted [sic] all wounded as it was not safe to leave them as they knifed everyone they could reach.'[30] Overall Denne regarded the three-and-a-half-hour battle as 'a very tough job much worse in my opinion than our great Tel el Kebir . . .'.[31]

He was much less impressed by the subsequent advance on Tokar (1 March), which was entered without a shot being fired:

> The General made an ass of himself by having a sort of triumphal march with some cavalry round the town . . . It is just the sort of bunkum I should expect of him. The relief of Tokar was in fact all humbug, we were too late, the place had fallen & the guns been carried off. The enemy & Egyptians had been living on friendly terms inside together till we came up, when the enemy bolted & our friend the Egyptian remained as there was nothing to be afraid of in us . . . I imagine that the fact of our having been too late to really relieve the place will be hushed up.[32]

Graham, nonetheless, had accomplished his mission. He had safely evacuated 600 Egyptian men, women and children from the garrison to Trinkitat and buried the dead, not only the British and some 2,000 dervish dead at El Teb[33] but the decomposed bodies of the Europeans from the previous battle (an exhausting and nauseating burial detail undertaken by half of the Black Watch). He withdrew all his forces safely and, by 6 March, had the first of his units sailing for Suakin. For the next four days the soldiers worked from morning to night, unloading all their vessels at Suakin in temperatures that reached 110 degrees Fahrenheit in the shade.[34]

Graham now planned to advance on Osman Digna's camp at Tamai some 16 miles from Suakin, with 2 squares of infantry and 12 guns (116 officers and 3,216 men), supported by cavalry and mounted infantry (41 officers and 696 men). Major-Generals Davis and Buller commanded the two infantry brigades, and the force as a whole was to undertake short marches (to limit the risk of sunstroke) and to protect itself by constructing zarebas (defensive perimeters about 4-feet high and 6-feet deep made out of mimosa bush) whenever it halted. Graham chose the Black Watch to lead the advance on 10 March, but on the previous day publicly rebuked the battalion for its purported 'unsteadiness' at El Teb, both its 'wild firing' and then its failure to cease fire when ordered. He declared that the battalion would be able to restore its reputation by its advanced position on the line of march. Captain Andrew Scott-Stevenson was 'astonished' by the speech and appalled by its demoralising effect; Bandsman Barwood was surprised that a mutiny did not follow, especially as the general closed the canteen after his speech: 'we did not deserve it', he added.[35]

The travails of the Black Watch persisted on the march, where over fifty men fell out with exhaustion and sunstroke on the first day and the column had to wait until the stragglers were brought in. At 'Baker's zareba' where they were due to bivouac overnight, a carelessly tossed match caused a bush fire that had to be extinguished with coats and kilts. The Highlanders then constructed a large zareba for the following convoy that Graham condemned as too large and so they had to begin again. Barwood explained that they

> had to use nothing but green bush, as the black ones caught fire, being too dry; it was no easy job to get all green bush. After a good deal had been cut, we were given a rope which we had to tie to staples in the ground; besides this, we had to fill numbers of bags with sand and attach them to the rope, which was reeved into the bush . . . and then bury the bags in the earth with the rope round them, so that the bush could not be pulled away.[36]

After the remainder of the column reached the zareba on the following day, the advance was resumed on 12 March. Officers and men were issued with one pint of water each, which had been brought up from Suakin on camels and 'smelt horribly'.[37] They marched another 7 miles until they reached a slight hill within range of the enemy's camp, where they built another zareba and replied to enemy shelling and rifle-fire with fire from their 9-pounders and Gardner machine-guns. During the overnight bivouac men were issued with rum, and when Barwood found his 'fighting chum . . . insensibly drunk', he 'had an awful bother to get him to lie still and hold his tongue'.[38] The officers had other refreshments, with Scott-Stevenson, his subaltern and Captain Rolfe (RN), consuming two magnums of champagne.[39]

On 13 September, after the cavalry and mounted infantry had located the enemy masses, possibly 9,000 in number, Graham launched his attack at 8.30 a.m., with the 2nd Brigade (Black Watch,

Yorks and Lancs, Naval Brigade and Marines), screened by Abyssinian scouts, moving in advance of the 1st Brigade. Within half-an-hour the Hadendowa were fiercely engaging the scouts at the edge of a gully, and so Graham, who had assumed command from Davis, ordered the Black Watch to charge. The regiment, still smarting from his previous rebuke, responded with alacrity, but the ensuing engagement proved a disaster, as graphically recounted by Captain Scott-Stevenson, whose original letter has survived, as well as many anonymous, abbreviated and carefully edited or paraphrased versions in various newspapers.[40]

Scott-Stevenson explained how Graham had failed to order the Yorks and Lancs to charge and so a gap quickly opened on the right-hand corner of the square. On reaching the edge of the gully, the Black Watch, realised that the Hadendowa had cleared their front and were working their way round towards the right. Enfilade fire had only limited effect because the 'smoke was too awful' and the guns never came into action, so enabling the Arabs to pour through the gap and attack the Black Watch from the rear. Regimental survivors confirmed that a ferocious hand-to-hand combat followed; several guns, though locked, fell into the hands of the enemy as their naval officers perished; and 'victory', as Sergeant Connan claimed, 'seemed to hang in the balance'.[41] Much of Scott-Stevenson's prose proved too lurid for publication. 'My trusty claymore', he wrote, 'found its way to the hilt into several black devils. I clove a piece out of one of their heads just as one does an egg for breakfast & saw his white brain exposed. I was mad with rage and fury. . . I fought like a demon & only wanted to kill, kill, kill these awful plucky demons.'[42] Another soldier commented more dispassionately on the retreat of the broken square:

> Our men fought as well as they could, but were too crowded. The square now collapsed into a mass, with the Marines lumped in the middle, and the 65th and 42nd, on the right and left flanks respectively, moving slowly back – the outside men nearest the enemy turning to fire and bayonet as best they could . . . The enemy had never surrounded the square, but persistently pushed it back in front and flanks – a form of tactics most favourable for their object of keeping us crowded up, narrowed, and unable to use our weapons.[43]

As the broken square lurched 800 yards backwards, Denne deprecated the effects on the other brigade, especially the Egyptian camel drivers who mounted their animals and fled. 'The correspondents', he added, 'were no better as they legged it to a man, several were stopped by the cavalry but two got straight into Suakin without drawing rein & one [Cameron] went to the admiral [Sir W. Hewett] with news of the annihilation of one square'.[44] In fact, dismounted fire from the cavalry and mounted infantry assisted in dispersing the Arabs on the left flank of the retreating square, while case shot from Major Holley's battery on the right followed by enfilade fire from Buller's Brigade, once it had warded off an assault on itself, proved decisive on the right. 'Our square', wrote Denne,

> stood well all the time & bowled over the niggers in style without letting them get up close . . . I thought when I saw the square coming back it was all over & it was Isandula over again, but the second square not being moved at all by the attack saved us in my opinion.[45]

Davis's square was able to reform, recapture the guns and advance with the 1st Brigade to seize Osman Digna's camp by about 11.40 a.m. Once the brigades moved on to the offensive and crossed the gully, there was little resistance, save from the flanks, and the camp was almost unoccupied when taken. An estimated 2,000 of the enemy died, though the British casualties were relatively heavy, with over 100 killed and about the same number wounded.[46] The Black Watch had the largest number of killed and wounded (61 and 33, respectively), and some of the wounded had horrendous cuts to their legs. Many of their survivors blamed Graham, and most regimental comrades agreed: 'The Black Watch', noted Marling, 'were very bitter about Graham, and who can blame them?'[47] Scott-Stevenson blamed Graham, and also asked, in another unpublished aside: 'Who is to blame for this[?] I wish old Gladstone had been in that square.'[48]

After burning Osman Digna's camp, Graham withdrew his force to Suakin. Thereafter he launched some minor reconnaissance operations to Handub (10 miles north-west of Suakin), Otao (a further 8 miles westwards) and into the Tamanieb valley. On 25 March, he led his two brigades against an enemy force at Tamanieb, dispersing the Mahdists and burning the village (with the medical officers inconvenienced mainly by the number of men succumbing to the heat – 50 within a mile of Suakin and another 130 during the remainder of the operation).[49] The futility of these actions was all too obvious: Marling reckoned: 'We ought really to go right across by the desert route to help Gordon, but old Gladstone, they say, won't let us, or buy sufficient camels.'[50] On returning to Suakin (29 March), Graham was ordered to close the campaign, and, apart from leaving two battalions to assist in garrisoning the town, embarked the remainder of his force on 3 April.

Soldiers left the Sudan impressed by the enemy, if not the outcome of the campaign. Major Robert Coveny, a Black Watch veteran of the Asante and Egyptian campaigns, claimed: 'I never saw such fellows to fight as those Hadendowa Arabs; they know not what fear is in most cases.'[51] Another soldier graphically described their fearsome appearance at the battle of Tamai: 'The half-naked black savages, having heads huge with lumps of woolly hair on end upwards and sideways, brandishing their spears and curved sticks used as shields and clubs, dancing madly behind the retreating square looked through the smoke like real demons.'⁵² Several officers, including Scott-Stevenson and Graham, also recognised the tactical finesse of these warriors – their ability to use the ground and the cover of smoke to creep up close and then attack the corners as the weakest part of square formations.⁵³

While soldiers grumbled over the issue of medals – restricted to those who had not previously served in Egypt, and those with Egyptian medals received only clasps –⁵⁴ most were glad to leave the Sudan. Although they had avoided being lured into the desert and had twice defeated Osman Digna's forces, the Mahdists remained in Sinkat, commanded the route to Berber and reoccupied Tokar. Understandably, soldiers dwelt less on the strategic implications of the campaign than the experience itself. A Fifer wrote:

> For Britain's honour we have fought,
>   And suffer'd heat, fatigue, and toil;
> Defeated Osman's swarthy host,
>   And made them quick disgorge their spoil.
>
> While for companions loved we mourn,
>   Struck down by roving Arab's spear;
> To Britain we will glad return,
>   From Afric's deserts, dry and dear.⁵⁵

Characteristically, Denne was much more blunt: 'everyone is heartily sick of this useless waste of life to bolster up government & hopes we are to have no more'.⁵⁶ Ironically, even Gladstone admitted privately that the military operations round Suakin were a great mistake, and the ever-sceptical Baring agreed that the political and military outcomes were hardly commensurate with the lives and resources expended.⁵⁷

Notes

1 Matthew, *Gladstone 1875–1898*, pp. 143–6; Earl of Cromer, *Modern Egypt*, 2 vols (London: Macmillan, 1908), vol. 2, p. 443.
2 *The Diary of Sir Edward Walter Hamilton 1880–1885*, ed. D. W. R. Bahlman (Oxford: Clarendon Press, 1972), vol. 2, pp. 555–7; PP, *Further Correspondence Respecting the Affairs of Egypt (Further Correspondence, Egypt)*, C 3969 (1884), LXXXVIII, Earl Granville to Sir E. Baring, 12 February 1884, p. 54.
3 Lt.-Col. E. W. C. Sandes, *The Royal Engineers in Egypt and the Sudan* (Chatham: Royal Engineers' Institution, 1937) pp. 59–60; H. Keown-Boyd, *A Good Dusting: The Sudan Campaigns 1883–1899* (London: Leo Cooper, 1986), p. 26; D. Featherstone, *Khartoum 1885* (London: Osprey, 1993), p. 13.
4 There are only references to eight letter-writers in Emery, *Marching Over Africa*, pp. 188–9; Wilkinson-Latham, *From Our Special Correspondent*, pp. 178–9, and R.

Stearn, 'War Correspondents and Colonial War, c. 1870–1900', in J. M. MacKenzie (ed.), *Popular Imperialism and the Military 1850–1950* (Manchester: Manchester University Press, 1992), pp. 139–61.

5 R. Stearn, 'Bennet Burleigh Victorian War Correspondent', *Soldiers of the Queen*, 65 (June 1884), 5–10; 'British Victory at El Teb', *Daily Telegraph*, 3 March 1884, p. 5.
6 GHM, PB 173, Pte P. McRae to his aunt, 10 February 1884; BWA, 0203/1, Barwood, diary, 6 and 19 August 1883, pp. 31 and 35.
7 BWA, 0203/1, Barwood, diary, 9 May 1884, pp. 50–1; 'The "Black Watch" and Their Fallen Comrades at Tel-el-Kebir', *Strathearn Herald*, 15 March 1884, p. 4.
8 Marling, *Rifleman and Hussar*, p. 100; see also A. O. G. (Capt. A. O. Green), 'From Cairo to Trinkitat with the Suakin Field Force', *REJ*, 14 (1 April 1884), 75–6.
9 A. O. G., 'From Cairo to Trinkitat', 75–6, GHM, PB 173, Pte P. McRae to his mother, 26 February 1884.
10 Marling, *Rifleman and Hussar*, p. 101; BWA, 0203/1, Barwood, diary, 9 May 1884, p. 52; A. O. G., 'From Cairo to Trinkitat', 75; Sandes, *Royal Engineers*, p. 61.
11 A. O. G., 'From Cairo to Trinkitat', 76; Bahlman, *Hamilton*, vol. 2, p. 564.
12 Cromer, *Modern Egypt*, vol. 1, pp. 410–14.
13 GHM, PB 173, McRae to his mother, 26 February 1884.
14 A. O. G., 'From Cairo to Trinkitat and El Teb with the Suakin Field Force', *REJ*, 14 (1 May 1884), 99–102; see also BWA, 0203/1, Barwood, diary, 9 May 1884, p. 54.
15 GHM, PB 173, McRae to his aunt, 20 April 1884; 'Letter from a Soldier of the Black Watch', *Falkirk Herald*, 5 April 1884, p. 2; for the marching ordeal of the 10th Hussars, see NAM, Acc. No. 7003/2, Danby MSS, Sgt W. Danby to Adie, 28 February 1884.
16 PRO, WO 33/42, *Correspondence Relative to the Expedition to Suakim*, Graham to the secretary of state for war, 2 March 1884, pp. 43–6; A. O. G., 'From Cairo to Trinkitat and El Teb', 100.
17 A. O. G., 'From Cairo to Trinkitat and El Teb', 100.
18 'The Bluejackets at El Teb', *Western Morning News*, 31 March 1884, p. 8; see also BWA, 0203/1, Barwood, diary, 9 May 1884, p. 58.
19 GHM, PB 64/5, Denne to his father, 6 March 1884.
20 It was slightly less than a month: 'Letter from a Pontypridd Soldier', *Western Mail*, 27 March 1884, p. 3; Col. R. S. Liddell, *The Memoirs of the Tenth Royal Hussars* (London: Longman Green, 1891), pp. 436–7.
21 'Letter from a Soldier of the Black Watch', p. 2; see also PRO, WO 33/42, Graham to secretary of state for war, 2 March 1884, p. 45.
22 'Letter from Another Welsh Soldier', *Western Mail*, 10 April 1884, p. 3. The 75th was an English battalion until it was linked with the 92nd and given the kilt, becoming the 1/Gordon Highlanders, GHM, PB 173, McRae to his Aunt, 7 August 1884.
23 'Letters from Egypt', *Ross-shire Journal*, 4 April 1884, p. 3; see also 'Bluejackets at El Teb', p. 8.
24 GHM, PB 64/5, Denne to his father, 6 March 1884.
25 GRO, D 873/C110, Marling to his father, 3 March 1884; NAM, Acc. No. 7003/2, Danby to Adie, 1 March 1884.
26 GHM, PB 64/5, Denne to his father, 6 March 1884.
27 *Ibid.* and 'Letter from a Pontypridd Soldier', p. 3.
28 NAM, Acc. No. 7112/39/4, Coghill MSS, Maj. P. H. S. Barrow to Coghill, 11 April 1884.
29 NAM, Acc. No. 7003/2, Danby to Adie, 1 March 1884; GHM, PB 64/5, Denne to his father, 6 March 1884. On casualties, see PP, *Further Correspondence, Egypt*, C 3969 (1884), LXXXVIII, Graham to Lord Hartington, 1 March 1884, p. 121; Marquess of Anglesey, *A History of the British Cavalry 1816 to 1919*, 8 vols (London: Leo Cooper, 1973–97), vol. 3, p. 316.
30 GRO, D 873/C110, Marling to his father, 3 March 1884.
31 GHM, PB 64/5, Denne to his father, 6 March 1884.
32 *Ibid.*
33 *Ibid.* and Marling, *Rifleman and Hussar*, p. 104.

34 BWA, 0230/1, Barwood, diary, 8 July 1884, pp. 62–5, 68; PP, *Further Correspondence, Egypt*, C 3969, Graham to Lord Hartington, 4 March 1884, p. 140; Keown-Boyd, *A Good Dusting*, p. 29.
35 BWA, 0641, Capt. A. S. Scott-Stevenson to his wife, 16 March 1884; and 0230/1, Barwood, diary, 30 August 1884, p. 69; see also PRO, WO 33/42, Graham to the secretary of state for war, 2 March 1884, p. 45.
36 BWA, 0230/1, Barwood, diary, 30 August 1884, pp. 70–2.
37 Marling, *Rifleman and Hussar*, p. 110.
38 BWA, 0230/1, Barwood, diary, 14 September 1884, pp. 74–7.
39 BWA, 0641, Scott-Stevenson to his wife, 16 March 1884.
40 Compare *ibid.* with 'The Battle of Tamai', *Scotsman*, 2 April 1884, p. 7; 'Black Watch at Tamanieb', *York Herald*, 8 April 1884, p. 5; and 'The Battle of Tamai: Description by an Officer of the Black Watch', *Sussex Daily News*, 14 April 1884, p. 2.
41 'The Battle of Tamai in the Soudan', *Strathearn Herald*, 12 April 1884, p. 2; BWA, 0641, Scott-Stevenson to his wife, 16 March 1884; 'The Battle of Tamai', *Oxford Times*, 19 April 1884, p. 6; 'Description by a Private in the Black Watch', *Edinburgh Evening News*, 4 April 1884, p. 4.
42 BWA, 0641, Scott-Stevenson to his wife, 16 March 1884.
43 'Notes from Egypt', *Hampshire Telegraph and Sussex Chronicle*, 12 April 1884, p. 5.
44 GHM, PB 64/6, Denne to his father, 15 March 1884. Burleigh, Prior and Villiers could not flee because they were in the broken square: Wilkinson-Latham, *From Our Special Correspondent*, pp. 182–3.
45 GHM, PB 64/6, Denne to his father, 15 March 1884; Marling, *Rifleman and Hussar*, pp. 111–12; PRO, WO 33/42, Graham to the secretary of state for war, 15 March 1884, pp. 76–80.
46 GHM, PB 64/6, Denne to his father, 15 March 1884; Sandes, *Royal Engineers*, p. 64.
47 Marling, *Rifleman and Hussar*, p. 112; see also GHM, PB 173, McRae to his mother, 17 March 1884, and 'Description by a Private in the Black Watch', p. 4.
48 BWA, 0641, Scott-Stevenson to his wife, 16 March 1884.
49 PRO, WO 33/42, E. G. McDowell, report, 29 March 1884, pp. 93–4.
50 Marling, *Rifleman and Hussar*, p. 118.
51 BWA, 0204, Coveny, 'Letters from Egypt and the Sudan', 9 June 1884, p. 10.
52 'Notes from Egypt', p. 5.
53 BWA, 0641, Scott-Stevenson to his wife, 16 March 1884; and PRO, WO 33/42, Graham to the secretary of state for war, 15 March 1884, p. 79.
54 Marling, *Rifleman and Hussar*, p. 117; and BWA, 0204, Coveny, 'Letters from Egypt and the Sudan', 9 June 1884, pp. 12–13.
55 'A British Soldier in the Sudan', *Fife Herald*, 30 April 1884, p. 5.
56 GHM, PB 64/6, Denne to his father, 15 March 1884.
57 Bahlman, *Hamilton*, vol. 2, p. 747; Cromer, *Modern Egypt*, vol. 1, p. 416.

CHAPTER SIX

The Gordon relief expedition

From the outset of Gordon's mission doubts existed about whether it was an advisory or an executive role, about what Gordon could accomplish once appointed governor-general of the Sudan and about what would happen if his life became endangered. Whatever Gordon's motives,[1] he felt compelled to remain in Khartoum and the Government dared not order him to withdraw. As the Mahdist siege tightened, so the question of whether to relieve Gordon, an 'icon of his age', became a matter of press, parliamentary and cabinet debate. Gladstone still opposed any 'forward' policy from Egypt, described the Sudanese as 'a people struggling to be free and they are struggling rightly to be free', and dreaded the risks, costs and long-term implications of a relief expedition. Only at the beginning of August 1884 did he relent (primarily to avert resignations from his cabinet) and approve the moving of a vote of credit for a relief mission.[2] Thereafter the Government endorsed the plans of Wolseley and his Red River veterans for an expedition up the Nile (1,650 miles) as a purportedly less expensive, less risky and less difficult option than constructing a railway from Suakin to Berber (over 280 miles), with another 200 miles upstream to Khartoum.[3]

The ensuing expedition involved the despatch of 9,000 men and 40,000 tons of stores and munitions up the Nile.[4] On 9 September Wolseley arrived in Cairo with plans to send his soldiers by train and steamer to Wadi Halfa, then south of the second cataract by specially designed whale-boats. By Christmas he had sufficient forces at Korti to send a desert column mounted on camels and horses across the Bayuda Desert and a river column in 200 whale-boats, supported by mounted troops, up the Nile. Despite failing to relieve Gordon, who was killed in the storming of Khartoum (26 January 1885), Wolseley's forces remained in the Sudan until mid-summer, while Graham commanded another 13,000 soldiers in operations near Suakin (March–May 1885). After the withdrawal of both forces, residual units remained on the

Egyptian–Sudanese border, where they periodically engaged the Mahdists, notably at the battle of Ginnis (30 December 1885).

The protracted hostilities afforded many opportunities for letter-writing for the large number of soldiers involved. A 'Camel Grenadier' even wrote while riding on top of his camel as the 'difficult feat' prevented 'drowsiness' and distracted attention from saddle sores![5] Some

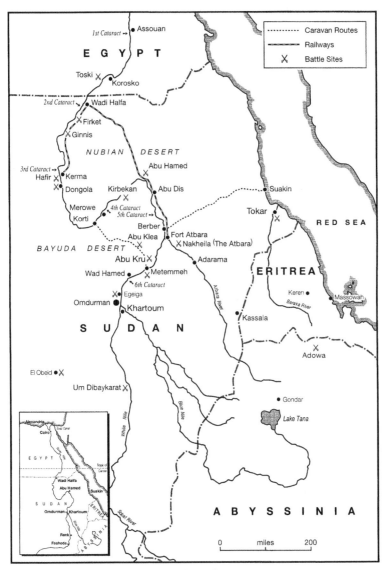

6 Egypt and the Sudan, 1885–99

[113]

doubted that letters would evade the attacks on the mails,[6] while Lieutenant-Colonel Philip H. Eyre (1/South Staffordshires), and perhaps others, saw little point in sending informative letters as 'crowds' of correspondents were present 'and no doubt every move is reported'.[7] Difficulties, though, bedevilled the despatch of all news from the front and so letters, if not too tardy, were generally welcome (and much more extensively reported than the seven cited by Emery).[8]

The expeditionary force, including a Naval Brigade, travelled slowly up the Nile by rail and Thomas Cook steamers, either carried or towed by the latter, covering the 793 miles to Wadi Halfa in about three weeks. Soldiers had ample time to gaze at the fertile country alongside the river (and the barren rock and sand hills between Shellal and Wadi Halfa), to barter with villagers and Greek traders for supplements to their diet of hard biscuits and preserved meat, and to write diaries and letters (some – to girls in Cairo – which were clearly not for publication).[9] They watched out for crocodiles, marvelled at the temples and ancient ruins, and some, like Telegrapher H. Emmerson, described the beauty of the Nile sunsets: 'As the sun dies away behind the yellow sand hills, the sky seems broken up into a veritable rainbow, the colours blending together splendidly, and the effect, once seen, remains vividly impressed on anyone for a lifetime.'[10]

Wadi Halfa, as Emmerson observed, became 'the headquarters of the Ordnance and Commissariat, and all stores for the front are made up and despatched from here',[11] but the railway track and rolling stock along the 33 miles to Sarras were not fully serviceable until mid-November (when two trains completed the journey on a daily basis). This slowed all movement, requiring boats to be hauled through the second cataract or carried round the rapids. The delays and damage suffered by so many boats (by 22 November sappers had overhauled 450 whalers[12]) meant that the advance upstream did not commence until 2 November.

Soldiers were delighted to leave Sarras – 'an awful place' where, as a Royal West Kent officer recalled, 'the duststorms and heat were fearful'.[13] They travelled in 30-foot whalers, each of which could carry ten fully equipped soldiers and a crew of two, later reduced to eight soldiers and a Canadian voyageur.[14] Each boat carried a prodigious weight in stores and rations – 'a little under 7,000 lbs.' in the first sapper boats to leave Sarras; 'about two tons of provisions, besides personal baggage' in boat No. 785 carrying Lance-Corporal W. Cook (2/Essex); and 'over 700 cases of provisions, varying in weight from 10 to 64 lbs', besides rations for fifteen days, in a West Kent boat. The West Kent officer added: 'The boat's gunwale when loaded is within a foot – in some cases less – of [sic] the water.'[15]

The boats travelled in groups of 4–5 and had to be hauled over various rapids (particularly the 7 major and many minor obstacles between the second and third cataracts). Cook recalled:

> Whenever we came to the cataracts we had to unload our boats and carry the provisions about a mile, and sometimes more. Then we had to go back and pull our boats over. We had to unload and do this eight times altogether. To get the boats over the cataracts we had to use a very long rope, and it took as many as 50 men to pull one boat over. Sometimes each boat took an hour to get over.[16]

Many soldiers found the work exhausting even when assisted in the portage by West African Kroomen. They travelled quite quickly in their whalers over the long stretches of clear water (the first sapper boats covered the 42 miles south of Dongola in less than 48 hours), and companies raced each other, seeking the £100 prize offered by Wolseley for the fastest boat to Debbeh.[17] Yet the stresses involved in hitting rocks, running aground or crossing rapids were all too memorable. After a day spent hauling his boat, Bandsman Barwood felt 'quite exhausted, my hands cut and blistered, wet through all day, scarcely any clothes whole, and my feet and legs also cut'.[18]

The work was frustrating and dangerous, too. Quite apart from the riverine hazards of cataracts, rapids, rocks, sandbanks and unpredictable currents, 'the boats' seemed to one officer 'absurdly unfit for their rough work and usage, being very fragile'.[19] They suffered broken rudders and holes from rocks, some capsized, and a handful broke up – all adding to the strains, delays and dangers of the expedition. Although remarkably few were seriously damaged, and relatively few men drowned,[20] the perception of danger was acute, particularly between the second and third cataracts. As a West Kent officer remarked: 'It is a great responsibility feeling one's way up a dangerous river, with little or no knowledge of it, and with men in the boat some of whom don't know the stern from the bow.'[21]

The Camel Corps, comprising volunteers formed into Guards, Heavy, Light and Mounted Infantry Camel Regiments, represented the fastest means of reaching Khartoum. Most of these forces, inexperienced in camel-riding, had ridden their animals from Wadi Halfa to Dongola where they practised column formations, fighting dismounted in squares and making bivouacs with their camels. A 'Camel Grenadier' (almost certainly Lieutenant Count Gleichen) found the journey from Wadi Halfa 'dismally monotonous' and distinctly uncomfortable on saddles so broad that his legs formed an angle of 120 degrees when the camels were fully loaded. He learned about the terrain that was composed of hard, often gravelly, sand – 'capital' for walking but so undulating that guardsmen often 'had to dismount' to lead their animals. He also found that camels' powers of endurance were distinctly limited (his own animal got 'a sore back after four days', needed water after 'five consecutive days', required 'a vigorous application of the koorbash' before it would run 'more than 250 yards at a time' and, in walking, never exceeded 'two and a half miles per hour').[22]

After an outbreak of smallpox at Dongola, Brigadier-General Sir Herbert Stewart led his mounted forces on to Korti where they rendezvoused with other elements of the Camel Corps. The latter included the 1/Royal Sussex, which had been a leading unit throughout the expedition, building forts at Dongola and Debbeh, and now at Korti, which Captain Lionel Trafford characterised as a 'hot dirty place'.[23] Those soldiers who spent a memorable Christmas at Korti (where imaginative puddings were made from ground biscuit, goat's milk and dates) soon found the location increasingly unhealthy. By 4 January a dragoon reckoned that 14–15 of the Camel Corps had already died at the base,[24] and, after a month at Korti, Private F. Daykin (18th Hussars) wrote: 'We are getting tired of this place, as it is very unhealthy, and the poor fellows are dying every day. It seems so sad to see such fine, strong fellows put under the sands of the desert in a blanket.'[25] By arriving relatively late at Korti, the Naval Brigade avoided these concerns but sailors had barely a week (and in some cases only a couple of days) to practise their camel-riding.[26]

On 30 December Stewart marched with a convoy of 1,000 soldiers, 200 natives and 2,000 camels to establish a forward base at Gakdul Wells, halfway across the Bayuda Desert, and then returned with the camels to bring forward the remainder of the Camel Corps. The time-wasting double trip, necessitated by the failure of Wolseley's staff to procure sufficient camels, left Corporal F. H. Middleton unimpressed: 'we returned . . . to Korti', he wrote, 'marching 182 miles in 126 hours – very good marching for camels; not much time for sleeping, I can tell you'.[27] Even worse was their first experience of the Bayuda Desert. Soldiers may have begun their marches 'in the highest spirits', buoyed by the novelty of riding camels and 'the expectation of seeing some hard fighting', as Trafford averred,[28] but their accounts dwelt on the 'appalling' heat and 'terrible' sandstorms.[29] During the marches to Gakdul Wells, a Bradford soldier recalled 'suffering for four days for want of water' (the allowance was 2 pints of water per day),[30] while an officer noted that the salt meat became 'very trying' in these conditions: 'it parches the lips and tongue. Some men's lips are quite blue.'[31]

Once revived at Gakdul Wells, Stewart resumed his advance on 14 January with some 1,800 soldiers, 350 natives, 2,900 camels, 150 ponies and three 7-pounder guns. After two days, they encountered a large *ansar* (Mahdist army) about 3 miles from Abu Klea Wells. Bivouacking within a zareba overnight, they endured an evening of long-range rifle-fire and enemy drumming. Although few men and animals were killed or wounded,[32] the experience was remembered as 'not very pleasant', 'very unpleasant', even as 'a night of terror' by Private Harry Etherington (1/Royal Sussex).[33]

At mid-morning on 17 January, Stewart left his baggage under guard in the zareba and advanced on Abu Klea. Trafford recalled how individual commanders, in the absence of any formal orders, had to send out skirmishers to protect their flanks and criticised the square as unbalanced and poorly aligned, with the rear face constantly broken by camels. Shortly after noon they reached the crest of a ridge and saw 'a sea of standards' as the *ansar* launched an assault on the left front, where the mounted infantry, once their skirmishers had retreated, responded with volley-firing.[34] The Mahdists wheeled off to attack and penetrate the rear corner where the Heavy Cavalry had broken formation, a naval machine-gun became exposed (with the Gardner jamming) and only a mass of camels blocked the enemy. Middleton claimed that the 'Cavalry on left face, Horse Guards, etc., made awkward infantry men', and Gunner Dixon asserted that Colonel Burnaby, though 'very brave and cool . . . exposed himself too much. If he had kept within the square he would not have been killed.'[35] The confusion became 'terrible', recalled Trafford, when the Heavy Cavalry 'retreated back to their proper place & came on the top of our men with the Arabs on the top of them', and the shooting of the 'Heavies' was 'very wild'.[36] Yet the square reformed and discipline held as the rear ranks turned about: 'For about ten minutes', wrote Marling, 'it was touch and go, but we beat them off & every nigger who got inside was killed. Our loss was very heavy, 9 officers and 66 men killed, 9 officers and 72 wounded.'[37] Trafford was mightily impressed by the 'glorious sight' of the Arab charge: 'one thought they were charging to certain death yet they not only reached the square but punctuated it'. Even when forced to retire by superior fire-power, they retreated not by running but by 'swaggering off'. Trafford was confident, nonetheless, that 'Gordon was as good as saved'.[38]

When soldiers reached the muddy water of the Abu Klea Wells, they spent an exhausting twenty-four hours, building defences, deepening wells, bringing forward the wounded and baggage, and filling water skins for the final advance to the Nile. Leaving another 100 Royal Sussex to guard the wounded, the march resumed at sunset, with many men sleeping in their saddles as they rode through the night. On the following morning confusion reigned: 'those on quick camels', noted Trafford, had 'got to the front, while those on slow animals [were] in the rear'.[39] As cavalry scouts detected another *ansar* gathering ahead, Stewart halted the corps under enemy fire near the village of Abu Kru (Gubat). Middleton laconically observed: 'Made a zareba, and stayed in it till two officers, one correspondent [Cameron], one conductor, and eight men were killed, and the general wounded [mortally]. Thought it was time to go out then.'[40]

Sir Charles Wilson, RE, assuming command from Stewart, left the Hussars, Naval Brigade, Royal Artillery and half the 'Heavies' to guard the zareba, and ordered an advance towards the river (under the executive command of Lieutenant-Colonel the Hon. Edward Boscawen) in a slow, tight, square formation. When the *ansar* charged the front face it met, as Middleton described, 'a beautiful little square this time; all infantry. Received charge without a wave in any flank. Enemy fell like rotten sheep. Glorious time. Fight over by sunset, 19th inst., no moon, marched on to river, about half a mile in the dark, rather dangerous proceedings, but had to be done.'[41] Half of the 'Heavies' had served in the rear face, but the engagement was over in five minutes and none of the Arabs got within 50 yards of the square.

There was immense relief at reaching the Nile after three days without a proper meal for the men, eight days without water for the camels and 56 hours without water for the ponies of the 19th Hussars. The remainder of the column was brought forward on 20 January; but the wounded, as Marling remarked, had 'an awfully bad time of it, most of them lying on the ground without any covering at all'.[42] Despite Wilson's abortive attack on Metemmeh (21 January) – a 'disgracefully mismanaged' affair in Marling's opinion[43] – hopes revived with the appearance of four steamers, packed with soldiers, from Khartoum. To the delight of one soldier, they had brought a message from Gordon 'saying he is quite well and can hold out till we get to him'.[44]

Once two vessels, the *Bordein* and the *Talahawiyeh*, were made ready (24 January), Wilson commanded a relief force of 240 soldiers, mainly Gordon's black Sudanese but including 24 Royal Sussex. Trafford noted that they followed Wolseley's orders and wore red serge jackets, in keeping with his belief that a small body of British troops (albeit 1,500 in number) would overawe the *ansar* and raise the siege.[45] Optimism persisted despite encountering rifle-fire within a couple of days, and then capturing an Arab who claimed that Khartoum had fallen and they would have to pass a fort with sixteen guns: 'We only laughed at him', recalled a sailor, 'and thought he was trying to frighten us . . .'.[46] However, on 28 January, spirits plummeted when Khartoum was sighted without an Egyptian flag flying, and, in the subsequent withdrawal under enemy fire, the *Talahawiyeh* foundered in the sixth cataract and the *Bordein* hit a rock, leaving Wilson's force stranded on an island. After a small boat, under Captain Gascoigne's command, left to seek assistance, a sailor commented: 'You may picture our position – twenty-three of us all told on an island, with two hundred niggers whom we could not trust, and some of the Mahdi's men on the mainland on either side of us. Two or three times we abandoned hope.'[47] After three days a crippled steamer appeared, under the command of Lord Charles Beresford, and, after repairing its boiler, carried Wilson's force to safety.

Meanwhile on 28 December advance elements of the river column began their journey up the Nile to establish a base at Hamdab, 40 miles from Korti. During the following month sappers built a fort and resumed their boat-repairing duties as the remainder of the column under the command of Major-General William Earle gradually followed in boats, on foot, or by horse and camel. By 16 January Captain J. E. Blackburn, RE, reported that the troops at Hamdab were 'in first-rate health and spirits' as the daytime heat was tolerable, the nights cool, and they had plentiful supplies of fresh meat, milk and Dhowra meal which made 'excellent porridge'.[48] The camp was alive with rumours, including one that the Naval Brigade had reached Khartoum: 'I should not be the least surprised', wrote Lieutenant-Colonel Coveny (1/Black Watch), 'to get the order to go back at any minute, because I don't think these people care to trifle with England's power'.[49]

Once Earle had a reasonably balanced force at Hamdab (24 January), he ordered the boats to tackle the fourth cataract, assisted by 400 Egyptian *fellahin* on the bank, and with a squadron of the 19th Hussars and the Egyptian Camel Corps scouting ahead. Day after day of excruciating effort followed as men hauled their boats over the rocks, rarely rowing for more than a mile at a time. 'For the most part', wrote Blackburn, 'it was the same monotonous grind, walking over slippery and sharp-pointed rocks or through deep sand, hauling on ropes, wading in the water to get boats off the rocks, and, on getting into bivouac, zeriba-making and cutting pathways and ramps up the steep banks to allow of horses and camels getting down to the water'. The rate of progress 'was very slow – for some time not more than three miles a day, due to the long column of boats and the necessity of getting all into the same bivouac by nightfall – so that the head of the column often halted about noon, the rear not reaching the same spot till nightfall'.[50]

News of the desert column's two actions hardly inspired confidence: 'the loss', asserted Denne, 'is enormous over 21 p[er] c[ent] in the 2 actions and though a junction has been effected with Gordon's steamers, the desert force is practically shut up on the banks of the Nile'. He regarded the loss of officers as 'utterly disproportionate' and suspected that 'the British Public will begin to appreciate that it is not a mere picnic'.[51]

After the leading boats reached the oasis of Berti, they halted unexpectedly (4–7 February) as Earle was informed of Khartoum's fall. He kept the news from his men but was subsequently ordered to resume his advance. In seeking to save time, he despatched the 1/South Staffordshires, 1/Black Watch and 19th Hussars across the desert towards Abu Hamed, where their path was blocked by some 1,500 Mahdists, armed with Remington rifles and deployed on hills near the village of Kirbekan. On 10 February Earle feigned a frontal assault with two companies of the South Staffordshires and a couple of guns, while the remainder of the battalion, dressed in red jackets, and six companies of Black Watch, in their kilts, and the Hussars moved round the ridge to its rear. 'As we neared the enemy's stronghold', recalled Corporal W. Walton (South Staffordshires), 'bullets were showered amongst us, and a lot of our men were killed or wounded before we could return a single shot.'[52] As the cavalry attacked the Mahdist camp, the Black Watch seized a knoll from which it enfiladed the enemy and covered any retreat to the river. The South Staffordshires, facing the highest ridge, sent D company forward advancing by sections in extended order with covering fire from other companies. When the latter followed as reinforcements, we 'charged the hill with a cheer', wrote Walton; 'a hand-to-hand conflict ensued', blood ran down the hill in streams, 'enough to sicken the heart of any man', and it was 'blow for blow, and stab for stab . . . They were brave men we fought with.'[53] An officer of the Black Watch described how his men marched across open ground 'as steadily as if on parade, notwithstanding the heavy fire', and then attacked the enemy's flanks before the Mahdists launched a charge: 'nearly all were shot dead and the others were shot as they tried to swim the river'. The Black Watch, with pipes playing, fought on from rock to rock 'against a most determined enemy',[54] and, after six hours, the position was secured.

In the only action fought by the river column, the Mahdists suffered between 200 and 700 dead whereas the column lost 3 British officers and 9 men killed, with 4 officers and 44 men wounded.[55] Once again senior officers – Earle, Coveny and Eyre – were slain in battle. Brackenbury assumed command and moved the column on to a point 26 miles from Abu Hamed before being ordered to return downstream. Soldiers greeted the order with 'woeful disappointment' as the men had recently learned of Gordon's death and were bent on revenge. They rightly sensed that the dilapidated condition of the desert column had confounded Wolseley's hopes of moving on to Khartoum,[56] and they remained depressed despite the quicker journey down river. On 13

March Private Robertson (Black Watch) asserted that 'This has been an awful sickener of a job . . . It is a great pity General Gordon being killed, and so many fine officers. I suppose it would cause a great consternation at home. I don't see what benefit is to be derived from this country. We all wish they would withdraw the troops from it altogether.'[57]

Feelings were as intense at Gubat when men received news of Khartoum's fall and Gordon's death. In a censored report Burleigh asserted: 'On all sides, among officers and men, there was universal dismay and indignation at the catastrophe', and, less plausibly, that there 'was no question of politics about the state of feeling'.[58] In fact, condemnation of Gladstone and his Government was widespread from Wolseley downwards,[59] but, unlike Wolseley, the desert column could not dwell on recriminations. It spent a month at Gubat, strengthening defences, mounting raids, and periodically attacking Mahdist positions downriver from a steamer. All these activities, as an officer of the 19th Hussars wrote, were undertaken in 'a state of glorious uncertainty', bereft of any mail from Korti or information from spies as the 'country all around is hostile'. Having 'anxiously awaited' Major-General Buller, the desert column's spirits revived with his arrival on 11 February and his prompt decision to withdraw in the face of a resurgent enemy.[60] Chronically short of camels, he had to order the jettisoning of many stores into the river and allow the commissariat to distribute portable 'luxuries such as cocoa, condensed milk, brandy, soups, an innumerable other things' to the troops.[61]

A convoy of the sick and wounded preceded the main body of 1,700 men, mostly on foot, in the slow, hazardous march across the desert. Harassed by skirmishers, the column struggled on to Abu Klea and Gakdul Wells, with several of the wounded, including Stewart, dying en route. At Gakdul they formed another 'sick convoy' for the last 104 miles, with the two doctors bringing a 'spade, pick, and shovel as part of their hospital gear'. The commanding officer had 20 dismounted hussars and 300 native auxiliaries to convey 26 stretcher cases, mainly amputees, and another 20–30 officers, 'more or less seedy, riding camels'. He described how the auxiliaries sometimes 'flatly refused to carry the wounded when they considered they had done enough; they were always shouting out for water . . . and the row they made carrying the wounded, which were all the worst cases, was just about calculated to finish most of them off. They dropped two poor fellows out of the stretchers.' Yet the convoy suffered only a single fatality and reached Korti after seven days.[62] By 16 March the main column arrived in a miserable state. A Scots Guardsman recalled:

Every man had bad boots; some had no tops to them, while most had soles worn through; some marching with their feet outside their boots, while others . . . contrived to make a pair of sandals . . . Our trousers were almost as bad, all patched over with red and yellow leather.[63]

Soldiers sent many letters thereafter, chronicling their exploits in the field, alluding to promotions for gallant conduct (Middleton was raised from corporal to lance-sergeant), and comforting the families of fallen comrades. Sergeant G. Baker (5th Lancers) wrote a poignant letter to Mrs Lovell about her son:

[H]e and I joined the regiment about the same time, and ever since we have been chums. We drilled together, and were made corporals together; in fact, we have been close friends since he joined till the day of his death. He was next to me all the battle till he was struck, and I can assure you there was no one who felt his death so much as I did. I lost a true friend and comrade.[64]

Meanwhile General Graham received instructions to destroy the forces of Osman Digna near Suakin and facilitate the construction of the Suakin–Berber railway line. He was given a substantial and well-balanced force of 13,000 men, with battalions at full strength, a cavalry brigade, balloon section and colonial contingents from India and New South Wales. He had equally impressive support – hospital ships, vessels able to condense 85,000 gallons of water daily, and 6,000 baggage and 500 riding-camels. Camp sites had to be found for this multitude outside the cramped and unhealthy confines of Suakin. 'Sanitary arrangements', as Surgeon Porter noted in his journal, 'governed the siting of the regimental camps, on dry sandy ridges' running out from Suakin. They were sufficiently elevated to benefit from the fresh sea breezes and to avoid both marsh fever near the coast and sandstorms in the desert; but 'these positions were inadequate for defence against incursions of a bold and predatory enemy'.[65]

Night after night Osman Digna's forces, in small groups, attacked the scattered camps, by-passing the guards and arc lamps to hack and kill soldiers asleep in their tents. Newly arrived units were particularly vulnerable (the Australians suffered on their arrival in late March just as the 1/Berkshires had done in early February) and the attacks had a demoralising effect. One soldier recalled being awakened by forty Sudanese rushing through the camp: their yell 'was something terrible – fairly froze the blood in one's veins. As our other tents faced us, we could not fire on them, so stood back to back with fixed swords . . .'. Later he had to treat the victims: 'one had his arm almost cut off' and later died; another 'had his stomach laid open, and half his head dragged off'.[66] Fortifying the camps with ditches, earthworks and bastions helped, but alerts frequently occurred and, amidst the confusion, crossfire was a recurrent hazard. By mid-March an officer recognised that the camps, though 'too far apart for mutual protection', were 'near enough to cause reciprocal damage'. He reckoned that 2,000 men 'were on guard every night, and what with fatigue duties all day we are nearly worked off our legs. The thermometer is eighty-seven degrees in the tents at night.'[67]

Even before Graham arrived in Suakin British forces had responded to the nightly raids, by reconnaissance actions and the burning of rebel villages. In scattering the bands of tribesmen, Private Charles Williams (1/Berkshires) boasted: 'We will make the Soudanese rue the day they killed poor Gordon'.[68] Graham planned to engage the main body of Osman Digna's army, located in the area of Tamai and Hashin, advancing towards the latter on 20 March where he bivouacked overnight. On the following morning the Beja tribesmen mounted a series of attacks from the surrounding hills. They inflicted significant losses on the Bengal Lancers: 'as the horsemen rode lance in rest', noted Porter, 'the Arab would suddenly fall prone, and as the lance missed would as suddenly spring up, hamstring the horse, and bring down the rider. In such a case it was sudden death to our men.'[69] However, the main squares of Guards, Indian Native Infantry, Sikhs and Marines stood firm: 'We shot them [the arabs] down like dogs', claimed a Coldstream Guardsman.[70]

In skirmishes lasting about nine-and-a-half hours, fire-power both kept the tribesmen at a distance and dispersed them from their vantage points overlooking the wells. Corporal Fred Bennett, (RE), described how the gunners pounded the enemy from two hillside redoubts, 'every shot except the first telling; and we could see the rebels leap into the air and fall never to rise again'.[71] Corporal R. Haslam (Medical Staff) saw the 'British rifle' wreak 'fearful havoc in that day', and praised the Berkshires, who worked with the Marines, to clear tribesmen from ridge after ridge.[72] The 5th Royal Irish Lancers dispersed some Arabs, claiming thirty-two kills and prompting Private Francis Ferguson (20th Hussars) to observe that 'Lances are the best to charge with. A sword is not the least bit of good with these fellows.'[73] Soldiers lauded the bravery of the enemy and their use of the bush, but not their marksmanship. The Berkshires had seized their summit, claimed one of their officers, despite 'a sharp fire' from the enemy, 'but luckily they are bad shots . . . our casualties were only two wounded'.[74] Ultimately Graham's force returned to its prepared zarebas, having lost 22 officers and men killed (and 43 wounded) compared with estimates of enemy losses ranging from 250 to 1,000 dead.[75]

On 22 March Major-General Sir John McNeill, VC, led two large square formations from Suakin to create an advance depot for supplies and water some 8 miles towards Tamai. Within one square he enclosed some 1,400 transport animals laden with food, water and ammunition, numerous water-carts, and litters for the sick and wounded. This cumbersome baggage train struggled through the thick and prickly bush, repeatedly breaking down and requiring frequent halts to reload the pack animals. 'Owing to the excessively rugged nature of the terrain', claimed Porter, 'the thick sand cloud always round the column and the mass of material to be covered, progress was necessarily slow.'[76] Having covered only 6 miles by noon, McNeill decided to halt and build a zareba before dusk, planning three separate squares of mimosa bush, placed diagonally like squares on a chess-board. The strategy would consume a large amount of space and time in hostile country, involving the creation of a large central square to hold the stores, animals and water, flanked by two squares to hold the fighting troops and machine-guns.

The defences were still incomplete, with groups of men either having their dinner or collecting brush wood, when the Mahdists launched their attack just after 2.30 p.m. As Captain C. Mackenzie Edwards (Berkshires) recalled: 'The whole rush was so sudden and everything so quick that it was a miracle how any of us got together; the cavalry videttes galloped through us with the enemy alongside.'[77] While the picket lines held firm to the north and west, they crumbled in the south: Lieutenant-Colonel H. W. L. Holman (Royal Marines) asserted that the dervishes, who followed the 5th Lancers through the lines of the 17th Bengal Native Infantry, 'outnumbered and outflanked the unfortunate Bengalis, who, firing wildly in the air, bolted'.[78] With camels, mules and horses stampeding amid clouds of dust, the tribesmen penetrated the incomplete zarebas. Soldiers rallied in separate squares, 'more like a mass of men in any shape', claimed Edwards, and four companies of the Berkshires fought as a group outside the zarebas.[79] 'Steady and incessant fire' prevailed, as Private Harold D. Smithies (Royal Marines) observed, but not before many men and camels were caught in the crossfire.[80]

In a battle lasting twenty minutes some 1,000 tribesmen died as well as over 130 British and Indian soldiers and 150 drivers. Particular groups suffered severely: sailors in the unfinished southern zareba, who were attacked before their Gardner guns were ready;[81] engineers, who had piled their arms while cutting bush, and were either caught in the open or found their arms taken by others;[82] and unarmed drivers and bearers who had tried running back to Suakin. On the following day an officer rode along the route, observing the 'sickening' sight and the smell of their corpses: it was 'a heavy butcher's bill truly', he added.[83] Osman Digna's forces had paid an even heavier price and proffered scant resistance when Graham's army subsequently occupied and destroyed the village of Tamai. The rebels, noted Smithies, 'are beginning to hang back ... finding the British are too good for them'.[84]

Nevertheless, some soldiers joined the critics of the Tofrik battle. 'The small skirmish at Hasheen was nothing compared to this', wrote Edwards. 'Of course someone blundered or it c[oul]d. never have happened . . . the surprise sh[oul]d. never have occurred.'[85] Surgeon E. H. Finn hoped that Wolseley would see

> what a disgracefully ignorant lot of Generals we have and withdraw us. No expedition was ever commanded so badly or so many gross errors made – the attack on the Zereba on the 22nd was entirely due to General McNeil's [sic] swaggering ignorance . . . General Graham is also a gigantic failure & everybody is thoroughly disgusted.[86]

Others defended McNeill, implying that the under-strength cavalry vedettes should have eschewed their drill book and fired warning shots while on horseback.[87]

Soldiers continued their dreary round of convoy duty (sometimes, if the wind was favourable, with a reconnaissance balloon above), sinking wells and felling trees for the railway line. As temperatures rose, morale sagged: Lieutenant Francis Lloyd (Grenadier Guards) regarded the long march to an evacuated Tamai as a 'fiasco' and reported widespread scepticism that the railway to Berber would ever be completed.[88] Those who had hoped to come 'home smothered in glory' were disabused; instead convoys regularly passed and repassed the 'sickening scene' near McNeill's zareba, where hundreds of kites and vultures fed on the 'festering bodies of camels and mules', and hands and feet lay thick on the ground, 'dragged from their graves' by hyenas.[89]

The arrival of the New South Wales contingent in its first imperial campaign aroused great interest. While most recognised the potential significance of the deployment, and some described the contingent as 'a fine body of men', Lloyd rated its soldiers as 'worse than any Volunteer regiment and [they] swagger more'. He deprecated their limited musketry skills and general indolence.[90] When not on duty, soldiers sampled the dubious delights of Suakin, dubbed by Corporal Haslam, as 'about the dirtiest place in existence'. In the bazaar, a long narrow street, 'all kinds of vendors' could be found, 'most of them indulging in opium smoking, the smell of which is enough to make one sick. Beer is "only" 1s [5p] a quart, while wines and spirits are very "cheap", and quite as "nasty".'[91] Fortunately British soldiers were soon spared these temptations: on 2 May, Wolseley arrived in Suakin to warn Graham that the Government was now more concerned with events in Afghanistan. On 17 May, Graham and his staff left Suakin and the withdrawal from the Sudan was underway.

As the process in northern Sudan was phased over several months, soldiers were none too sure when they would leave. 'The summer occupation', claimed a DCLI officer, 'is very unpopular; all the troops hate the prospect of it.'[92] Soldiers and sailors complained about the monotony of camp life, the misery of sheltering in bell tents when the temperature soared to 120 degrees Fahrenheit, and the mounting toll of sickness and death. Within five weeks of forming a camp at Kurot, an officer reported 7 deaths from typhoid fever and 150 men sick. 'It is a disgrace', he affirmed,

> to keep us in such a fiendish country. Nothing can excuse it. The food is bad, and we are still in rags . . . For God's sake write about it, and get other correspondents to take it up. They are generally the best friends the troops have; and now they have gone, everything is concealed, and there is no one to say a word for the soldiers.[93]

Even when soldiers returned to Cairo, they still grumbled: 'For the last two campaigns', wrote Barwood, 'the men have received no decorations, and the bitter feeling among the men is something awful. They have simply put two honours on one bar, what a mean thing to do . . .'.[94]

Despite all these complaints, when the soldiers faced lengthy encampments, as the Cameron Highlanders did, they made the best of it. Based at Korosko for ten months, the Highlanders spent the summer building mud huts, playing games of cricket and football, and rowing on the river. They enjoyed fresh bread and fresh meat 'in abundance', formed their own theatrical company and enjoyed cordial relations with the natives, many of whom liked the bagpipes, even if soldiers were banned from entering any native village.[95] In October 1885 the battalion was sent upriver to occupy the small fort of Kosheh, the most southerly frontier post protecting the 87-mile railway from Wadi Halfa to Akasheh.

As Khalifa 'Abdullah, the Mahdi's successor, had resolved to expel this infidel presence and invade Egypt, he sent a large *ansar* (possibly 6,000 strong) northwards to invest Kosheh and a flying column to cut the vulnerable railway. Hitherto the Camerons had patrolled the river in a stern wheeler, the *Lotus*, but, by early December, Kosheh and the other frontier posts came under sporadic attack. Parts of the rail track were destroyed, the telegraph cut and villages like Firket briefly occupied, prompting the despatch of flying columns from Akasheh to disperse the tribesmen. Meanwhile as the Kosheh fort was effectively besieged, the Camerons engaged enemy snipers, mounted sorties to dislodge their marksmen (notably on 16 December), gathered intelligence from spies and deserters, and supported counter-battery fire from artillery and machine-guns.[96] By 19 December, the enemy came so close that officers 'distinctly heard the dervish cry – weirdly it sounded in the stillness of night – summoning the faithful to prayer'. By Christmas the battalion had lost three killed and nineteen wounded out of the fort's casualties of eight dead and twenty-five more or less severely wounded.[97]

The Camerons had bought sufficient time for General Sir Frederick Stephenson and Brigadier William Butler to bring two brigades, with mounted support, into action. In a pre-dawn advance (30 December 1885) their forces extended round the Mahdist positions at Ginnis and Kosheh before launching a massive bombardment. Ferguson, whose 20th Hussars protected the left flank and assisted the Egyptian Camel Corps, recalled 'the rattle of the Gatling & the volleys of the Infantry & the Artillery & us firing', it was 'terrific at one time'.[98] Six companies of Camerons (about 450 men), flanked by 150 Sudanese blacks, launched the frontal attack on the village of Kosheh. One of the Cameron officers recounted their delight at ending their 'imprisonment' and their desire to advance 'at the double' in a 'thin red line' (this was the final action fought by British soldiers wearing red):

> When the order was given to fix bayonets, the ready click and the fierce determined look of the men unmistakably told of pent-up revengeful passion about to find an outburst. The thought of comrades killed and wounded like rabbits in a warren during all those harassing days in the fort worked with revengeful fierceness in the mind of each . . . I had seen the same set teeth, flushed cheeks, and wild glare in the eyes of the men on the 16th December when they shot, bayonetted, and madly re-bayonetted the marksmen and others on the Rock.

The officer felt thwarted when the enemy retreated to the houses: 'there was now nothing for it but attack the houses from loop-holes . . . It was nasty work. There was a good many inside, and it was a desperation stand with them.'[99] The Sudanese blacks cleared 'the Rock' and cover close to the river, and so: 'When we met in the rear of the houses, and had captured the enemy's guns, we gave them a cheer to which they lustily responded. It was a strange but hearty comradeship in arms.'[100]

Overwhelming fire-power, and Butler's adroit manoeuvring of the brigades and camel corps, had produced a decisive outcome. After three hours the *ansar* was in full retreat, leaving 500 dead and 300 wounded compared with British losses of 7 killed and 30 wounded. The victors, all of whom were entitled to the Egyptian medal and the Khedive's star, had thwarted the immediate threat of invasion and so facilitated the final withdrawal from the Sudan.[101] This process took several months until the fortification of Wadi Halfa, the new frontier outpost, was completed. Meanwhile British soldiers felt immensely frustrated about the outcome of the relief expedition. If they were less critical of Wolseley's planning and staff system than some historians have been,[102] many felt that their mission had begun too late, and that they had struggled up the Nile and defeated the Mahdi's forces in several battles to little effect. These frustrations were felt most keenly by those left on the frontier. By 24 January, when over 200 men were in hospital with dysentery and typhoid fever, at least one officer, uncertain about the future, complained:

> Alas, alas, it looks like another summer in Halfa with its accompanying plagues of dust, heat, flies, and smells. After near a year and a half one gets very sick at the thought of a further prolonged residence . . . Oh, why did we ever meddle in Arabi? Oh, that the bondholders had been left to burn their fingers. As for danger to the Suez Canal there never was aught to be apprehended.[103]

Notes

1 For theories about Gordon's motives, see C. Chevenix Trench, *Charley Gordon: An Eminent Victorian Reassessed* (London: Allen Lane, 1978), pp. 246–50; A. Nutting, *Gordon: Martyr and Misfit* (London: Constable, 1966), pp. 207–29; Cromer, *Modern Egypt*, vol. 1, pp. 446–7, 562–8; R. Neillands, *The Dervish Wars: Gordon and Kitchener in the Sudan 1880–1898* (London: John Murray, 1996), pp. 104–7.

2 Matthew, *Gladstone*, pp. 145–7; Bahlman, *Hamilton*, vol. 2, pp. 556, 570, 602, 610, 659, 662, 664; *Parliamentary Debates*, 3rd series, vol. 288 (12 May 1884), col. 55.

3 A. Preston (ed.), *In Relief of Gordon: Lord Wolseley's Campaign Journal of the Khartoum Relief Expedition 1884–1885* (London: Hutchinson, 1967), pp. xxviii–xxxii; Sandes, *Royal Engineers*, pp. 88–90; B. Holland, *Life of the Duke of Devonshire*, 2 vols (London: Longman, Green & Co., 1911), vol. 1, pp. 459–62, 466–72; J. Symons, *England's Pride: The Story of the Gordon Relief Expedition* (London: Hamish Hamilton, 1965), pp. 65–72.

4 Sandes, *Royal Engineers*, p. 103.

5 'The Khartoum Expedition', *Army and Navy Gazette*, 20 December 1884, p. 949.

6 BWA, 0203/1, Barwood, diary, 17 May 1885, p. 140; 'Letter from a Soldier in the Soudan', *Kinross-shire Advertiser*, 2 January 1886, p. 2.

7 'Lieutenant Colonel Eyre's Last Letter', *Evening Standard*, 13 February 1885, p. 5.

8 'The Battle of Abu Klea', *Daily Chronicle*, 25 February 1885, p. 5; Wilkinson-Latham, *From Our Special Correspondent*, p. 195; Emery, *Marching Over Africa*, p. 189.

9 BWA, 0203/1, Barwood, diary, 30 October 1884, pp. 90, 93–4, 97–8; GHM, PB 173, McRae to his mother, 2 December 1884.

10 'The Egyptian Campaign', *Auckland Times and Herald*, 27 February 1885, p. 5.

11 *Ibid.*

12 'Diary of an Officer with the Khartoum Expedition', *REJ*, 15 (1 January 1885), 13–14; Sandes, *Royal Engineers*, p. 102.

13 'Egypt and the Soudan', *Western Morning News*, 13 January 1885, p. 8.

14 These boatmen were hired in Canada but bore little resemblance to the voyageurs who had served with the Red River expedition, Preston, *In Relief of Gordon*, p. xxxiii; Symons, *England's Pride*, pp. 106–8.

15 'Egypt and the Soudan', p. 8; Capt. J. E. Blackburn, 'From Gemai to Debbeh in a "Whaler"', *REJ*, 15 (2 February 1885), 23–6; 'An Essex Soldier's Letter from the Soudan', *Colchester Chronicle*, 21 March 1885, p. 7.

16 'An Essex Soldier's Letter from the Soudan', p. 7; Symons, *England's Pride*, p. 139.

17 Blackburn, 'From Gemai to Debbeh in a "Whaler"', 25.

18 BWA, 0230/1, Barwood, diary, 30 November 1884, p. 121.

19 'Egypt and the Soudan', p. 8.
20 Symons, *England's Pride*, p. 144.
21 'The Nile Expedition', *Western Morning News*, 5 February 1885, p. 8.
22 'Khartoum Expedition', p. 949; compare with Count Gleichen, *With the Camel Corps Up the Nile* (London: Chapman & Hall, 1888), chs 2 and 3.
23 West Sussex Record Office (WSRO), RSR, MS 1/85, Capt. L. Trafford, 'A Diary of the Sudan Campaign, 1884–5', p. 8.
24 'A Soldier's Letter from Korti', *Dover Express*, 30 January 1885, p. 5.
25 'Camp Life at Korti', *Bradford Daily Telegraph*, 28 February 1885, p. 2.
26 'An Engine-Room Artificer's Experiences', *Western Morning News*, 18 March 1885, p. 8; 'The Naval Brigade in the Sudan', *Portsmouth Times and Naval Gazette*, 18 April 1885, p. 5; Brooks, *Long Arm of Empire*, p. 189.
27 'A Soldier's Letter', *Daily Telegraph*, 12 March 1885, p. 5; Symons, *England's Pride*, pp. 173–7.
28 WSRO, RSR, MS 1/85, Trafford, 'A Diary of the Sudan Campaign', p. 8; H. M. L. (Lt H. M. Lawson), 'Desert Notes from Korti to El Goubat', *REJ*, 15 (1 April 1885), 71–3.
29 H. Etherington, 'Sent to Save Gordon', in Small (ed.), *Told from the Ranks*, pp. 195–206; 'An Engine-Room Artificer's Experiences', p. 8.
30 'A Bradford Soldier's Letter', *Illustrated Weekly (Bradford) Telegraph*, 7 March 1885, p. 7.
31 'A March from Korti to Gakdul Wells', *Western Morning News*, 26 March 1885, p. 8.
32 PRO, WO 33/44, 'Diary of the Suakin Operation, 1885', no. 297, Wolseley to secretary of state for war, 26 January 1885, enclosing Stewart's despatch on Abu Klea.
33 'Naval Brigade in the Soudan', p. 5; 'A Soldier's Letter', p. 5; Etherington, 'Sent to Save Gordon', p. 201.
34 WSRO, RSR, MS 1/85, Trafford, 'A Diary of the Sudan Campaign', p. 15; 'A Bradford Soldier's Letter', p. 7.
35 'A Soldier's Letter', p. 5; 'Another Letter from a Melton Man in the Soudan', *Leicester Chronicle and Leicestershire Mercury*, 18 April 1885, p. 3.
36 WSRO, RSR, MS 1/85, Trafford, 'A Diary of the Sudan Campaign', p. 16.
37 GRO, D873/C110, Marling to his father, 28 January 1885.
38 WSRO, RSR, MS 1/85, Trafford, 'A Diary of the Sudan campaign', pp. 17–19.
39 *Ibid.*, p. 19.
40 'A Soldier's Letter', p. 5.
41 *Ibid.*
42 GRO, D873/C110, Marling to his father, 28 January 1885.
43 *Ibid.*
44 'A Bradford Soldier's Letter', p. 7.
45 WSRO, RSR MS 1/85, Trafford, 'Diary of the Sudan Campaign', p. 22; Preston (ed.), *In Relief of Gordon*, pp. 90 and 103.
46 'Naval Brigade in the Sudan', p. 5.
47 *Ibid.*
48 Capt. J. E. Blackburn, 'From Debbeh to Hamdab with the "Nile Column"', *REJ*, 15 (2 March 1885), 50–2.
49 BWA, 0204, Coveny, 'Letters From Egypt and the Sudan', 16 January 1885, p. 16.
50 Capt. J. E. Blackburn, 'With the Nile Column from Jan. 17 to March 7, 1885', *REJ*, 15 (1 July 1885), 151–5.
51 GHM, PB 64/8, Denne to his father, 26 January 1885.
52 'The Battle of Kirbekan', *Midland Counties Express*, 11 April 1885, p. 8.
53 *Ibid.*; see also Staffordshire Regiment Museum (SRM), Acc No. 7648, Capt. Morris Bent, 'From Korti to Huella in a Whaler', n.d., pp. 9–10.
54 'The Battle of Kirbekan', *Daily Telegraph*, 10 March 1885, p. 3.
55 *Ibid.*; PRO, WO 33/44, Brig.-Gen. Brackenbury to Wolseley, 10 February 1885; Symons, *England's Pride*, p. 256.
56 Blackburn, 'With the Nile Column', 154–5.
57 'The Black Watch at Abu Dom', *Scotsman*, 11 April 1885, p. 7.

58 He bypassed the censor by sending this part of his report by letter: 'Press Censorship at Korti', *Western Morning News*, 27 March 1885, p. 8.
59 Preston (ed.), *In Relief of Gordon*, pp. 141, 147 and 154; *Memoirs of Sir Hugh McCalmont*, p. 249; Gleichen, *With the Camel Corps Up The Nile*, pp. 190, 192, 215; 'The War in the Soudan: Letters from a Local Officer', *Newcastle Courant*, 3 April 1885, p. 8; Marling, *Rifleman and Hussar*, p. 148.
60 'The Campaign in the Soudan: Letters from a Local Officer', *Newcastle Courant*, 20 March 1885, p. 5.
61 *Ibid.*
62 *Ibid*; 'War in the Soudan: Letters from a Local Officer', p. 8.
63 'Our Ragged Regiments', *Birmingham Weekly Post*, 18 April 1885, p. 6.
64 'Letters from the Soudan', *Leicester Chronicle*, 18 April 1885, p. 3; 'A Soldier's Letter', p. 5.
65 Royal Gloucestershire Berkshire and Wiltshire Museum (RGBWM) (Salisbury), 004/28, 'R. Marine Surgeon's Views on the Campaign', n.d., p. 12; see also FACT, 'The Berkshire Regiment at Suakim', *Reading Mercury, Oxford Gazette, Newbury Herald & Berks County Paper*, 14 March 1885, p. 4.
66 'A Letter from the Soudan', *Surrey News*, 18 May 1885, p. 6; 'Letter from a Sailor', *Scotsman*, 3 April 1885, p. 5; and 'A Taunton Volunteer with the Australian Contingent', *Somerset County Gazette*, 2 May 1885, p. 11.
67 'The Soudan War', *Yorkshire Gazette*, 25 March 1885, p. 4.
68 'Characteristic Letter from a Welsh Soldier', *Western Mail*, 13 March 1885, p. 3; 'Berkshire Regiment at Suakim', p. 4.
69 RGBWM, 004/28, 'R. Marine Surgeon's Views on the Campaign', p. 14.
70 'Letter from a Soldier', *Scotsman*, 16 April 1885, p. 6.
71 'Letter from the Soudan', *Oxford Times*, 25 April 1885, p. 7.
72 'Letter from a Birkenhead Soldier at Suakin', *Birkenhead and Chester Advertiser*, 16 May 1885, p. 6.
73 NAM, Acc. No. 6807/269, Ferguson MSS, Pte F. Ferguson to his parents, 21 March 1885.
74 FACT, 'The Berkshire Regiment in Action', *Reading Mercury, Oxford Gazette, Newbury Herald & Berks County Paper*, 18 April 1885, p. 2; 'Further Severe Fighting Near Suakim', *Manchester Courier*, 23 March 1885, p. 8.
75 Featherstone, *Khartoum 1885*, p. 86.
76 RGBWM, 004/28, 'R. Marine Surgeon's Views on the Campaign', p. 15; see also 004/17, Col. A. S. Cameron, 'Action at Tofrik', 22 March 1885, p. 1.
77 RGBWM, R 4659, Capt. C. Mackenzie Edwards to 'Colonel', 16 April 1885.
78 RGBWM, 009/7, Lt-Col. H. W. L. Holman, 'The Battle of Tofrik or McNeill's Zeriba', n.d., p. 11.
79 RGBWM, R 4659, Edwards to 'Colonel', 16 April 1885; 'Berkshire Regiment in Action', p. 2.
80 'A Sheffield Marine's Account of Recent Fighting', *Sheffield Daily Telegraph*, 30 April 1885, p. 5; 'Letter from the Soudan', p. 7.
81 Brooks, *Long Arm of Empire*, p. 193.
82 'Suakin, 1885, Field Operations', *REJ*, 16 (1 May 1886), 97–101.
83 'Letter from an Officer at Suakim', *Oswestry Advertizer*, 22 April 1885, p. 5; see also 'A Private on the Soudan Campaign', *Uttoxeter New Era*, 22 July 1885, p. 5.
84 'A Sheffield Marine's Account of Recent Fighting', p. 5.
85 RGBWM, R 4659, Edwards to 'Colonel', 16 April 1885.
86 RGBWM, 004/24, Surgeon E. H. Finn, letter, 7 April 1885; see also NAM, Acc. No. 7709/43, Lloyd MSS, Lt F. Lloyd to his wife, 24 March and 25 April 1885.
87 'The True Story of McNeill's Zereba', *Pictorial World*, 16 July 1885, pp. 51–2; RGBWM, 009/7, Holman, 'Battle of Tofrik', p. 9; Marquess of Anglesey, *A History of the British Cavalry*, vol. 3, p. 360.
88 NAM, Acc. No. 7709/43, Lloyd to his wife, 5, 6, 17 and 23 April 1885; see also 'A Taunton Volunteer with the Australian Contingent', p. 11; 'Suakin, 1885, Field Operations', 99–100.

88 'A Letter from the Soudan', p. 6; 'A Hideous Experience', *Western Morning News*, 7 May 1885, p. 8.
90 NAM, Acc. No. 7709/43, Lloyd to his wife, 1 May 1885; 'Letters from the Soudan', p. 3.
91 'Letter from a Birkenhead Soldier at Suakin', p. 6.
92 'A Cornish Officer's Experiences', *Western Morning News*, 2 April 1885, p. 8.
93 'Our Soldiers in the Soudan', *Auckland Times and Herald*, 7 May 1885, p. 3; see also 'Letter from a Naval Officer', *Western Morning News*, 11 April 1885, p. 8, and 'A Cornish Officer's Experience' *ibid.*, 13 May 1885, p. 8.
94 BWA, 0203/1, Barwood, diary, 1 July 1885, p. 142.
95 'A Soldier's Letter from Korosko', *Scotsman*, 18 April 1885, p. 7; 'Korosko', *The 79th News*, no. 198 (April 1932), 171–3.
96 'Letter from a Soldier in the Soudan', *Kinross-shire Advertiser*, 2 January 1886, p. 2; 'A Letter from the Soudan', *Surrey News*, 11 January 1886, p. 3 and 'In the Soudan', *ibid.*, 18 January 1886, p. 3; 'Egypt and the Soudan', *Scotsman*, 19 January 1886, p. 5.
97 'Egypt and the Soudan', p. 5.
98 NAM, Acc. No. 6807/269, Ferguson to his parents, 18 January 1886.
99 'Egypt and the Soudan', *Scotsman*, 3 February 1886, p. 8.
100 *Ibid.*
101 S. G. P. Ward, *Faithful: The Story of the Durham Light Infantry* (Edinburgh: Thomas Nelson, 1964), pp. 274–5.
102 Preston (ed.), *In Relief of Gordon*, pp. xx–i; Symons, *England's Pride*, pp. 128–30, 174–7, 286–7.
103 'In the Soudan', *Surrey News*, 15 February 1886, p. 3; Sandes, *Royal Engineers*, p. 119.

CHAPTER SEVEN

Trekking through Bechuanaland

Several African campaigns did not involve skirmishes, sieges, battles or engagements of any significance. Whereas the British Army had to mount offensives and seek rapid, decisive military outcomes to disperse and demoralise its enemies (while minimising its own logistic burdens and likely losses from sickness and disease),[1] African adversaries responded to these offensives in different ways. If facing overwhelming odds, they sometimes avoided engagement and opted for manoeuvre (or even complete dispersal), luring the British and their auxiliaries across an inhospitable landscape and leaving them tired, thirsty and despondent. Inevitably these expeditions attracted less attention at home, especially if they coincided with major campaigns elsewhere – as happened to the Bechuanaland expedition (1884–85) and the two Asante expeditions of 1896 and 1900 – and so few letters from them survive. Nevertheless, the Bechuanaland campaign at least demonstrated the degree of British adaptation since the Anglo-Boer War of 1881.

The expedition was occasioned by Boer freebooters exploiting the rivalry among Bantu clans along the border from Vryburg to Mafeking and proclaiming the two semi-independent republics of Goshen and Stellaland in Bantu territory. The Gladstone Government regarded these incursions as breaches of the London Convention (1884), and resolved to protect the Bantu chiefs and retain control of the trade route from Cape Colony to Central Africa. It despatched Major-General Sir Charles Warren (RE), as a special commissioner with some 4,000 men, including 1/Royal Scots, the 6th Inniskilling Dragoons, three batteries of field artillery, a battery of Gardner machine-guns, three regiments of mounted rifles (recruited partly in Britain and partly in the Cape), balloon and field telegraph sections, a pioneer corps, and a corps of Bantu guides. Warren was required to evict the Goshenites from Bechuanaland (the Stellalanders had accepted British rule) and re-establish order.[2]

The first units of regulars and volunteers reached Cape Town on 19 December 1884 and left by train the same day for the Orange River, disembarking near Hope Town. They struggled over 12 roadless miles through deep sand, and waded the Orange River, to reach a camp site at Langford Rest. An old volunteer recalled that the dust and sand was so thick that 'we could not see five yards forward', so arriving 'with our tongues sticking to the roofs of our mouths'.[3] They found the camp infested with snakes, scorpions, ants and beetles, and temperatures that reached 112 degrees Fahrenheit in their tents. Life was made even more miserable by the sandstorms which repeatedly swept the site, the ban on 'intoxicants', and the cost of extras (including Bass pale ale, which was presumably not regarded as an 'intoxicant', at 2s 6d, or 12.5p, a pint bottle). Yet one trooper was impressed by the 'good many troops here', particularly the batteries of artillery and machine-guns and the many mounted men (all distinct improvements on the preparations of 1881), while another correspondent regarded the men of Colonel Paul S. (later Lieutenant-General Lord) Methuen's Horse as 'admirable, both physically and in *morale*'.[4] Almost as impressive was the health of the incoming men: by 4 January 1885 when half the force had arrived, there were under a dozen men in hospital and, after eleven days, only one of the Royal Scots, 740-strong, had fallen sick. Of more immediate concern was the 'want of water, transport and supplies', especially the lack of native labour, so the burden of 'constructing kraals, loading and unloading waggons, etc., falls on the soldier'.[5] However, by 13 January, Warren had sufficient mule-carts, wagons and drivers to march towards the Vaal River, where a forward base was established at Barkly West.

Although sunstroke took an increasing toll on the line of march, and many of the gentlemen troopers suffered 'severely from the heavy marching' (as their horses had yet to arrive from Natal), soldiers rapidly recovered at the camp site which had ample water, trees, shrubs and plenty of fresh meat from nearby sheep, goats and cattle.[6] Visitors were surprised to see British soldiers (apart from the Royal Scots) wearing 'rough corduroy' suits with their formerly white helmets 'travel-stained to a dirty brown'.[7] Julius M. Price, a volunteer of Methuen's Horse, confirmed this image of soldiers wearing inconspicuous kit and adapting to local conditions by sketching, for the *Illustrated London News*, officers in slouch hats and living in makeshift accommodation.[8]

Engineers, including the telegraph-laying section, and mounted rifles led the way into the disputed territory, with men aware that they had 'to march up the country to show the natives and Boers our strength'.[9] Writing on 4 February, some 80 miles north of Barkly, a trooper acknowledged the sensitivity of the mission: 'It is a most difficult thing to find out anything about the Boers. We absolutely don't know if we are going to fight or not . . . Stellaland seems to be quiet; and if we can manage to capture or kill the Freebooters we shall have easy work. But if, on the other hand, we kill a Transvaal Dutchman, there will be a general rising.'[10]

As the field force pressed on to the village of Taungs, it established an extensive line of communications, with telegraphic connections, wells dug at 12-mile intervals, and detachments posted along the route. The Royal Scots based its headquarters and four companies at Taungs, with detachments at Bank's Drift, Barkly and Langford 'holding wells and fords'.[11] After two months of trekking northwards, a Port Elizabeth volunteer affirmed that 'we are in excellent health. We have very fine horses. I do not think that the enemy can fly from their pursuers. The men here who are making money are the parties following the corps selling everything except liquors . . . Our haults [sic] have all been made on the open veldt so as to avoid inebriation'.[12] As patrols and outposts failed to find any freebooters in Stellaland, speculation mounted: what had become of them, wrote a colonial volunteer, 'goodness only knows, though we hear they talked big up to a fortnight of our arrival. They have entirely disappeared. They and their friends confess to being quite funked by the force – so I hear.'[13]

Warren, accompanied by 600 dragoons and mounted riflemen, rode north to Vryburg and thence over rolling grassland and through woods of acacia trees to Mafeking, where he sought to restore order in Goshen. He arrived on 9 March and Carrington's Horse moved up to the frontier at Rooi Gronde on the following day. Only a few Boers remained in the vicinity: as a trooper observed, 'They generally refuse to speak to an Englishman or at best answer in monosyllables; but the natives seem genuinely pleased to have us among them.'[14] As the expeditionary force now languished, patrolling along the frontier until October 1885, officers indulged their passion for shooting and some old soldiers found solace in drink. Several troopers insisted: 'We are all tired of the bloodless campaign', and claimed that 'more than one longed to return as speedily as possible'.[15] Warren, though, had to establish a British protectorate over Bechuanaland, and in doing so demonstrated another means of surveillance and control by deploying a balloon on the veld. Major Henry Elsdale, RE, was delighted that his team was able to spend a week in April, often 'in very unfavourable gusty weather', conducting reconnaissance operations. 'We pulled it off by a very narrow margin', he wrote, 'for our balloons were designed for Egypt at a low elevation above sea level, and the great elevation here (about 5,000 feet above sea level) is so much against them . . .'.[16] The whole exercise was given maximum publicity as colonial reporters described the size and scope of the balloon (20 feet in diameter, containing 10,000 cubic feet of hydrogen gas, and able to float steadily at 1,000 feet), and noted that Elsdale could scan a horizon of over 30 miles' radius while communicating with the ground by telephone. At least one correspondent concluded that 'henceforth no army in the field will be complete without its ballooning detachment'.[17]

If the campaign had demonstrated that some lessons had been learned about campaigning in South African conditions, particularly in respect of dress, fire-power and mobility,[18] the outcome was scant consolation for the soldiers involved. If they were well fed (graphically depicted by Price in his sketch of a sentinel standing on 2,000 cases of corned beef), generally healthy, and able to enjoy shooting game in the environs of Taungs,[19] they had little to show for the expedition itself. Bored and isolated (hence the anxiety about the receipt of post and newspapers from Britain),[20] they endured the heat, thunderstorms, and the ordeal of African campaigning without the excitement of engaging an enemy and the accompanying opportunities to earn medals and promotions in the field. In writing to his wife, Methuen, a veteran of the Asante and Egyptian campaigns, deeply resented his exclusion from the Nile expedition. 'It is hard to see the chance gone', he had written in September 1884;[21] six months later he still thought 'of the chance I lost', adding:

> It is a very bitter disappointment having toiled here for nothing particularly for the others, who have never seen service: had a shot been fired, my feeling is that there could have been heavy losses, as the Boers shoot so well, and the hatred here is intense. We all long to wipe out the shame inflicted on us, though at a heavy sacrifice.[22]

Notes

1 Maj.-Gen. Sir C. E. Callwell, *Small Wars: A Tactical Textbook for Imperial Soldiers* (London: HMSO, 1896; reprinted by Greenhill Books, London, 1990), pp. 75–6, 85, 91, 159, 170–1.
2 *Diary of Sir Edward Walker Hamilton*, vol. 2, pp. 695, 699; Tylden, 'The British Army and the Transvaal', 169; S. M. Miller, *Lord Methuen and the British Army: Failure and Redemption in South Africa* (London: Frank Cass, 1999), p. 44.
3 'The Bechuanaland Expedition', *Surrey Mirror*, 7 March 1885, p. 2.
4 *Ibid*; and 'With the Bechuanaland Field Force', *Scotsman*, 31 January 1885, p. 7.
5 *Ibid*.
6 'Bechuanaland Expedition', p. 2; 'With the Bechuanaland Expedition', *Natal Witness*, 3 February 1885, p. 3.
7 'With the Bechuanaland Expedition', p. 3.
8 'Bechuanaland Expedition' and 'With the Expedition to Bechuanaland', *Illustrated London News*, 14 March 1885, pp. 273–4.
9 'Bechuanaland Expedition', p. 2.
10 'Sir Charles Warren's Expedition', *Morning Post*, 6 March 1885, p. 5.
11 'Affairs of Bechuanaland', *Times of Natal*, 2 April 1885, p. 3; PP, *Further Correspon-*

dence Respecting the Affairs of the Transvaal and Adjacent Territories, C 4432 (1884–85), LVII, Sir C. Warren to the Earl of Derby, 28 February 1885, p. 21.

12 'News from Bechuanaland', Eastern Province Herald, 11 March 1885, p. 3.

13 'Affairs of Bechuanaland', p. 3; see also 'The Bechuana [sic] Expedition', Leeds Mercury, 13 March 1885, p. 3.

14 'The Bechuana Expedition', Leeds Mercury, 16 April 1885, p. 8.

15 'Affairs of Bechuanaland', p. 3; 'Warren and the Rooi Gronders', Natal Witness, 4 April 1885, p. 3; PP, Further Correspondence, Transvaal, C 4432 (1884–85), LVII, Warren to High Commissioner, 11 March 1885, p. 83; PRO, WO 106/264, 'Report from Colonel Methuen on the Organization and Recruiting, 1st Mounted Rifles', 20 June 1885, in 'Report of Proceedings of the Bechuanaland Field Force', pp. 177–9.

16 'Balloon Work on Active Service', REJ, 15 (1 June 1885), 119.

17 'Ballooning in Bechuanaland', Times of Natal, 15 May 1885, p. 3.

18 But Methuen advocated further improvements in some pieces of kit: see PRO, WO 106/264, Col. P. Methuen to Assistant Adjutant-General, 12 June 1885, in 'Report of Proceedings of the Bechuanaland Field Force, 1884–5', pp. 209–10.

19 'Affairs of Bechuanaland', p. 3; 'The Bechuanaland Expedition', Illustrated London News, 28 March 1885, pp. 328 and 334.

20 'Bechuanaland Expedition', p. 2.

21 Wiltshire and Swindon Record Office (WRO), Methuen MSS, WSRO 1742/8564, Col. P. S. Methuen to his wife, 17 September 1884.

22 Ibid., WSRO 1742/8565, Col. Methuen to his wife, 16 March 1885.

CHAPTER EIGHT

Reconquering the Sudan

After the costly failure of the Gordon relief expedition, successive British governments retained only a small army of occupation in Egypt and withdrew forces from the southern frontier, the defence of which was left increasingly to the Egyptian Army. The latter was reformed and trained by a cadre of British officers and NCOs and was periodically supported by British units, notably a squadron of the 20th Hussars at the battle of Toski (13 August 1889; and in engagements with Osman Digna's forces near Suakin. British units were even more prominent in the Sudanese campaigns of the late 1890s; the 1/North Staffordshires served in the Dongola campaign of 1896 and another eight battalions, supported by the 21st Lancers, two batteries of artillery, a machine-gun battery and a flotilla of gunboats served in the Anglo-Egyptian army at Omdurman (2 September 1898). As all these campaigns involved protracted journeys and tedious days spent in barracks or under canvas, soldiers kept diaries, drew sketches, and took numerous photographs.[1] They were also prolific correspondents, and, in some cases, wrote campaign histories based partially on their first-hand experience.[2] They explained how the logistic problems of operating in the Sudan were overcome and how an Anglo-Egyptian army defeated the forces of the Khalifa. Some of these letters have been reproduced,[3] others have embellished well-known accounts of the campaign, particularly those commemorating the centenary of the battle of Omdurman;[4] but the surviving correspondence is even more voluminous than these sources suggest. Although most material derives from the 1898 campaign, the earlier letters and diaries provide a comparative context, indicating how the experience of soldiering in the Sudan evolved over a decade.

As most of the Gordon relief expedition began to depart, Private Francis Ferguson (20th Hussars) reconciled himself to a long tour of duty in Egypt. He anticipated another twelve months but would ultimately spend the remainder of his five years with the colours in Egypt, where he liked 'the fighting if it were not for the cursed climate . . .'. He had already succumbed to dysentery and knew that his regiment, despite receiving regular drafts of men from England, had 'been weakened by a lot of men being invalided home with Dysentry & Enterick fever'.[5] Within two months of the battle of Ginnis he was again invalided down to Assouan from Wadi Halfa, which he regarded as 'the most unhealthy station' in Egypt with '3 or 4 funerals every day sometimes as many as 9'.[6] After returning to Wadi Halfa, where he remained until May 1886, Ferguson feared the risks of illness above anything else whenever the prospect of frontier service recurred. In April 1887 he noted reports of 'a good many of our men dying' at Assouan, and, after the battle of Toski, berated the medical authorities for failing to provide any water purification: 'the Nile is rising & we have to drink the water like mud as we have no means to clear it'. By now well acquainted with Sudanese conditions, he regarded the medical department as '[v]ery thoughtless . . . as they ought to know the state of the Nile at this time of the Year & I think that is the cause of all the sickness here at present'.[7]

Egyptian service had its attractions, nonetheless. Ferguson liked the barracks at Abbassiyeh, some 3 miles from Cairo, describing the rooms as 'large & lofty, each capable of holding over fifty bed cots and are very cool considering the climate'. He regarded the stables, about a mile from the barracks, as 'much better than English stables', with plenty of water and troughs 'about fifty feet long & six feet wide'. The troops enjoyed beer at 7d (3p) a quart in a 'very decent canteen with a stage' and could supplement their rations with plentiful supplies of cheap local produce. While the charms of Cairo were only a donkey ride away, a local bazaar had formed near Abbassiyeh 'kept by French people & girls & some Greek but no English'.[8] Periodically the temptations of the canteen proved too much, and there was a drunken Christmas brawl between the Shropshire Light Infantry and the 20th Hussars: 'Iron bed legs were flying about in all directions & one of our men is a lunatic in the hospital caused by a bayonet going through his head. Several more got bayonet wounds & 18 of the infantry are in with sword wounds but all is quiet now.'[9]

Ferguson, like many of his comrades, never formed a high opinion of the Egyptian soldiery (other than the black Sudanese). When the garrison at Wadi Halfa was handed over to the Egyptians, he remarked: 'It is nearly time they were able to shift for themselves' and, in departing for Suakin in December 1888, he recalled the debacle of Hicks Pasha's army, claiming that 'The Egyptians cannot be trusted as they run away if a few men chase them'.[10] In fact, the Egyptian Army had been reformed and would fight effectively in the Sudan: at Gemaizah (20 December 1888) the Sudanese cleared the Mahdist trenches before the cavalry charge. Both Corporal Wakefield and Ferguson described the 'awful' crash of the two mounted forces as they charged each other over 'terribly rough ground'. Whereas Ferguson thought that we 'emptied about 30 saddles', Wakefield reckoned that most of the enemy dismounted to fight alongside 'hundreds of rebels on foot'. The 20th Hussars, he claimed, were handicapped by the quality of their sabres: in the first clash of arms, he saw one trooper killed and another slashed from shoulder to nearly his waist while at least three British sabres 'broke over the Arabs' spears'. He himself 'cut one man full on the head, but it had no effect on him'. After a couple of charges the troopers retired, dismounted 'and commenced firing, which ultimately made the enemy retire'.[11]

During the cavalry charge three troopers and trumpeter Newton were killed and mutilated, prompting not merely feelings of rage and vengeance but the reflections of Trooper E. P. Wedlake:

> It was, indeed, a glorious charge, though marred with grief and pain,
>   For Newton, Thomas, Jordan, Howes, were numbered with the slain.
> We bore them from the field of strife with tenderness and love,
>   And trusted that their souls had found a resting-place above.
> Then our thoughts returned to Cairo's camp, with its mottoes and its
>   flowers,
>   With saddened recollections of its gay and festive bowers.
> We wept for our gallant comrades, as still in death they lay,
>   And in the camp of our beaten foes we spent our Christmas Day.[12]

Ferguson's letter largely chronicled his own exploits, particularly in protecting Private Knowles from an Arab wielding a double-edged sword. When copies of the *Evening News* containing this letter and an advertising placard were sent to him, soldiers posted the material on the stable door and ribbed him about his tale. Ferguson defended 'every word' by referring to various witnesses, including Private Knowles, memories of his blood-stained horse and the deep cut in his sword hilt, 'So they said no more to me about it'. He also explained to his parents that the hussars had spent the month after the battle constantly on parade and vedette duty, capturing the odd rebel and scouring hills near Tamai for the enemy. Ferguson was particularly impressed with Colonel H. Herbert Kitchener, whose linguistic gifts had enabled him to operate as a spy in Metemmeh during the Nile campaign: 'he is a very brave man & well liked by all Troops'.[13]

Finally, Ferguson left his impressions of the battlefield at Toski where the 20th Hussars was the only British unit present and assisted in the final rout of Wad Nejumi's invading army. After all his previous engagements, Ferguson was gratified that 'hardly any fighting men of the Rebels escaped', and that all the leaders, save one, were killed. In killing Nejumi, who he thought, erroneously, had killed Gordon and defeated King John of Abyssinia, they had disposed of 'the ablest & best leader & bravest of the Mahdi's Generals'. He had never seen 'so many Dead after a Battle, and so close together . . . They were in heaps as they were shot down', with more women, children and animals slain in the two camps, including a women killed in the act of childbirth, 'a horrible sight'.[14] The last Mahdist invasion of Egypt had been repulsed.

Although Ferguson made scant reference to the role of the Egyptian Army at Toski, it had proved its worth in repelling a Mahdist assault and then in advancing to seize the enemy's camp. Some eighteen months later, in February 1891, Egyptian and Sudanese forces reoccupied Tokar without the assistance of any British troops (other than their British officers and NCOs). Nevertheless, in March 1896, the 1/North Staffordshires were sent forward in support of the Egyptian Army when the cabinet approved a limited incursion into the northern province of Dongola. This decision was a response to Italian pleas for a military diversion to ease the pressure on their garrison at Kassala (after the catastrophic defeat of the Italian forces at Adowa on 1 March). Cromer advised Lord Salisbury, then prime minister and foreign secretary, that it would 'be a serious business, from a military point of view, to get to Dongola'. He doubted 'whether it can be achieved without employing English troops'.[15]

At Abbassiyeh barracks the North Staffordshires greeted news of their impending action with 'wild excitement': 'officers and men', recalled Lieutenant (later Major) J. J. B. Farley, dashed 'about, throwing helmets in the air and shouting "Wady Halfa in a week"'.[16] After rigorous medical examinations in which 10 per cent of the strength were turned down, the battalion left Cairo by train on 22 March to a tremendous ovation from friends and well-wishers. On the next day the 912 men were crammed on to two steamers and completed a journey of 800 miles to Wadi Halfa in ten days. Thereafter they languished in barracks for several months as Kitchener concentrated on extending the railway and the telegraph south of Sarras while moving stores and supplies forward to the base at Akasheh.[17] Colonel Archibald Hunter (Egyptian Army) later explained that: 'More than two-thirds of the work is calculating the quantity of supplies required and where to have them and by what time. In fact, war is not fighting and patrolling and bullets and knocks; it is one constant worry about transport and forage and ammunition and seeing that no one is short of stuff.'[18]

Although the North Staffordshires had come to Egypt from Malta in the previous October, they were not prepared for the heat, flies and general discomfort of serving on the Sudanese frontier. 'We are grow-ing weary', wrote Captain Somerset Astell, 'horrible rumours come in that the Dervishes are starving, their allies deserting, so they may cave in & then we shall have borne the burden & heat of the day for nought.'[19] They endured a daily routine of early morning drill, includ-ing attack and square formations, and musketry practice before spend-ing most of the day in barracks. In the extreme heat water fatigues were particularly arduous, and the medical staff tried to prevent their ther-mometers from bursting. Officers sought to occupy bored men, some-times by reading aloud to their companies. As Astell recalled: 'Slatin's Fire & Sword in the Soudan held the Palm & was a veritable gold mine to us, both as instruction and interest to men & officers.'[20] In the late afternoon soldiers played football or, like the officers, bathed in the Nile and attended concerts or smoking concerts at night. Officers, find-ing little scope for riding or shooting, experimented at fishing, while some sailed on the river, and most enjoyed the company of the hard-drinking and garrulous war correspondents. Everyone appreciated the receipt of mail from home.[21]

None of the regiment apart from Captain Goldfinch's Maxim bat-tery took part in the major battle of the campaign at Firket (7 June 1896). They learned at second hand of the night march by the three brigades of the Egyptian Army, the co-ordinated strike on the village, and the house-to-house fighting before the Mahdists retired. 'The plan', reckoned Astell, was 'as ably thought out, as it was brilliantly executed.'[22] Farley agreed: 'The whole operation was a perfect example of careful planning on the part of the Sirdar and Colonels Rundle and Hunter and it was brilliantly carried out by the troops.'[23] Hunter, who commanded one of the Egyptian brigades, attributed the success to the element of surprise after the 'silence' of the night march. He doubted that they could achieve another surprise and expected 'a great fight at Dongola'. Despite being critical of his soldiers for their 'wild, badly aimed' shooting, he was glad they had seized this 'chance to belie the croakings of their detractors'.[24]

Of more immediate concern was the typhoid fever and cholera that began to sweep through English and Egyptian ranks from mid-June onwards. Lieutenant-Colonel Beale, Lieutenant Hutchinson and sev-eral North Staffordshires were invalided to Cairo, and, on 1 July, the battalion moved camp to Gemai. Within a day of their arrival another man was struck down and over the next six weeks cholera took a heavy toll of officers and other ranks. Astell grimly noted: 'Funerals, for obvi-ous reasons took place as quietly as possible, generally at night.'[25] While officers praised the efforts of the medical staff, Farley noted how the latter had struggled without water filters and wood for boiling

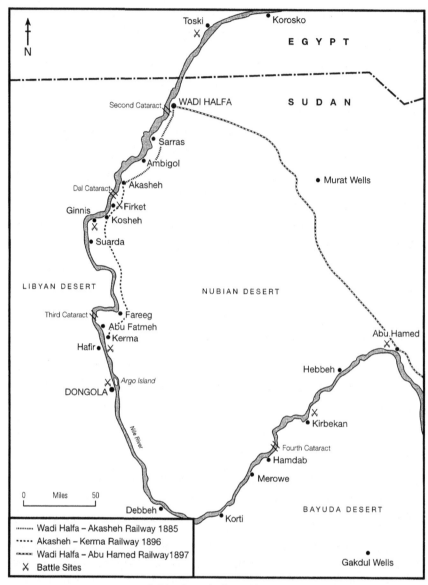

7 Northern Sudan, 1884–98

water.[26] The battalion was now dispersed into three locations, with the sick being treated in a separate hospital from Gemai and an increasing number being invalided to Cairo. The two local Methodist preachers, Conductor Linnington (Ordnance Service Corps) and Sergeant Forde (North Staffordshires) conceded that they could no longer hold reli-

[142]

gious gatherings; but Forde consoled himself: 'Not a single abstainer has been attacked, and there is not a single abstainer in hospital up here. This speaks for itself.'[27]

Fortunately the cholera abated by mid-August but a massive storm and flooding ruined a section of the railway on 25 August, so many of the available soldiers were sent to Sarras to repair the track. Although the railway work 'was very hard', Astell claimed that the men 'rejoiced' at anything that gave them some relief from 'the utter stagnation' they had endured for 'so long'. He observed, too, that 'the Soudanese & our men were always great friends' but 'one never saw any mingling of the white & Egyptian troops'.[28] Officers and other ranks were even more pleased when the orders came to move forward by train to Kosheh. The North Staffordshires were now somewhat depleted as 44 had died, 120 had been invalided to Cairo, and, at Kosheh, another 150 had to be left behind as the steamer *Zafir* burst its cylinder.

At Hafir (19 September) they were largely spectators as the gunboats and a brigade of artillery under Colonel C. Parsons bombarded the enemy's defences. 'The Dervishes', wrote Farley, 'certainly deserved and obtained our highest admiration for the way they stuck to their position.'[29] When the Mahdists eventually withdrew, the North Staffordshires marched on without any food, rations or water, covering the next 23 miles 'on empty stomachs' and losing only one man on the line of march. On 23 September the battalion marched on Dongola in the centre of the front line of the 15,000-man army, with gunboats providing fire support. Once again the bulk of the Mahdist forces withdrew, although Baggara horsemen and a few individuals proffered token resistance. By 11.30 a.m. the town had fallen without any casualties among the English soldiers.[30] While soldiers appreciated Kitchener's words of praise on the following day, and the opportunity to acquire 'dervish loot', this was scant comfort for their state of health: when the North Staffordshires returned to Cairo on 9 October, another seventy-six men entered hospital, of whom twenty, including Captain J. Rose, died.[31]

In a subsequent interview Kitchener admitted his 'great surprise' that the enemy had bolted from Dongola 'in utter rout'. He attributed this collapse of morale to the stories from Firket, the presence of gunboats and the overwhelming numbers of the Anglo-Egyptian army, but warned against underestimating the power of the Khalifa.[32] Hunter agreed, claiming that the Egyptian Army had only overwhelmed the enemy's positions at Toski, Tokar and Firket because it had English officers and 'we were always in superior numbers. We have never asked him to do anything that was not within the easy compass of attainment'.[33] Such reasoning would ensure that once the Sudan Military Railway (SMR) was built from Wadi Halfa across the Nubian desert, British forces would again be required for the advance on Omdurman. Despite appalling climatic conditions, construction of the railway began on 1 January 1897, involving gangs of native labourers under the energetic direction of Lieutenant E. P. C. Girouard, RE, and his staff. On 7 August 1897, Hunter in command of a flying column secured the terminus for the 230-mile railway at Abu Hamed,[34] and then pressed on to establish a forward base at Berber. The railway, completed on 4 November 1897, was rightly regarded by Hunter as 'the all important factor of this expedition'. It shortened the journey to Abu Hamed from eighteen days by camel and steamer to twenty-four hours (depending on the serviceability of the engines) and enabled Kitchener to move his forces and gunboats into the heart of the Sudan independently of season or the height of the Nile. As Hunter added: 'That Railway from Halfa to Abu Hamed is a monument of the skill & resources of the Sirdar. It is his idea & his only.'[35]

Railway construction continued during 1898. By February, when the railway from Cairo reached Assouan, Colonel A. O. Green (RE) reckoned that even with a delay the boat and rail journey to Wadi Halfa took only six days; by August, when the SMR reached Atbara – 385 miles from Wadi Halfa – Sergeant-Major Clement Riding (Royal Army Medical Corps – RAMC), claimed that it took only seven days to reach Atbara from Cairo.[36] Soldiers sometimes erred in recalling the length and duration of journeys – Corporal George Skinner (RAMC) added 120 miles to the rail journey from Wadi Halfa to Abu Hamed[37] – and the travelling experiences often varied from unit to unit. Of the four battalions of the First British Brigade (the 1st Battalions of the Lincolns, Royal Warwicks, Cameron Highlanders and Seaforth Highlanders) only the late-arriving Seaforths and some drafts for the other units, including Private H. Matthews (Lincolns), experienced the delights of riding through the night on camels to their camp site. 'After this camel ride', grumbled Matthews, 'we could hardly walk', and the experience was even less agreeable in a kilt: as Sergeant Roderick Morrison complained, 'It was by far the worst journey I ever undertook.'[38]

Travel was only one of several new experiences for the short-service soldiers, many of whom had never served in Egypt and the Sudan before.[39] Coming from Malta, Lance-Sergeant Colin Grieve (Seaforths) was franker than most in his description of Cairo as 'one of the finest cities in the world to look at, but the wickedest place on God's earth . . . As far as I can see the majority of the people in these Eastern Countries live on Villany [sic] & their wits, and immorality is looked on as quite a respectable trade.'[40] Many recalled the enthusiastic crowds that had greeted their departures and the cheering from passing steamers, the experience of being 'packed like herrings in a box' on Nile vessels, the spectacle of the ancient ruins at Luxor, and the first sight of the Sudan Military Railway as its 'shimmering rails disappeared into the mirage'.[41] Yet battalions were shocked as the strain of the logistic arrangements took its toll, with two elderly quartermasters committing suicide: a Cameron Highlander 'blew out his brains', reportedly 'through a choking off that the Colonel gave him';[42] and Quartermaster Sergeant Haines of the Lincolns cut his own throat. Another Lincolnshire sergeant explained: 'He had had a lot of work to do of late, and was not in good health, nor had he been used to a life such as this'.[43]

Any gloom over these suicides soon dissipated once soldiers completed their journeys, pitched camp near the railhead 22 miles south of Abu Hamed, and began a hectic round of daily fatigues and training. The arrival of their commanding officer, Major-General William F. Gatacre, a 55-year old martinet from India, ensured that they would not languish in camp as the North Staffordshires had done.[44] A Lincolnshire sergeant wrote:

> Our daily routine [is] as follows: Running drill to the Nile and back, bathing parade, battalion drill in fighting formation, attack and defence, outpost duty by night and day, camp fatigues, wood and water fatigues, unloading railway trucks of stores, and pitching and striking camp; also marching drill during the warm part of the day.[45]

Gatacre added to these labours by insisting that everyone wore their full kit, boots and ammunition, by night and day: 'what little sleep we got for fully a month', wrote Private Matthews, 'was with our boots and clothes on'.[46] If officers were more sceptical of Gatacre's excessive precautions, hectoring speeches and constant interference – 'He is one of the fussiest men going', claimed Lieutenant William Stewart (Camerons)[47] – the men appeared more tolerant of 'Old Back-acher', as they described him, other than his proscription of beer. Occasional tots of rum were scant comfort: 'the men began to moan', noted Skinner, 'especially when it was known that the officers were getting as much as they wanted'.[48] 'As regards rations', Matthews admitted, 'we cannot grumble. We each get 2lbs. of bread each day, and if we do not get bread we get a pound of biscuits and a pound of meat. We also have to drink tea four times a day.'[49] Soldiers appreciated, too, that some of Gatacre's additional fatigues would enhance their prospects in battle, particularly filing the tips off their bullets to make them similar to Dum Dum ammunition: by 19 February, a Cameron Highlander could report: 'we have just finished the last box to-day; so that is 300 boxes of Dum Dums for Fuzzy Wuzzy to stomach'.[50]

Officers and men were less impressed when Gatacre ordered them to undertake a forced march to Berber and thence to Darmali, some 122 miles in 5 days with a day's rest (25 February–2 March), reputedly to save the advance units of the Egyptian Army from Mahdist attack. Whether marching at night or early morning, the soldiers struggled through deep sand and then over hard rocky desert. The latter, wrote Sergeant Murphy (Lincolns), 'was very trying. It hurt the men's feet badly, the stones were so sharp. We marched 32 miles on this day with only the water in our bottle . . . I never saw one tree on this march; nothing met the eye except now and again the bleached bones of a camel. After this long march we received a ration of rum.'[51] 'What made the marching worse', added Private D. MacDonald (Camerons), 'was that most of it was done on our bare feet, as we had no shoes or sox [sic] on.'[52] Lieutenant Ronald F. Meiklejohn (Warwicks) agreed that 'some had no soles on their boots: many had the skin off their feet: & others were worn out. We left about 150 men & two officers (Caldecott & Christie): the Lincolns left 180: the Camerons 200: and these waited for two gunboats to arrive & bring them on.' He was even more incensed when the battalions reached Berber to an enthusiastic reception and the realisation that they had not been expected for a week at least. 'Our confidence [in Gatacre]', wrote Meiklejohn, 'is shaken. He has the reputation of wearing out his troops unnecessarily.'[53]

Nevertheless, soldiers were pleased with the issue of fresh boots from the Egyptian Army and a more varied diet from Berber (including bacon, rice and other vegetables). While the Seaforths joined the Camerons at Kunour on 16 March, the Lincolns and Warwicks encamped in the village of Darmali, some 15 miles south of Berber. Cordial relations were again forged between the British and Sudanese soldiers, with the 10th Sudanese greeting the Lincolns with cheers and cups of tea, its band playing a rendition of the 'Lincolnshire Poacher', and soldiers shouting in broken English: 'You, 10th Inglesey, we 10th Soudanese.'[54] The Sudanese even found a mess table for the Warwickshire officers, whereupon the latter were able to host a dinner for Gatacre, involving 'soup, stewed beef, rice and green peas, asparagus, rice pudding, and damsons, coffee, champagne and port', all the produce being acquired in Berber.[55]

More importantly British, Egyptian and Sudanese battalions were now able to practise combined movements, forming squares and completing other manoeuvres under Kitchener's observation. When news arrived that Emir Mahmud was leading an *ansar* of 16,000 men towards the River Atbara, Kitchener ordered his entire army to advance on the Atbara (20 March). Within two days the army reached Ras-el-Hudi, where Sergeant Murphy described the scene: 'We are lying

close on the Atbara river which is teeming with fish, gazelle are plentiful in the woods, while quail, geese, wild ducks, and pigeons, hares,
rabbits, etc., are in abundance . . . Palm and mimosa trees are thick
here, and milk trees are in abundance.'[56]

Having waited in vain for a Mahdist attack, Kitchener eventually
resolved to advance on Mahmud's zareba. After a series of cautious
marches his army deployed some 600 yards from Mahmud's stronghold
(6 a.m. on 8 April), whereupon the Egyptian artillery began pounding the
enemy's position for three-quarters of an hour. Thereafter three brigades
walked towards the zareba, with the Camerons deployed in line at the
front of the British Brigade, followed by the Seaforths, Warwicks and
Lincolns in column. As the units advanced firing volleys, many remembered the Sirdar's final exhortation: 'Remember Gordon.'[57] Private H.
Pexton (Lincolns) recalled: 'The bullets from the Dervishes were like
hailstones flying about', while Private J. Turnbull (Camerons) admitted:
'It felt a bit funny at first hearing the bullets whistling round a fellow's
ears, and seeing a chum drop beside a fellow, and never having time to
think when your own time was coming'. A comrade added that once the
Camerons ripped open gaps in the zareba, they never waited for 'orders
to charge, but went for them for all we were worth like devils'.[58]

Sergeant Morrison was 'astonished' by 'the heavy and continuous
fire kept up by the enemy, but it all went high, and a good job too'.[59]
They found the Mahdists fighting from a maze of deep trenches and a
central stockade, with many slaves, as observed by Private Arthur
Hipkin (Lincolns), 'unable to retreat because they were chained by the
ankles'.[60] 'They are a very tough lot of men', claimed Sergeant Murphy,
not least those who survived multiple wounds from Gatacre's bullets
before succumbing to the bayonet. However, their shamming of death
or injury before shooting or stabbing passing soldiers provoked fierce
retribution: 'After that', wrote Drum-Major David Nelson (Seaforths),
'they got no mercy. They got bayonetted every time.'[61]

British soldiers praised the Sudanese for their zeal in close-quarter
fighting, if not always the accuracy of their shooting, and for capturing
Mahmud: Private George Young (Lincolns) even 'pitied the Dervishes
that showed any signs of life, as the Soudanese soon put an end to their
misery'.[62] Another Lincoln, Corporal D. W. Anderson, deplored the
'slaughter' of the battle:

> [I]t was a horrible sight to see those trenches full of dead and dying
> Dervishes, and as we drove them to the river they were properly
> butchered, and hundreds of them were fairly blown to pieces . . . The
> smell was awful, for the huts, which were made of large palm leaves,
> were burning (from the shells and rockets) and it was horrible to see lots
> of Dervishes burning in these fires.[63]

[147]

Compounding the stench of battle were the odours of a camp bereft of sanitary arrangements: 'The Dervishers [*sic*]', asserted Hipkin, 'are a dirty tribe',[64] but the dangers of the battlefield, especially from 'ammunition constantly exploding' in the fires, prompted a withdrawal of the victorious units and their wounded. They had to bivouac in the desert with 'absolutely no shade', burying their dead and remaining until 5 p.m. whereupon they could march back to camp. 'If it was bad for us', wrote one Seaforth officer, 'it was a thousand times worse for the wounded, who suffered much.'[65]

The sufferings of the wounded, many of whom had injuries from explosive bullets, were a source of continuing anxiety. Corporal Skinner explained that the under-staffed and ill-equipped medical team 'had plenty of work' with ninety-four patients (there were a few less seriously injured). They lost 5 of their patients after the battle (adding to the 19 killed outright) and another 3 in the coming weeks. Even transporting the wounded on litters and stretchers by night, with the less serious cases on camels, was a 'very trying' experience – 'the worst march of the whole lot', in Skinner's opinion.[66] Lincolns praised their 'brave old colonel', T. E. Verner, who was shot through the jaw 'but led us on to the finish',[67] while several Seaforths lauded officers either killed or mortally wounded when leading from the front. Bandsman P. Learmonth grieved for 'one poor young officer, Lieutenant Gore', who died with 'a smile on his face', and Private Thomas R. Clarke composed a poem about 'our brave young captain', Alan Baillie, who died after an amputation. The poem testified to the strength of officer–man relations, ending

> We'll march no more together,
>   We'll miss his kindly care,
> Until we meet our captain
>   In yonder land so fair.[68]

If good officer–man relations underpinned regimental *esprit de corps*, rivalry between the battalions added a competitive dimension. As the Scots incurred most of the casualties, with Camerons suffering the bulk of the fatalities and nearly half of the wounded, they joined war correspondents in extolling their own achievements. Even Lance-Sergeant Grieve, who was not present at the battle, concluded that 'the Lincolns & Warwicks had scarcely any wounded as the Jocks were in the trenches first'.[69] A Warwickshire soldier was not alone in complaining that 'according to one paper, anyone would think the Warwicks and Lincolns had not taken part in the affair – but we have, and we did our duty'.[70]

The veterans of Atbara returned to their respective camps – the Camerons and Seaforths to Darmali, the Lincolns and Warwicks to Es Sillem – gratified by the Khedive's promise of a medal and clasp, and pleased by the improvements in food and accommodation, and by the delivery of mail.[71] For four months the brigade languished in its 'summer quarters', with officers and men trying to occupy themselves with hunting, fishing, smoking concerts and sports, including an Atbara 'Derby' in June. Marches and drills were largely confined to the early morning as daytime temperatures soared above 100 degrees Fahrenheit. Dysentery became prevalent from late April onwards and later typhoid fever took an increasing toll (leaving fifty dead at Darmali and probably more among those who had to be evacuated). Lance-Sergeant W. Briggs (Seaforths) was almost certainly trying to reassure relatives when he claimed: 'All the troops at Darmali are in good heath'; others were more candid about the state of the camps.[72]

By early August reinforcements began to arrive, notably the 2nd British Brigade (1/Grenadier Guards, 1/Northumberland Fusiliers, 2/Rifle Brigade and 2/Lancashire Fusiliers), the 32nd and 37th field batteries RA, a battery of Maxim machine-guns manned by Royal Irish Fusiliers, 16th company Royal Garrison Artillery, and ultimately the 21st Lancers who joined the army on 23 August. Given the rapidity of their travel from Cairo, the forces struggled to acclimatise and to practise their drills and fighting formations: as Private Walter Pickup observed, 'the sweat rolls out of you if you walk only about half a dozen yards out of your tent', but fellow Grenadier Lance-Sergeant George Shirley insisted that spirits were high and that all were 'very anxious to get a fight'.[73] Kitchener was keen to oblige and had sent the Sudanese ahead, followed by the 1st British Brigade to establish a vast camp at Wad Hamed, just above the sixth cataract. When the Warwicks arrived on 16 August after a three-day journey, one of their officers remarked: 'From this date campaigning started again in real earnest, sleeping in our boots, and patrols going all night.'[74] On this part of the advance the Lancers, following the caravan trail south from Fort Atbara in a succession of early morning rides, had several cases of sunstroke and exhaustion, including two fatalities and the loss of 18 horses.[75] They arrived after Kitchener's review of 23,000 soldiers at Wad Hamed but in time to screen the ensuing march over the remaining 60 miles to Omdurman.

Even seasoned soldiers from the Egyptian Army and the 1st Brigade struggled in the daily marches which, though short, were extremely slow on account of the number of soldiers involved. Conducted over undulating terrain and through patches of deep sand and scrub, the marches were, according to Lance-Corporal Whiting (Lincolns),'worse' than the pre-Atbara march, 'for instead of sandstorms we had a thunderstorm about every other night'.[76] If a 'great many men fell out', as Lance-Corporal A. Unsworth (Seaforths) recalled, most fell out from the 2nd Brigade, where grumbling persisted about the lack of food and water. Unsworth reckoned that most bore their discomforts 'cheerfully, and with resignation . . . resolved to make the Khalifa pay dearly' for them; others testified to the inspirational support of the regimental bands and Reverend Watson's sermon on the Sunday before Omdurman, in which he likened their mission to a crusade to avenge the death of Gordon.[77] Sergeant W. G. Moody (Lincolns) expressed confidence in Kitchener and fatalism about the battle to come: 'There was nothing left to chance by the Sirdar, and he will carry this through all right. Of course, we shall probably leave a good few behind us, but that can't be helped, and everyone stands the same chance of getting through all right.'[78]

On reaching the village of Egeiga (1 September), soldiers were impressed by the Sirdar's preparations for battle. While gunboats and howitzers travelled upriver to pound the defences of Omdurman and the Mahdi's tomb, Lancers posted signallers on Jebel Surgham, a hill about two miles away, to report on the movements of the Khalifa's army. The remainder of the Anglo-Egyptian army formed a horseshoe-like formation with its back to the Nile, and, as a Warwickshire officer explained, this semi-circle stretched for 4,000 yards and each front-line battalion deployed six companies in the firing line, with two in reserve. The British constructed a zareba (unlike the shallow shelter trench and parapet built by the Egyptian troops), placed range-markers out to 2,000 yards, and, after the cavalry withdrew, sent out spies to check on the Khalifa's movements.[79] After an anxious night in which an alert sounded, and the men stood to arms from 3.30 a.m. onwards, Lance-Corporal J. Gibson (Lancashire Fusiliers) claimed: 'I was glad when morning came, as I wanted to have a rub at the dervishes.'[80]

Once the dawn patrols of cavalry and horse artillery returned to the zareba, they heard the 'awful noise' of the advancing army[81] and then saw, as Grenadier Drill-Sergeant Morgan described,

> the sight of countless black men clad in white – an enormous host with spears and swords that glittered in the early sun, and hundreds of coloured banners. The big drums boomed – the small ones gave a peculiar liquid tone. The sight and sounds seemed to create a queer feeling among the younger chaps, but they immediately stiffened up and remembered they were Britons.

This was an organised foe, he recalled, 'in five lines, in good formation, and they were led by chiefs mounted on splendid horses'.[82] As they charged across open ground, Guardsman Percy Thompson recalled how 'a murmur of admiration ran through British ranks'.[83] 'We waited with breathless intensity', wrote Corporal Fred Monks (Rifle Brigade), 'for the first shot, which we knew would be delivered by the artillery.' First the gunners 'with their coats off for some hot work',[84] then some infantry firing long-range volleys at 2,000 yards, the Maxims and the remaining infantry at about 1,500 yards, sustained a fusillade of gun and rifle fire all along the line for at least an hour-and-a-half. 'We knew', claimed Private Lison (Camerons), 'that we were all right so long as we kept them at a distance', and none of the enemy reached the zareba.[85]

Most praised the bravery and tenacity of the Mahdists, particularly the leader of the Baggara horsemen, whom Unsworth thought bore a 'charmed life' as he charged on alone after all his comrades had fallen before being killed.[86] 'It was a fearful slaughter', wrote Drum-Major Cordial (Northumberland Fusiliers), 'more like a butcher's killing house than anything else. Although the Dervishes are very brave men, our magazine fire was too much for them, and the Maxims and big guns actually mowed them down.'[87] Morgan agreed: 'The slaughter was dreadful. I thought it was like murder. Men fell in heaps, and corpses were piled up.'[88]

Soldiers were delighted when the first phase of the battle was over. 'My arms were aching', recalled Lison, and the barrel was 'too hot . . . to hold'; he welcomed the rest, a biscuit and water as ammunition pouches were refilled (the Seaforths had fired 56 volleys, the Warwicks between 60 and 70 rounds per man).[89] When the British moved forward at about 9 a.m., they 'got orders', as Colour-Sergeant Eastwood (Rifle Brigade) observed, 'to bayonet and shoot everyone we saw': this was 'horrible' if 'absolutely necessary' work in the opinion of some – a fore-taste of the controversy that would later rage in the press – but it was a task relished by others, like Gibson, who killed 'about twenty-five, I think, and every shot I fired I said "Another one for Gordon"'.[90] Thompson found it 'a peculiar sensation bayonetting a man. I shut my eyes the first one I struck, but I got used to it by the time I reached the next one.'[91]

The 21st Lancers advanced under orders to harass the enemy on their flank and head them off from Omdurman. The regiment, as Captain F. H. Eadon admitted, was 'keen to make some mark in history in this our first campaign',[92] and after encountering some 150 riflemen guarding the Khalifa's line of retreat and coming under fire, Colonel Roland Martin wheeled his four squadrons into line and ordered a charge. He subsequently claimed that patrols had given 'correct information' about the enemy's numbers, that the khor over which they jumped was not as deep as 'represented in some quarters', and that 'We charged because it was our duty to do so'.[93] Trooper Fred Swarbrick, however, whose patrol had initially sighted the enemy, confirmed that the reconnaissance had been minimal: 'I pointed with my lance towards them, and immediately afterwards they opened fire. The regiment wheeled into line.'[94]

As they galloped forward, Lieutenant Frederick Wormald realised that they had been lured into a trap (prepared by Osman Digna), and 'that instead of a mere handful of men there were about 1,500, armed with rifles and swords'.[95] Trooper Thomas Abbot described the ensuing clash:

> Wild with excitement, we galloped for all we were worth, lances down at the 'Engage'. Shots were flying in all directions and you could see nothing else but a mass of black heads appearing from the ground. We charged with all our might right to the hilt of our steel. After we had finished our first man the lance was only in the way, and we had to draw our swords, and then I completely lost my senses in the midst of them. It was a dreadful fight for about ten minutes – a fair hand to hand.[96]

The 'horrors of those moments', as Trooper Clifford Thompson recollected, varied in intensity and duration from troop to troop, with the bulk of the fighting falling upon the central B and D squadrons: Eadon's squadron had 'eleven killed and thirteen wounded' out of total casualties of 21 killed and 50 wounded.[97] Lancers reflected upon their own luck, deeds of great gallantry (three VCs were won), the misfortunes of wounded comrades (Sergeant Freeman was unrecognisable with his nose cut off and face covered in blood), and the mutilation of fallen comrades. When they dismounted and opened fire with carbines, 'we had the pleasure', as Trooper M. Bryne observed, 'of seeing the enemy flying out of the trench', but afterwards it was a 'ghastly sight' gathering up the dead.[98] Few dwelt on the futility of a charge that left the regiment with 119 horses killed or wounded and thereby incapable of harassing the enemy.

On the main battlefield Hector Macdonald's brigade of Sudanese and Egyptian soldiers (and the Camel Corps) fought off the final attacks from the Khalifa's reserve forces. Compelled to change front in dealing with the separate attacks, 'our men behaved splendidly', wrote Major Nason; they moved 'quickly . . . and without the slightest confusion', virtually completing the fighting by the time the 1st British Brigade arrived: 'Our Brigadier has been given, I am glad to say, great credit for it.'[99] With the enemy scattered, the Anglo-Egyptian army pressed on to Omdurman, a city whose size impressed the victors but not the rows of mud huts nor the stench from a multitude of dead and decomposing bodies, both animal and human. 'What a sickening march', recalled

Guardsman Thompson, 'through five miles of dirty, foul, smelling streets, and us dead beat, too', but there was a welcome, especially from the women who 'ran out and kissed the officers' hands and sword scabbards'.[100]

After a night bivouacked outside or near the edge of the city, British units moved to more sanitary camp sites and buried their dead. On the following day, soldiers from each unit attended 'an imposing little ceremony' in Khartoum where flags were raised, and Kitchener wept as laments were played, a service conducted and guns fired in memory of Gordon.[101] Meanwhile, each battalion sent an officer and sixteen men to count the dervish dead: as a Warwickshire officer remarked, this was 'not a pleasant occupation', especially as they counted 10,800 corpses. They also carried biscuits and water for the enemy wounded and marvelled at their resilience despite some horrendous wounds: 'it is wonderful the way they hang on'.[102]

For the vast majority of the British soldiers the campaign was now over, but 'E' Company of the Cameron Highlanders was chosen with the 11th and 13th Sudanese battalions to accompany Kitchener in three gunboats up the White Nile to confront Major Marchand's force at Fashoda. Although they were all sworn to secrecy, several officers, kept diaries and the account of Captain the Hon. Andrew Murray was used by Bennett Burleigh in his famous 'scoop' on the expedition. As Murray recorded, they had 'a very miserable journey' south, for it rained heavily every night as they travelled through tropical country, with heavily forested river banks. They used all their Maxims and guns to disperse a Mahdist camp at Renk and disable an enemy vessel before the fateful meeting between Marchand and Kitchener on board the *Dal*. The Camerons then had the honour of providing an escort ashore, whereupon the Khedive's flag was raised and his anthem played before they marched back to the tune of the 'Cameron Men'. Sudanese troops were left to provide garrisons at Fashoda and Sobat, but Murray doubted they 'cared much to be back in their native country'. The Camerons returned directly to Omdurman and thence to Cairo.[103]

After the declaration of the Anglo-Egyptian Condominium, Sir F. Reginald Wingate was left with the task of pacifying the country and suppressing the last embers of Mahdism. This would involve several fruitless expeditions in attempts to apprehend the Khalifa before encountering his remaining forces at Um Dibaykarat (24 November 1899). Egyptian fire-power duly overwhelmed the enemy, leaving the Khalifa dead with his emirs alongside him. One of Wingate's staff regarded it as 'a truly touching sight, and one could not but feel that, however great a beast he and they had been in their lifetime, their end was truly grand'.[104]

Notes

1 'The Fall of Khartoum: Notes from an Officer's Diary during the Campaign, 1898', *Pall Mall Magazine*, 17 (January-April 1899), 61–76; P. Harrington, 'Images and Perceptions: Visualising the Sudan Campaign', in Spiers (ed.), *Sudan*, pp. 82–101.
2 H. S. L. Alford and W. Dennistoun Sword, *Egyptian Soudan: Its Loss and Recovery* (London: Macmillan, 1898); 'An Officer' (Lieut. H. L. Pritchard), *Sudan Campaign 1896–1899* (London: Chapman & Hall, 1899).
3 M. Barthorp, 'A Letter from Omdurman', *Soldiers of the Queen*, 89 (June 1997), 2–5; and seven letters in Emery, *Marching Over Africa*, pp. 161–74, 189.
4 Keown-Boyd, *A Good Dusting*; P. Ziegler, *Omdurman* (London: Collins, 1973); P. Harrington and F. A. Sharf (eds), *Omdurman 1898: The Eye-Witnesses Speak. The British Conquest of the Sudan as Described by Participants in Letters, Diaries, Photos, and Drawings* (London; Greenhill Books, 1998); E. M. Spiers, 'Campaigning Under Kitchener', in Spiers (ed.), *Sudan*, pp. 54–81; J. Meredith (ed.), *Omdurman Diaries 1898* (Barnsley: Leo Cooper, 1998).
5 NAM, Acc. No. 6807/269, Ferguson MSS, Ferguson to his parents, 1 July 1885.
6 *Ibid.*, Ferguson to his parents, 8 February and 8 April 1886.
7 *Ibid.*, Ferguson to his parents, 20 May 1886, 30 April 1887 and 18 August 1889.
8 *Ibid.*, Ferguson to his parents, 2 June and 1 July 1885.
9 *Ibid.*, Ferguson to his brother and sister, 14 January 1887.
10 *Ibid.*, Ferguson to his parents, 20 May 1886 and 11 December 1888.
11 'Narrative of the Fight by a Wounded Hussar: The Broken Sabres', *Leeds Mercury*, 7 January 1889, p. 5. Wakefield is identified as the man who saved Major Irwin's life in 'The Charge of the 20th Hussars: A Trooper's Narrative', *Evening News*, 26 January 1889, p. 3.
12 NAM, Acc. No. 6807/269, Ferguson MSS, press cutting.
13 *Ibid.*, Ferguson to his parents, 14 February 1889.
14 *Ibid.*, Ferguson to his parents, 18 August 1889; Keown-Boyd, *A Good Dusting*, p. 129, n. 6.
15 Hatfield House Muniments (HHM), Salisbury MSS, 3M/A, Cromer to Lord Salisbury, 15 March 1896.
16 Sudan Archives Durham University (SAD), 304/2/2, Maj. J. J. B. Farley, 'Some Recollections of the Dongola Expedition', n.d.
17 *Ibid.*; Alford and Sword, *Egyptian Soudan*, pp. 50–1, 57, 59, 61–2; Lt. M. E. G. Manifold, 'The Field Telegraph, Dongola Expedition, 1896', *REJ*, 27 (1897), 3–5.
18 SAD, Hunter MSS, D/S 13, Col. A. Hunter to Captain Beach, 23 July 1896.
19 SRM, Capt. S. Astell, 'Diary of Dongola Expedition 1896', p. 3.
20 *Ibid.*, p. 4.
21 *Ibid.*, pp. 3–4; SAD, 304/2/5, /7, /10, Farley, 'Some Recollections'.
22 SRM, Astell, 'Diary', ch. 3, p. 4.
23 SAD, 304/2/13, Farley, 'Some Recollections'.
24 SAD, Hunter MSS, Hunter to Beach, 23 July 1896.
25 SRM, Astell, 'Diary', ch. 4, p. 2.
26 *Ibid.*; SAD, 304/2/15, Farley, 'Some Recollections'.
27 'Our Weslyan Soldiers in the Soudan', *Methodist Times*, 27 August 1896, p. 594.
28 SRM, Astell, 'Diary', pp. 17–18.
29 SAD, 304/2/23, Farley, 'Some Recollections'; see also Alford and Sword, *Egyptian Soudan*, pp. 110, 122–33. Alford stated that another eighty men were 'weeded out' at Hafir and Sadek but Farley claimed that all but one of these men rejoined the battalion, so 599 marched on Dongola: SAD, 304/2/28, Farley, 'Some Recollections'.
30 *Ibid.*, 304/2/24–6. Wad Bishara was actually bound by his emirs and led from the battle: I. H. Zulfo, *Karari: The Sudanese Account of the Battle of Omdurman* (London: Frederick Warne, 1980), pp. 66–7.
31 SAD, 304/2/28, Farley, 'Some Recollections'; Alford and Sword, *Egyptian Soudan*, pp. 146–7, 152.
32 'The Soudan Campaign: Interview with Sir Herbert Kitchener', *Leeds Mercury*, 10

November 1896, p. 3.

33 Liddell Hart Centre for Military Archives, King's College London (LHCMA), Maurice MSS, 2/1/2, Col. A. Hunter to Sir F. Maurice, 12 July 1896.

34 Col. A. O. Green, 'Cairo', *REJ*, 28 (1898), 131–3.

35 LHCMA, Maurice MSS, 2/1/4, Hunter to Maurice, 15 February 1898; see also E. M. Spiers, 'Introduction', in Spiers (ed.), *Sudan*, pp. 1–10.

36 Green, 'Cairo', 131; 'With the Army Medical Corps', *Sheffield Daily Telegraph*, 4 October 1898, p. 6.

37 NAM, Acc. No. 7909/15, Cpl G. Skinner, diary, 15 January 1898.

38 'A Horncastrian at the Battle of the Atbara', *Horncastle News and South Lindsey Advertiser*, 28 May 1898, p. 5; 'Letter from a Seaforth', *Northern Weekly*, 19 May 1898, p. 2; 'Letter from a Nairn Man at Atbara', *Nairnshire Telegraph*, 25 May 1898, p. 3.

39 Some veterans of Ginnis still served in the Cameron Highlanders, and senior officers, like A. G. Wauchope (Black Watch), had served in previous Sudanese campaigns.

40 NAM, Acc. No. 7906/139, Grieve MSS, L/Sgt C. Grieve to Tommie, 16 February 1898.

41 'A Lincolnshire Sergeant on the Nile', *Grimsby News*, 22 March 1898, p. 6; 'A Horncastrian at the Battle of Atbara', p. 5; Brig.-Gen. A. J. McNeill, 'A Subaltern's Reminiscences', *Caber Feidh: The Quarterly Magazine of the Seaforth Highlanders*, 6:46 (1933), 338–41; Spiers, 'Campaigning Under Kitchener', pp. 54–6; Meredith, *Omdurman Diaries*, pp. 9–15.

42 NAM, Acc. No. 7906/139, Grieve MSS, Grieve to his mother, 20 January 1898; Meredith, *Omdurman Diaries*, p. 29.

43 'A Lincolnshire Sergeant on the Nile', p. 6; NAM, Acc. No. 7909/15, Skinner diary, 11 January 1898.

44 HHM, Salisbury MSS, vol. 109, no. 98, Cromer to Salisbury, 14 October 1896.

45 'A Lincolnshire Sergeant on the Nile', p. 6.

46 'A Horncastrian at the Battle of Atbara', p. 5.

47 J. W. Stewart, 'A Subaltern in the Sudan, 1898', *The Stewarts*, 17:4 (1987), 223–8; see also NAM, Acc. No. 7704/36/3, Lt R. E. Meiklejohn, 'The Nile Campaign' (a transcript account based on his campaign diary), pp. 5–6.

48 NAM, Acc. No. 7909/15, Skinner diary, 20 February 1898; see also 'An Inverness Soldier', *Highland News*, 21 May 1898, p. 2 and 'Letter from a Seaforth', p. 2.

49 'A Horncastrian at the Battle of Atbara', p. 6.

50 'Amusing Letter from a Cameron Highlander', *Edinburgh Evening News*, 22 March 1898, p. 4.

51 'Lincoln Lads in the Desert', *Gainsborough Leader*, 30 April 1898, p. 7.

52 'The Camerons in the Soudan', *Inverness Courier*, 17 May 1898, p. 5.

53 NAM, Acc. No. 7404/36/3, Meiklejohn, 'Nile Campaign', pp. 9, 11. Regimental comparisons must be treated with reserve: Lieutenant-Colonel G. L. C. Money, in admitting that many Camerons fell out, claimed that 'we had far fewer than other regiments': 'The Soudan Campaign', *Leeds Mercury*, 31 March 1898, p. 7.

54 'Lincoln Lads in the Desert', p. 7.

55 'With the British Army on the Nile', *Hampshire Independent*, 23 April 1898, p. 2.

56 'Lincoln Lads in the Desert', p. 7.

57 '"Remember Gordon"', *Grimsby News*, 17 May 1898, p. 5; 'Camerons in the Soudan', p. 5; 'Our Lincolnshire Lads', *Gainsborough Leader*, 21 May 1898, p. 9.

58 'Khartoum in July', *Grimsby News*, 27 May 1898, p. 2; 'Inverness Soldier', p. 2; 'The Atbara', *Evening News*, 16 June 1898, p. 2.

59 'Letter from a Seaforth', p. 2; see also 'A Horncastrian at the Battle of Atbara', p. 5, and 'A Further Letter from the Soudan', *Grimsby News*, 20 May 1898, p. 2.

60 'A Further Letter from the Soudan', p. 20.

61 'Our Lincolnshire Lads', p. 9; 'Highlanders' Experiences at Atbara', *Edinburgh Evening News*, 14 May 1898, p. 4; see also '"Remember Gordon"', p. 5.

62 'Our Lincolnshire Lads', p. 9; 'A Further Letter from the Soudan', p. 2; NAM, Acc.

No. 8305/55/10, Cameron MSS, R. Brooke to Sir W. Cameron, 29 May 1898.

63 'Our Lincolnshire Lads', p. 9, parenthesis added; 'An Inverness Soldier', p. 2; 'A Further Letter from the Soudan', p. 2.

64 'A Further Letter from the Soudan', p. 2; see also 'An Officer', Sudan Campaign, p. 158.

65 'The Battle of Atbara', Scotsman, 18 May 1898, p. 11.

66 NAM, Acc. No. 7909/15, Skinner diary, pp. 35–7; 'An Aberdeen Soldier at Atbara', Aberdeen Journal, 14 May 1898, p. 4; Spiers, 'Campaigning Under Kitchener', pp. 61–2; Keown-Boyd, A Good Dusting, pp. 200–2.

67 'Our Lincolnshire Lads', p. 9; 'A Further Letter from the Soudan', p. 2.

68 'In Memory of Captain A. C. D. Baillie', Nairn County Press and Advertiser, 25 June 1898, p. 3; 'A Soldier's Experiences of the Battle of the Atbara', Nairnshire Telegraph, 18 May 1898, p. 3.

69 NAM, Acc. No. 7906/139, Grieve to his father, 14 April 1898; see also 'The Camerons', Evening News, 11 April 1898, p. 2; 'Highlanders' Experiences at Atbara', p. 2; 'The Atbara', p. 2; G. W. Steevens, With Kitchener to Khartum (Edinburgh: Blackwood, 1898), pp. 146–7.

70 'A Leamington Soldier in the Soudan', Leamington, Warwick, Rugby and County Chronicle, 28 May 1898, p. 8; see also 'The Bravery of the Lincolnshire Regiment', Grantham Journal, 28 May 1898, p. 7; 'The Battle of Atbara', Horncastle News and South Lindsey Advertiser, 21 May 1898, p. 6.

71 'Our Lincolnshire Lads', p. 9; 'A Horncastrian at the Battle of Atbara', p. 5; 'Khartoum in July', p. 2; '"Remember Gordon"', p. 5; 'The Advance on Khartoum', Grantham Journal, 1 October 1898, p. 3.

72 'British Soldiers in the Soudan', Edinburgh Evening News, 9 June 1898, p. 2; 'A Further Letter from the Soudan', p. 2; 'The Advance on Khartoum', Coventry Standard, 12 August 1898, p. 8; Spiers, 'Campaigning Under Kitchener', p. 63.

73 'The Campaign in the Soudan', Bury Times, 10 September 1898, p. 6; 'In the Soudan Campaign', Hampshire Observer, 8 October 1898, p. 3; 'The Khartoum Campaign', Manchester Evening Chronicle, 30 September 1898, p. 4.

74 'A Southampton Officer in the Soudan Campaign', Hampshire Independent, 8 October 1898, p. 7.

75 'Lieut. "Fritz" Wormald's Graphic Account of the Lancers' Charge at Omdurman', (Dewsbury) Reporter, 15 October 1898, p. 5; Maj. J. Harris (ed.), 'The Nile Expedition of 1898 and Omdurman – The Diary of Sergeant S. W. Harris, Grenadier Guards', JSAHR, 78 (2000), 11–28; Spiers, 'Campaigning Under Kitchener', p. 66.

76 'Letters from the Soudan', Grimsby News, 4 October 1898, p. 6; 'The Great Battle in the Soudan', Strathearn Herald, 1 October 1898, p. 2; 'The Advance on Khartoum', p. 3.

77 'An Account by a Manchester Man', Manchester Courier, 28 September 1898, p. 9; 'The Soudan War', Salford Journal, 1 October 1898, p. 4; 'In the Soudan', Bradford Daily Argus, 30 September 1898, p. 4; 'Khartoum Campaign', p. 4; Harris, 'Nile Expedition of 1898 and Omdurman', 19–20; 'Advance on Khartoum', p. 3; Spiers, 'Campaigning Under Kitchener', pp. 66–7.

78 'Sergeant and Sirdar', Manchester Courier, 28 September 1898, p. 9.

79 'A Southampton Officer in the Soudan Campaign', p. 7; 'Advance on Khartoum', p. 3; 'An Account by a Manchester Man', p. 9.

80 'At Omdurman', Manchester Evening Chronicle, 11 October 1898, p. 4.

81 'Khartoum Campaign', p. 4.

82 '"Single Men in Barracks"', Evening News, 7 October 1898, p. 2.

83 'The Fight at Omdurman', Bradford Daily Argus, 19 October 1898, p. 4.

84 'The Battle of Omdurman', Manchester Evening Chronicle, 28 September 1898, p. 4.

85 'Letters from the Soudan', p. 6; see also 'A Southampton Officer in the Soudan Campaign', p. 7; Harris, 'Nile Expedition of 1898 and Omdurman', 21.

86 'An Account by a Manchester Man', p. 9; 'Letter from a Manchester Man', Manchester Evening Chronicle, 29 September 1898, p. 4; 'A Keighley Soldier on the

Omdurman Fight', *Yorkshire Post*, 5 October 1898, p. 5.

87 'A Letter from Omdurman to Alnwick', *Alnwick and County Gazette*, 8 October 1898, p. 8.

88 '"Single Men in Barracks"', p. 2; see also 'The Battle of Omdurman', p. 4; Harris, 'Nile Expedition of 1898 and Omdurman', 21.

89 'Letters from the Soudan', p. 6; 'An Account by a Manchester Man', p. 9; 'A Southampton Officer in the Soudan Campaign', p. 7.

90 'A Derbyshire Soldier at Omdurman', *Gainsborough Leader*, 8 October 1898, p. 3; 'Battle of Omdurman', p. 4; Harris, 'Nile Expedition of 1898 and Omdurman', 21; 'At Omdurman', p. 4; Keown-Boyd, *A Good Dusting*, p. 240.

91 'Fight at Omdurman', p. 4.

92 'The Omdurman Charge', *Grimsby News*, 18 October 1898, p. 3.

93 'Colonel Martin', *Evening News*, 11 October 1898, p. 2.

94 'A Gallant Lancer's Description of the Charge', *Yorkshire Post*, 8 October 1898, p. 9.

95 'Lieut. "Fritz" Wormald's Graphic Account', p. 5; see also 'The Charge of the Lancers', *Gainsborough Leader*, 8 October 1898, p. 6.

96 'Letters from the Soudan', p. 6.

97 'Charge of the Lancers', p. 6; 'Khartoum Campaign', p. 4; 'Lieut. "Fritz" Wormald's Graphic Account', p. 5; 'Omdurman Charge', p. 3.

98 'A Berwick Trooper in the Lancers' Charge', *Edinburgh Evening News*, 14 October 1898, p. 2; see also 'Omdurman Charge', p. 3; 'Gallantry of One of the 21st', *Sussex Daily News*, 12 October 1898, p. 5; 'Charge of the Lancers', p. 6.

99 'Great Battle in the Soudan', p. 2.

100 'Fight at Omdurman', p. 4; see also 'A Letter from Omdurman to Alnwick', p. 8; 'A Derbyshire Soldier at Omdurman', p. 3; 'Letters from the Soudan', p. 6.

101 'Great Battle in the Soudan', p. 2.

102 'A Southampton Officer in the Soudan Campaign'. p. 7.

103 Although Murray's account broadly confirms the particulars in Lt R. L. Aldecron's diary, there are discrepancies about dates: compare 'Full Account of the Sirdar's Expedition to Fashoda', *Daily Telegraph*, 4 October 1898, p. 7, with R. L. A., 'A Diary of the Fashoda Expedition', *The 79th News*, 42 (1 March 1899), 8–10.

104 'The Khalifa's Last Stand', *Cheltenham Chronicle*, 16 December 1899, p. 6.

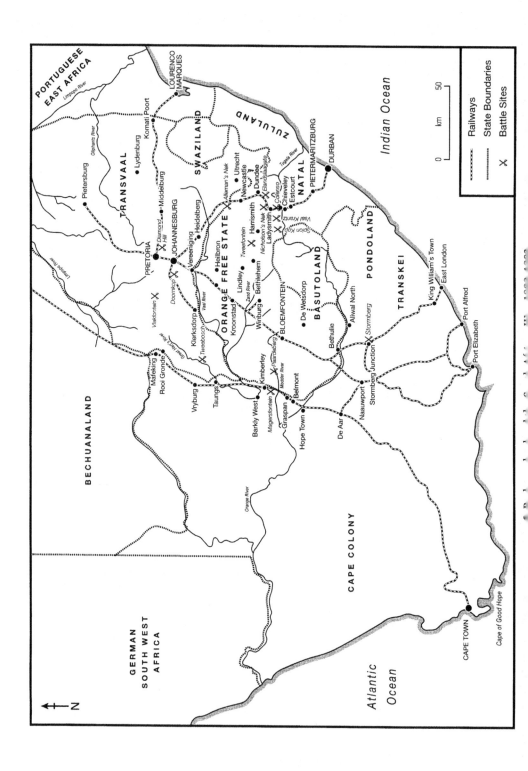

CHAPTER NINE

Re-engaging the Boers

The South African War (1899–1902) posed an unprecedented challenge for the Victorian army and eventually involved the services of 448,435 British and colonial troops in a series of major battlefield engagements, sieges, relief operations and protracted counter-guerrilla campaigns. The volume of correspondence from British soldiers was prodigious, and some of these letters have been used in campaign accounts, regimental histories, local studies and an analysis of the Scottish military experience.[1] If many of the letters were largely descriptive, they also testified to the immense difficulties presented by a well-armed and highly mobile adversary, operating over vast terrain and capable of mounting strategic offensives, conducting sieges, fighting from formidable defensive positions and engaging in guerrilla warfare. Although a single chapter, utilising largely unused correspondence, cannot review the entire war, it can shed light on how British soldiers responded and reacted to the unique demands of this conflict. It does so by comparing the experiences of a sample of soldiers, specifically those from Scotland and the west country (Cornwall, Devon, Somerset, Dorset and Gloucestershire). Soldiers were chosen from these parts of the United Kingdom as they served in distinguished local regiments and other arms, and came from localities with strong military connections,[2] ensuring coverage of their exploits in the provincial press. Some had served previously in Africa or on the North-West Frontier, so facilitating comparisons with previous wars; they also fought in many of the major battles of the war, thereby attracting the attention of metropolitan as well as local newspapers. Sometimes Scots and west countrymen fought together, as at Elandslaagte, Colenso, Paardeberg and the siege of Ladysmith, and, like others, they endured the demands of the counter-guerrilla campaign.

When war began on 11 October 1899, the Boers launched their invasions of Natal and Cape Colony and began the investment of the strategic border towns of Mafeking and Kimberley (14 October). The 2/Gordons, 1/Gloucesters and 1/Devonshires were among the reinforcements sent from India and already deployed in Natal; further Scots and west country units would serve in the 47,000-man army corps sent from Britain under the command of Sir Redvers Buller. As Buller arrived in Cape Town on the day after 'Mournful Monday' (30 October, when Sir George White's forces in Natal suffered defeats at Lombard's Kop and Nicholson's Nek, and fell back on Ladysmith), he decided to split his army corps. He led a relief force into Natal, sent a division under Lord Methuen along the western railway to relieve Kimberley, and another division under Gatacre with Major-General J. D. P. French's cavalry division to repulse the invasion of Cape Colony. Although Scots and west countrymen served with all these forces, they were most prominent in Methuen's command and in Buller's relief force.

Even before they faced the new realities of warfare, especially fire-zones swept by smokeless fire from magazine rifles, British soldiers had to adapt to the rigours of campaigning in South African conditions. Apart from the small garrisons in Cape Colony and Natal, and the seasoned soldiers sent from India and the Mediterranean garrisons, many short-service soldiers and reservists from Britain were new to the demands of colonial service. They appreciated the welcome from the English-speaking community, particularly in Natal where 'the people', claimed Lieutenant George Smyth Osbourne (2/Devons), 'are very loyal, much more so than at Cape Colony',[3] and, in Durban, added Private L. Graham (2/ Somerset Light Infantry), they gave 'us fruit, fags, tobacco, and made a great fuss of us'.[4] Yet soldiers had to acclimatise, and they struggled when required to march, often on short rations of bully beef and biscuit, in the heat (and flies) of the day before enduring cold nights and periodically heavy fogs or severe storms.[5] Corporal Devas (2/Somersets), posted with his heliograph on top of Mount Umkolomba, Natal, described how he had never 'been in such a funk before; a thunderstorm is no joke on top of these mountains'.[6]

The 1/Devons and five companies of 2/Gordons (formerly the 92nd Highlanders who fought at Majuba) were soon in action at Elandslaagte (21 October 1899), serving with half a battalion of the Manchesters and the Imperial Light Horse. Many of the Devons had recently fought on the North-West Frontier, and so appreciated the extended formation adopted by another Tirah veteran, Colonel Ian Hamilton. 'We were advancing in single rank', wrote Private J. Isaac (Devons), 'about 15 paces interval from one another, so we could not form a big target for them.'[7] While the Devons with close artillery support launched a frontal attack across the veld, some 2 miles distant the Gordons and Manchesters advanced, again with artillery support, in 'open column' with intervals of 'about 100 yards' between companies round the horseshoe ridge towards the enemy's left flank. Private S. Anstey (Devons) described how bullets rained 'down on us like large hailstones', but when they 'were within 200 yards of their position . . . the order to charge was given, and every man rushed as for revenge into the enemy, who did not face the bayonet'.[8] Devons and Gordons then recalled bitterly how the Boers waved the white flag, prompting a British cease-fire, before launching another charge 'with an awful fire, killing a lot of our chaps'.[9] Having rallied his men to repulse these 'treacherous marksmen', Captain (then Lieutenant) Matthew F. M. Meiklejohn (Gordons), who lost an arm in the action and earned the VC, observed that two squadrons of cavalry (5th Dragoon Guards and 5th Lancers) completed the rout.[10]

Like others, Meiklejohn reflected on the difficulty of seeing any Boers during the advance and the futility of volley-firing: 'Men fired as they saw something to fire at.'[11] Equally significant were the differential casualty rates, with far fewer injured (about thirty-four) and none killed in the Devons compared with five officers and three rankers killed in the Gordons, eight officers and ninety-eight other ranks wounded. A Teignmothian suspected that the Gordons must have got 'too close together', and Meiklejohn confirmed that it had proved difficult to restrain the supporting soldiers, eager to avenge Majuba, from running into the firing line. The officers of the Gordons, wielding claymores and wearing distinctive uniforms, had also proved far too conspicuous.[12] In the aftermath of battle a Devonian colour-sergeant reckoned: 'The sight would turn you cold – headless bodies, limbs lying around everywhere . . . I found one young fellow badly wounded, talking about his mother and his home, and it touched me, for the enemy are white people like ourselves.'[13] Nevertheless, Devonians were proud of their regiment's achievement at Elandslaagte; some insisted that they had gained 'a very good name, better than the Gordons did at Dargai'.[14]

Conversely, there was deep despair after the six-hour battle at Nicholson's Nek when 850 soldiers surrendered from five-and-a-half companies of 1/Gloucesters and six companies of Royal Irish Fusiliers (another 33 'Glosters' were killed and some 80 officers and men were wounded). Surviving 'Glosters' said little about the feasibility of their mission (a night march into the rear of Boer forces who were beginning to invest Ladysmith) or their maldeployment when they occupied Tchrengula Hill overnight or the folly of constructing sangars (stone breastworks) that served as targets for covering fire while other Boers scaled the hillside.[15] Rather they dwelt on several misfortunes, including the stampede of their mules on the previous evening removing much of their ammunition and rendering the mountain guns useless,[16] and how the surrender of an isolated and heavily wounded advance party triggered the wholesale surrender of the entire force.[17] Inevitably some exaggerated the numbers of casualties and of the Boers who attacked from three sides: a soldier asserted, 'if we had not given in then we would all have been slaughtered'.[18] As inquiries were made into the raising of the white flag, and recriminations persisted between the Fusiliers and the 'Glosters',[19] Captain Stephen Willcock (1/Gloucesters) praised the Boers for their 'devilish' fire, 'wonderful' use of the ground and generous treatment of the prisoners.[20]

Unable to break the Boer lines, some 12,000 soldiers withdrew into Ladysmith which, along with Kimberley and Mafeking, would endure protracted investment. When the soldiers retreated into Ladysmith, Dr Harry H. Balfour saw 'men wandering in, so tired that they could hardly crawl and had to fall out to have a rest, sitting or lying on doorsteps . . .'.[21] Soldiers could not dwell on their misfortunes as they had to fortify outposts along an 11-mile perimeter. A sergeant of the Gordons described this work as harder 'than would have been necessary under normal circumstances', labouring 'for several days from four to six hours a day, and then most part of the night amongst rocks and cactus trees of a horrible kind tearing your hands and legs, breaking off nails, etc.'. Many of these untreated sores tended to swell and fester amid the heat, sweat and flies, so making life 'miserable': 'Scarcely a man escaped suffering from diarrhoea and dysentery, and some pitiable sights were to be seen.'[22] Under regular shelling from the Boers (other than on Sundays), men kept in their trenches by day and worked building or repairing the fortifications by night.[23]

The besieged took comfort from information gleaned by their balloon and signallers (other than in periods of torrential rain), from the odd sortie against the Boer positions, and retaliatory fire from their own artillery, especially the naval 4.7-inch guns, but morale soon flagged. By 16 November, Lieutenant-Colonel Cecil W. Park (Devons) confirmed that 'everyone is most deadly sick of the monotony of the siege', and later that his men had hardly been encouraged by news of Buller's defeat at Colenso.[24] Yet the defenders fought off the enemy, particularly during the seventeen-hour attack on Wagon Hill and Caesar's Camp (6 January 1900). Once again the 1/Devons had the dramatic, if costly, privilege of launching the final bayonet attack to clear the Free Staters from Wagon Hill. 'The gallant Devons', wrote Private Lyons, 'showed how we could fight with fixed bayonets', an achievement relished by Private W. Parminter because 'before our regiment charged, the Gordons and the Rifles had a go at it, but failed in the attempt, losing many killed and wounded'.[25] The defenders suffered heavy

losses in this close-quarter fight (17 officers and 158 men dead, 28 officers and 221 men wounded), but in the hospital throughout the siege
only 59 of the wounded died compared with 510 deaths from typhoid
and dysentery.[26]

Men clearly weakened as the siege dragged on and provisions
became increasingly scarce. By February 1900 Devonshire soldiers
recorded both the escalating prices at auction – £25 for a bottle of
whisky, 10s (50p) to £10 for tins of condensed milk, 22s 6d (£1 12.5p)
for a dozen potatoes – and the cuts in their own rations: sometimes
bread and horse meat per day, or biscuit and bully beef, 'very old and
nasty' porridge, and ultimately a daily allowance of some 3oz of mealie
bread and over 1lb of horse meat.[27] The horse flesh, added a Gordon,
was 'very often putrid … crawling with maggots and stinking, of
course'.[28] With the siege lifted on 28 February 1900, the relief column
subsequently marched through the town and the beleaguered garrison
provided a guard of honour: 'The poor fellows', wrote Gunner H. Lambert, 'were too weak to stand up and so they sat down, looking thin and
haggard, not a smile to be seen except when they happened to see a face
they knew.'[29]

If protracted sieges were a rarity in the African experience of the Victorian army (other than in conflicts with the Boers), so were the three
major defeats in the 'Black Week' of 10–15 December 1899. Scots and
west countrymen were involved in two of these defeats. At Magersfontein (11 December) the Highland Brigade incurred the vast majority
of some 948 killed, wounded and missing, and many survivors vented
their spleen on the generalship of Lord Methuen. Anonymous claims
of a mutinous spirit within the brigade may have been far-fetched,[30] but
soldiers, aggrieved at the death of their own commander Major-General Andrew Wauchope, denounced Methuen's 'blundering', 'bad generalship' and 'almost criminal negligence'.[31] Corporal W. G. Bevan
(1/Argylls), a veteran of an earlier, costly ordeal at Modder River (28
November), and Private Walter Douglas (2/Black Watch) were more
specific: they berated the lack of reconnaissance, a laborious night
advance in quarter-column formation (which made an ideal target for
the Boers before it could deploy in intervals of five paces), and an
inability to cross an open field of fire against an unseen, entrenched
and well-armed enemy: 'It was not fighting', wrote Bevan, 'it was
simply suicide.'[32] Some conceded that the brigade, after several
thwarted attacks and ten hours pinned to the ground under a fierce sun,
compounded its predicament by retiring in daylight. An HLI soldier
admitted that after the shout 'Retire!' a 'stampede' ensued – '4,000 men
like a flock of sheep running for dear life' – and many soldiers were shot
in the retreat.[33] Methuen, though revered by many of his Guardsmen,[34]

deeply alienated the Highlanders by sympathising with 'their terrible loss' in his post-battle speech, and Lord Roberts, the new commander-in-chief, quickly removed the brigade from his command.[35]

Buller had never encountered such difficulties in Natal, despite his relief force suffering an even heavier defeat at Colenso, a disaster at Spion Kop (24 January 1900) and another reverse at Vaal Krantz (5–7 February 2000) before eventually breaking through the Tugela defences. Scholars have speculated on how he retained the enduring affection of his troops, whether it was respect for his personal bravery and endurance; or his attention to the comforts of the men, including their food, supplies and mail from home; or his readiness to withdraw rather than push on recklessly; or recognition that the campaign in Natal was extremely daunting.[36] Soldiers' letters support all these claims, but those written immediately after Colenso – a failed frontal attack across open ground against an unseen enemy – reflected the shock of young soldiery, many of them in their first battle. Soldiers of the 2/Devons described how they survived a 'hailstorm' of bullets, lying behind anthills for eight hours under a blazing sun before withdrawing in daylight 'under a murderous fire' or managing to evade capture.[37] If some grossly exaggerated the enemy's numbers ('22,000' rather than 3,000) and their casualties ('2,000' killed rather than 38), and described their positions as 'impregnable',[38] others were more perceptive. Scots Fusiliers, who escorted the guns forward, testified to the lack of reconnaissance: 'we got a surprise, as they hid in their trenches until we came near them', and the 'mistake' of taking the 'artillery so near the enemy's position'.[39] A Cameronian, who observed the battlefield from high ground in the rear, where he escorted the naval guns, saw the target presented by Hart's brigade as it advanced in a 'close mass of columns', the heavy casualties caused by withdrawing in daylight, and the vulnerability of Barton's more extended brigade when it advanced without artillery support.[40] Soldiers tended to blame Colonel C. J. Long for losing the ten guns and Major-General Fitzroy Hart for his choice of formation rather than Buller, who was lauded for remaining in the firing line.[41]

Similarly Buller evaded much of the blame for Spion Kop but earned plaudits for breaking off the attack, a decision repeated at Vaal Krantz. Sergeant A. Kean (2/Somerset Light Infantry) affirmed:

There is no doubt General Buller deserves the greatest praise for the way in which he has manoeuvred the troops about from one place to the other . . . I think it is General Buller's great motto to manoeuvre and take the positions with as few casualties as possible and not to rush a position which means sure death, especially against such positions and fortifications as our enemy possessed.[42]

Inevitably there was grumbling about the withdrawals and sarcasm about Buller's claim to have found the 'key' to the road to Ladysmith,[43] but many soldiers resented the domestic criticism of Buller, arguing that their commander had the toughest task in breaking through the Tugela line, showed 'bull-dog tenacity' in that, 'checked three times, he yet went for them a fourth', and deserved every credit for the relief of Ladysmith.[44] Devonians, identifying with one of their own, were probably more supportive than most, but Sergeant-Major William Young (2/Dorsets) was delighted by Buller's praise of the Dorsets after Spion Kop as 'our Regt was the only one that did not run away'.[45] Soldiers appreciated, as Private H. Easterbrook (2/Devons) argued, that Buller had shared their hardships: 'where the fighting was the fiercest there he was to be found' and ensured that they lived 'very well; even better than I ever lived in barracks. Plenty of biscuits, tinned meat, cheese, jam, fruit and bread, and fresh meat whenever it is possible to get it.'[46] Some lauded his tactics in the final push on Ladysmith with a sustained onslaught, and heavy use of artillery and Maxims, over eleven days (16–27 February); many remained fiercely loyal to him thereafter.[47]

Veterans of previous wars were equally forthright: 'My Soudan experiences', wrote Father Matthews, 'were mere child's play in comparison'; any action in the Tirah, argued Private H. Worth (2/Devons), was eclipsed by Colenso; and 'Omdurman was a picnic', claimed Private Louis Wilshaw (2/Lancashire Fusiliers), by comparison with Spion Kop.[48] Egyptian veterans told Private F. Hughes (2/Black Watch) that this campaign was far more stressful as they were always on the march or look-out, while Tirah veterans praised the supply services in South Africa inasmuch as rations (and presents from home) were far more plentiful than in India. They observed, too, that their khaki kit served as excellent camouflage in South African conditions, and that the wounded could be left on the battlefield, as they were at Magersfontein, 'in the knowledge that they will receive the best treatment at the hands of their enemies and not the "coup de grace" from the Afridis'.[49] Yet soldiers recognised that they were being tested as never before: after Magersfontein Private Bain (1/Argylls) admitted that 'a lot more troops from home' were 'badly' needed; many gunners, drivers and troopers complained that 'our horses are badly in want of rest' or 'are dropping down like dead sheep every day as they can't stand the heat'; and some protested that the army needed 'more modern and quick-firing guns' as well as a rifle to match the Mauser.[50] Soldiers acknowledged, nonetheless, that the army was adapting to the constraints of modern war. Modifications of kit aroused intense debate as Highlanders placed aprons over their kilts, while officers, as Smyth

Osbourne described, discarded their swords and dressed 'as much like the men as possible' to make themselves less conspicuous.[51] Another officer in Natal indicated that the soldiers were developing new skills in field-craft to beat the Boer at 'his own game', adding: 'What a lot they are teaching us, these farmers! When we have settled them we shall be the most magnificent army in the world.'[52]

Meanwhile Scots and west countrymen would be involved in the worst day's fighting of the war, the assaults launched by Kitchener on Cronjé's beleaguered forces at Paardeberg (18 February 1900). Soldiers recalled the gruelling marches over several days that preceded those attacks. 'Some days', wrote Bandsman P. Kelly (Argylls), 'we did 18 miles, and went off at night, marching by moonlight, and for about four days we never had four consecutive hours' sleep'; Colour-Sergeant G. Fry (2/Gloucesters) recollected 'marching day and night, on half rations . . . Of course we had no tents; we simply lay on the ground, just where we halted . . .'.[53] Barely recovered from such exertions, the Highlanders were thrown into an early morning attack on the Boer trenches. While other assaults were launched from upstream and against the front of the Boer positions, with gunners pounding the Boer positions from 5 a.m. to 7 p.m., the Highlanders and later the 'Dukes' attacked from the south-east. The Highlanders were soon halted by Boer fire-power across open ground, whereupon a company of Seaforths accompanied by two companies of the Black Watch forded the river and charged to within 300 yards of the Boer trenches. 'When I got across', recalled Lance-Corporal Wallace Maxwell (2/Seaforths), 'I had to advance, soaked through as I was, and with 150 rounds of ammunition in my pouches, I was not very comfortable.' Unlike 155 Seaforths (the largest number of casualties suffered by any battalion on that day) Maxwell avoided injury, but ruefully observed: 'Our regiment is once more reduced to very small numbers, so there will be some more gruesome reading at home'.[54] On the other bank of the river, Major-General Hector Macdonald ordered the Argylls, who had been guarding the guns, to join the firing line and 'give a good account' of themselves: as Bandsman Kelly recalled, once bullets began whistling 'round our ears', the infantry were soon pinned to the ground; and another Argyll, Private William Johnston, admitted: 'It is cruel work lying in the sun all day.'[55] At least they did not panic and remained prone, desperate for water and tantalisingly close to the Modder River until dusk.

The 'Dukes' only arrived at the battlefield in early morning and had one company posted on outpost duty and the other six guarding the baggage. At 10.30 a.m. Lieutenant-Colonel William Aldworth was required to send the right half of the battalion to support the Highland Brigade on the southern bank of the river, and, three hours later, to launch the other three companies in a direct attack from the northern bank. The colonel, as Lieutenant Hugh Fife recalled, gave an inspirational speech to the officers and men, assuring them that their first action would take the form of a 'Cornish charge': it would earn them lasting fame, and he would give £5 to the first man who bayoneted a Boer.[56] Officers and men were allowed some food, and then forded the river, using a rope, with water 'up to our waists'.[57] By about 4.45 p.m., they formed three extended lines with intervals of 150 yards between each company and then charged with fixed bayonets across open ground into a 'most terrific hail of bullets, pom pom fire and shrapnel'.[58] Forced to take cover behind 'a goodly sprinkling of ant-hills', some claimed that the 'Dukes' made a second charge (covering about 300 yards in all, or barely half the requisite distance); but few disputed that once their colonel fell mortally wounded, 'the men', as one private asserted,'acted more for themselves, rushing to the front one at a time for about 50 yards or so and getting under cover'.[59] The fighting ceased about 7.30 p.m., whereupon soldiers began ferrying the wounded across the river: 'their groans', claimed Private D. James, 'were sickening'; he would not have 'cared so much' had he been able 'to see some Boers to fire at' and had the 'Dukes' received any support.[60] In their first action the two parts of the battalion had lost 3 officers and 24 men killed and 74 wounded, a 'very heavy loss', in Fife's opinion, for which Kitchener was responsible. Their brigadier, Major-General H. L. Smith-Dorrien, 'knew nothing of it', further testimony of the poor staff work and lack of communications during the attack.[61]

Soldiers were certainly relieved when Lord Roberts resumed command on 19 February and replaced the costly attacks on Cronjé by siege operations. Lieutenant Lachlan Gordon-Duff, whose 1/Gordon Highlanders had observed the battle on the previous day, regarded the mission set for the DCLI as an 'impossible feat', while Private H. Haughton described the Canadian charge, over a distance similar to that attempted by the 'Dukes', as 'ridiculous', since 'after running 700 yards, a man would hardly push a bayonet through a sheet of paper'.[62] During the ensuing siege Haughton, like his Cornish comrades, had horrible memories of nights in the muddy trenches, with an all-pervading stench of dead men and animals, or on outpost duty often in torrential downpours.[63] Conditions were even worse in the Boer laager, and when Cronjé surrendered on the anniversary of Majuba Day (27 February) soldiers were able to inspect the Boer defences. Lieutenant R. M. S. Gardner (2/Gloucesters) found a 'wonderful collection of rifles' in the laager, a less pleasant sight in soft-nosed (or explosive) ammunition and 'marvellous' trenches, explaining how they held out so 'well behind them'.[64]

After the loss of Cronjé's wagon laager with over 4,000 men, women and children, a joint council of the two republics resolved on 17 March 1900 to rely thenceforth on mounted commandos, a new method of warfare in which the Boers exploited their increased mobility. Although they abandoned both capitals without resistance (Bloemfontein on 13 March and Pretoria on 5 June), they engaged in fixed battles until the end of August 1900 before embarking on a protracted guerrilla war. At first British soldiers seemed unaware that they would have to adapt once again to altered conditions of warfare. When they captured Bloemfontein, and received a hearty reception from the British inhabitants, many were convinced that Lord Roberts had decisively transformed their fortunes. They now had a chance to rest and re-equip: 'We are nothing but a bundle of rags now', wrote Private Tom Wood (2/DCLI), 'our clothes are nearly dropping off us; we have not had them off since January . . .', while Private W. James (2/Gloucesters) was even more relieved, thinking that the war was nearly all over, 'for we have been on the march this last five weeks, and we are all half-starved and ragged – just like a lot of tramps'.[65]

The optimism proved short-lived: as Private Wood described, typhoid soon swept the large encampment at Bloemfontein and British forces, though re-equipped, were required to mount 'long and tedious marches into the surrounding country on look-out for the enemy'.[66] The 'hit-and-run' tactics of the Boer commandos, led by Christiaan de Wet, Louis Botha and Koos De la Rey, increased their frustration. Even those soldiers, like Private Stinchcombe (2/DCLI), who had enrolled in the growing ranks of the mounted infantry, complained that his company never got 'much rest', was 'nearly roasted in the day' and had 'to keep on all the time'.[67] Others were exasperated by de Wet's ability to harass convoys, burn farms, attack trains and still elude his pursuers. After de Wet captured a major convoy en route to Heilbron (4 June 1900), and then attacked the railway, destroying the mails at Roodewal station (7 June), Sergeant William Hamilton (1/HLI) emphasised 'how disgusted and wild we we all felt on receiving this news'.[68]

Roberts resolved to assume the initiative when he left Bloemfontein on 3 May, advancing in concert with forces from Kimberley in the west and Buller's forces from Ladysmith in the east as they drove towards Pretoria. A Tauntonian gunner, Harry Verrier (82nd Battery, Royal Field Artillery) chronicled his exhausting itinerary:

> action on 4th of May; captured Wynburg 10th May; Zand River in action the whole of the day; 12th of May captured Kroonstad; 18th of May captured Lindley; 20th of May had a rearguard action with De Wet . . . 23rd of May captured Heilbron; 26th of May crossed the Vaal River into the Transvaal; 29th of May in action at the battle of Doornkop; 30th of May

in the gold district of Florida; 31st of May captured Johannesburg; 5th of June captured Pretoria after some fighting, had a grand march past for Lord Roberts; 11th and 12th of June had a severe battle at Diamond Hill, which I shall never forget: I worked like a slave that two days fixing and setting fuses, but we kept them at bay.[69]

New units and tactics were employed to overwhelm Boer positions. At Doornkop (29 May 1900) Hamilton launched his assault with the City of London Imperial Volunteers (CIV) and the Gordons, supported by the Cornwalls, up sloping ridges burnt black by the Boers to remove any cover and render the khaki uniforms more easily targeted. The Gordons included a Volunteer company in their second line, and attacked in extended order, covered partially by artillery fire. Many of the casualties occurred near or at the crest where there was a fierce fire-fight among the rocks before the Boers withdrew. While the 'Dukes' suffered only two casualties, including Lieutenant Fife who was fatally wounded, the Gordons incurred 97 (about 20 of whom would die from wounds caused by explosive bullets). Even so, Lieutenant Gordon-Duff thought: 'Luckily they were not first class shots, otherwise not so many of us would have come off, Scot free'.[70]

On 11 June 1900, the 2/Dorsets undertook their first major action at Alleman's Nek, where they were required to seize two hills overlooking the pass. After languishing in Natal where many had succumbed to fever, the men were reportedly jubilant at the prospect of action. They were deployed in the centre of the advance (flanked in a wedge-shaped formation by Middlesex soldiers on the left and Dublin Fusiliers on the right). Under Major-General J. Talbot Coke's instructions, companies had to advance across the open plain without firing in a succession of lines, each occupying 120 yards in width and with 150 yards in depth between each line. Supported by naval guns and artillery, the Dorsets, led by Lieutenant-Colonel Cecil Law, stormed Conical Hill before pursuing the Boers onto Alleman's Hill, and during this pursuit, as Corporal A. E. Robinson observed, 'we lost most of our men'.[71] Given the lack of cover and the height of the hills, the loss of 2 officers and 10 men killed and 52 wounded (2 of whom would die of their wounds) testified to the value of a rapid assault. A Boer prisoner described the Dorsets as not men but 'devils' since they had moved so quickly past their range markers and had not stopped to fire in the assault; even more gratifying, added Corporal R. Abbott, was the fact that the enemy not only evacuated Alleman's Nek but fled from their positions on Laing's Nek and Majuba, thereby enabling Buller to break through the rear of the Boer defences.[72]

Capturing Pretoria unopposed did not, as Lord Roberts hoped, bring the war to a 'rapid conclusion'.[73] His extended lines of communication and dependence on the railway left British forces vulnerable to attacks in the renamed Orange River Colony, the Transvaal and, later, Cape Colony. Countering these attacks proved difficult, as Private George C. Fraser (1/Royal Scots Mounted Infantry) conceded, because 'the marvellous energies and skilful tactics of Christian De Wet' were 'leading our men a dance and no mistake . . .'. He believed, nonetheless, that the mounted infantry were becoming more proficient as horsemen, skirmishers and snipers, and claimed: 'The Dutchmen have taught us many useful military lessons since the commencement of the war.'[74] Infantry and artillery were also involved in chasing the Boers, and, after a fortnight's action in July 1900, Robert McClelland (chaplain, 1/Cameron Highlanders) described how the Camerons, as part of the 21st Brigade, had become proficient in the use of cover, in extended operations, and in fire and movement with artillery support. 'The Cameron Volunteers', he noted, 'particularly distinguished themselves, advancing at the double up the face of almost inaccessible cliffs'.[75] However, the futility of infantry chasing commandos soon became apparent: 'it is impossible', wrote Private Ross (2/Seaforths), 'for infantry to follow them up', and packing soldiers into carts, as described by Lieutenant John Bryan (2/Gloucesters), 'had no luck, as usual . . .'.[76] Even mounted patrols floundered in pursuit of de Wet, with a Truro soldier in Lieutenant-Colonel H. C. O. Plumer's column acknowledging: 'It's a marvel how he gets about so rapidly. We are all mounted, and it takes us all our time to keep up with him'.[77]

Facing repeated attacks on detachments, patrols and convoys, the British forces had to protect their lines of communication. Battalions, already depleted by mounting tolls of sick, were often split up, with companies assigned to garrison duty in towns, stations and depots, while others manned armoured trains, guarded bridges and escorted convoys. These duties varied considerably: in some garrisons and rear-area postings, officers and men enjoyed, as Captain F. M. Peacock (Somersets) remarked, 'fairly easy times', with hospitality from friendly civilians and opportunities for shooting; but, in more isolated posts, men endured extremes of temperature, restricted rations and often monotonous duty.[78] Patrolling was often arduous, and after four companies of the Somersets completed 240 miles of marching from Vryburg 'through blinding dust, scarcely any water, and often only half rations', Sergeant Edward E. Husband was pleased that 'the Somersets have pulled through, and had only three men fall out the whole time'.[79] The engineers, as a Devonian sapper, C. Bowden, affirmed, were particularly busy: his company not only engaged the enemy periodically but built redoubts and roads, cleared dynamite from bridges, repaired railway tracks and marched on to Komati Poort, covering 800 miles in 6 months. There they built huts and roads in temperatures of '110 degrees in the shade all through the fever months'.[80]

Small detachments, too, were vulnerable to enemy attack. Three companies of the unlucky 'Glosters' were among 480 soldiers mounting a garrison at De Wetsdorp when de Wet's forces surrounded them, captured their two guns, and killed or wounded some 96 soldiers. When the widely dispersed and poorly fortified garrison surrendered (23 November 1900), Private Bray reflected: 'We had been in the trenches three days and two nights without rest, and thirty hours without water, so you can guess what state we were in . . .'.[81] By February 1901 Private E. Eyers was delighted to learn that another 30,000 soldiers were due to arrive in South Africa: 'They are badly wanted, for this is a great country, and it takes a lot of men to fight, while others hold all the towns and look after the railway lines and escort convoys, etc.'[82] Despite the reinforcements, including imperial troops and auxiliary forces, regular units still struggled to operate effectively: by May 1901, Peacock admitted: 'The companies are not strong now; in fact, very weak, and as we had to find a detachment of twenty men, under Harrison, to guard the railway bridge, we cannot muster much more than eighty men for duty, and as thirty men is the minimum we can do with for picquet and outpost duty, the nights in bed are few'.[83]

Soldiers also engaged in active counter-guerrilla operations: farm-burning, the destruction of Boer livestock and the removal of Boer families into concentration camps – policies begun under Roberts and continued under Kitchener.[84] Soldiers had mixed feelings about these tasks: some, like Captain Boyd A. Cunningham (4/Argyll and Sutherland Highlanders Militia), regarded 'orders to ravage some farms . . . [as] great fun';[85] others regretted the destruction of livestock or emphasised that they only burnt farms from which they had been fired upon. Whereas an Australian officer of Cornish stock found it 'very disagreeable work', another officer justified farm-burning as necessary because the Boers used 'their women and children' as cover and their farms as arsenals.[86] The implacable hostility of many Boer women only compounded these difficulties: 'The women', wrote Peacock, 'are at the bottom of the war.' 'They loathe us', added a Bristolian officer, 'the first thing they teach their children is to hate the British.'[87]

The bitterness of the guerrilla engagements, coupled with the seemingly endless conflict, exacerbated feelings towards the enemy. Soldiers and chaplains retold accounts of the Boers using explosive bullets, firing on ambulance wagons, destroying loyalist farms, killing wounded men at Vlakfontein and shooting blacks.[88] Some soldiers attributed this resistance to the lenient policies adopted by Roberts when he first entered the republics and allowed Boers who surrendered, and took an oath of 'neutrality', to return to their homes (where-upon some resumed combat). Reverend C. E. Greenfield (acting chaplain with the Scots Greys) maintained that the British should have grasped the nettle 'strongly' from the outset: 'our weak efforts have only resulted in us being grievously stung'.[89]

Soldiers adapted to Kitchener's more systematic methods of counter-guerrilla warfare; they constructed, with native assistance, a vast network of blockhouses and barbed wire entanglements within which to mount drives against the Boers. Sergeant H. Hurley (2/DCLI) was impressed with the 'craze' of 'hemming ourselves in with barbed wire and also building blockhouses, which are great things in guarding the line . . .'.[90] If blockhouse duty was less onerous than trekking, soldiers had to stay alert, particularly at night, despite a daily routine which Lance Corporal G. Hill (Somersets) aptly described as 'very quiet and monotonous . . .'.[91] The drives yielded variable returns: after a seven-day trek in May 1901, F and H companies of the Argylls brought in '24 prisoners of war, 8 surrenders, 3 undesirables, 36 rifles, 2,300 rounds of small ammunition, 37 women, 124 children, 80 wagons, 26 Cape Carts, 200 horses, 12 mules, 1,300 cattle, 5,500 sheep'.[92]

Despite the mounting number of surrenders and the assistance afforded by blacks (both armed and unarmed) and Boers who joined the British as scouts,[93] soldiers despaired of an end to hostilities. 'The "war"', argued Major Mackintosh (Seaforths), 'may go on forever at this rate',[94] a fear that partly explained the intense resentment of the pro-Boers at home. As Lieutenant-Colonel Law (2/Dorsets) commented: 'I am sorry to say the war drags on, our greatest enemies being the size of the country and the traitors at home who give the Boers every encouragement to continue this struggle with a view to getting their independence.'[95] Many soldiers deplored the expression of pro-Boer opinions in Britain. Private W. Willis (2/Devons) reckoned that the pro-Boers knew 'nothing' about the war: 'They want to come here and see what is going on. It is perfectly disgraceful.'[96] Corporal Chin (2/DCLI) reported that his regimental chaplain, Reverend H. K. Southwell, vicar of Bodmin, was planning to send samples of explosive bullets to Leonard H. Courtney, a local Member of Parliament and prominent pro-Boer.[97]

Soldiers were even more incensed by criticisms of their counter-guerrilla operations, especially of the concentration camps where, according to a Gordon Highlander, 'every facility' was offered to the Boers and they were 'treated as well, if not better, than Tommy Atkins himself'.[98] This was a recurrent military refrain,[99] and those more directly acquainted with the camps ascribed much of the 'distressing' mortality rate to the insanitary habits of the Boers in confined quarters and their lack of co-operation with the medical authorities. Reverend F. J. Williams insisted that there was 'no cruelty, no neglect, no unkindness' in the management of the camps, while Dr H. A. Spencer of the Middelburg camp praised his nursing sisters who were trying to 'convert some scores of irresponsible and careless women into better mothers'. Just as Spencer deplored the criticisms of Emily Hobhouse,[100] Trooper Lambert argued:

> It is very annoying for us poor fellows, who have been out here just two years and have been in the stiffest of battles, to have to read in English papers that so-called English gentlemen have the soft headedness to stand up before the British public and say that it has been a most barbarous war, accusing British Generals and Tommy Atkins of the same.[101]

Whether these fulminations reflected more than momentary outbursts of anger, triggered by incidents in the field, articles in the press or frustrations over the length of the war, is difficult to discern. At least one officer admitted being 'a bit rabid on this question',[102] but others proffered more considered judgements: Lieutenant M. H. Grant (2/Devons) would not overlook the 'many white flag incidents' but insisted that the Boers were not cowards but 'brave men', capable of acts of 'collective heroism . . . astonishing in a soldiery brought up in a school of pure individualism'.[103] A Dorset Lancer conceded: 'The Boers are awfully clever, though . . . both deceitful and treacherous', adept at the use of cover; several engineers commended the trenches of the Boers and their long-range shooting; and Corporal Philip Littler (2/Gordons) insisted that 'it is a mistake to look upon the Boers as poor ignorant farmers . . . They will take some beating'.[104] A Devonian officer agreed, describing fighting that began at 3,000 yards:

> You never see your enemy, even at 900 or 500; and the Boer is a busy fellow if he feels so inclined. He will stay and fire 300 shots at you before you can clap your hands. If he wants to go to a better place he will go, but you can't see him move. Taking one consideration with another, the Dutchman is a fine enemy, and if he did not misuse the white flag he would be universally respected.[105]

Whatever their feelings towards the enemy,[106] many tired of the war and yearned to go home. Neither news of Boer surrenders nor reports of convoys capturing large numbers of refugees, animals and wagons deflected the desire of Corporal F. Hawkins (Somersets) and others to leave 'this miserable place'.[107] Once the peace conference at Vereeniging began, hopes of a complete Boer surrender rose and a sergeant in the South Wales Borderers was delighted to see Kitchener 'in particularly good spirits. He actually smiles, and that is a thing he does not often do.'[108] Relief was certainly the overwhelming sentiment when the peace was signed on 31 May 1902, but soldiers had expressed hopes that lessons would be learned from the new methods of warfare. As a Gordon Highlander claimed after Paardeberg: 'Our generals have learnt their lesson in the harsh school of adversity. The dangers attending misdirected strategy and antiquated tactics have been recognised.'[109]

Notes

1 Pakenham, *The Boer War*; Jackson, *The Boer War*; Downham, *Red Roses on the Veldt*; W. J. P. Aggett, *The Bloody Eleventh: History of The Devonshire Regiment*, Volume 2: *1815–1914* (Exeter: Devonshire and Dorset Regiment, 1994), chs 15–16; V. Peach, *By Jingo! Letters from the Veldt* (Totnes: Totnes Community Archive, 1987); Spiers, 'The Scottish Soldier in the Boer War', in Gooch (ed.), *The Boer War*, pp. 152–65 and 273–7.

2 Even in Cornwall, where the 'Dukes' struggled to raise men for two battalions and so recruited heavily from Birmingham and London, Lt-Col. Aldworth had taken a portion of the 2nd Battalion on a lengthy tour of the county in early 1899 and so 'nearly all Cornishmen are now acquainted with their territorial regiment and regard it with feelings of pride and affection': 'The Departure of the 'Dukes'', *Cornish Times*, 4 November 1899, p. 4; 'Cornwall & the War', *Cornish Telegraph*, 9 May 1900, p. 5, and 3 October 1900, p. 6; 'Where Are the Cornishmen?', *Cornish Telegraph*, 18 September 1901, p. 3; and A. W. Rose, *The Diary of 2874 L/Cpl. A. W. Rose 2nd D.C.L.I.: His Experiences in the South African War 9th October, 1899–28th December 1901*, ed. H. White (Bodmin: DCLI Museum, n.d.), p. 2.

3 'Letter from the Front from a North Devon Officer', *Western Times*, 18 December 1899, p. 4.

4 'Interesting Letters from a Somerset in South Africa', *Somerset County Gazette*, 10 March 1900, p. 2.

5 *Ibid.*; see also 'News from the Somersets at the Front' and 'Yeovil Men at the Front', *Somerset County Gazette*, 30 December 1899, p. 9, and 13 January 1900, p. 3; 'A Letter from Estcourt', *Reading Mercury*, 6 January 1900, p. 4; 'From One of the "Cornwalls" at the Front', *Launceston Weekly News*, 3 February 1900, p. 4.

6 'A Somerset's Experiences in the War', *Devon and Somerset Weekly News*, 25 January 1900, p. 6.

7 'A Torrington Soldier's Letter', *Devon Weekly Times*, 24 November 1899, p. 5; GHM, PB 182, Capt. M. F. M. Meiklejohn, 'Rough Account of the Action at Elandslaagte 21 October 1899', 23 February 1902, p. 10; and PB 175, Lt-Col. Sir N. Macready, diary, October 1899, p. 3.

8 'With the Devons at Elandslaagte', *Western Times*, 22 November 1899, p. 4; see also 'A Crediton Man in a Bayonet Charge', *Western Morning News*, 24 November 1899, p. 8; 'Wounded Devon's Story of Elandslaagte', *Devon Weekly Times*, 12 January 1900, p. 7; 'A Wounded Shaldon Man's Experiences', *Mid-Devon and Newton Times*, 23 December 1899, p. 3; GHM, PB 175, Macready, diary, p. 3.

9 'Wounded Devons' Stories of Elandslaagte', *Devon Weekly Times*, 5 January 1900, p. 5; GHM, PB 175, Macready, diary, p. 5.

10 GHM, PB 182, Meiklejohn, 'Rough Account', p. 10.

11 *Ibid.*, p. 5.

12 *Ibid.*, pp. 5, 7; GHM, PB 175, Macready, diary, p. 4; 'Teignmouth Man at Elandslaagte', *Western Morning News*, 24 November 1899, p. 8.

13 'The Battle of Elandslaagte, Touching Incidents', *Cheltenham Chronicle*, 2 December 1899, p. 5.

14 'Crediton Man in the Fighting' and 'Crediton Private at the Front', *Crediton Chronicle*, 25 November, 1899, p. 5, and 2 December 1899, p. 5.

15 'Nicholson's Nek Described by a Gloucestershire Officer' (Capt. S. Willcock; see n. 20), *Gloucestershire Chronicle*, 16 December 1899, p. 7; L. S. Amery (ed.), *The*

Times History of the War in South Africa 1899–1902, 7 vols (London: Sampson Low, Marston, 1900–9), vol. 2, pp. 253–5.

16 'Bristolians in Battle', *Bristol Observer*, 2 December 1899, p. 4; 'The Spirit of the Gloucesters', *Gloucestershire Chronicle*, 23 December 1899, p. 7.

17 'The Surrender of the Gloucesters', *Gloucester Journal*, 22 September 1900, p. 3.

18 'The Gloucesters at Pretoria', *Devon Weekly Times*, 15 December 1899, p. 7; 'An Officer's Home-Letter', *Cheltenham Chronicle*, 16 December 1899, p. 5.

19 'Why the Gloucesters Surrendered', *Gloucestershire Chronicle*, 18 November 1899, p. 7; Soldiers of Gloucestershire Museum (SGM), Capt. S. Duncan to Lovett, 29 July 1900.

20 SGM, Capt. S. Willcock, letter, 9 November 1899.

21 GHM, PB 605, Dr H. H. Balfour, 'A Diary Kept During the Siege of Ladysmith', p. 33.

22 'Letters from a Ladysmith Defender to Friends in Crieff', *Strathearn Herald*, 21 April 1900, p. 3.

23 GHM, PB 66, 'War Diary of Lt-Col. W. Harry Dick Cunyngham (2 Bn), 1899', p. 3; 'Ladysmith After the Siege', *Morning Leader*, 12 April 1900, p. 2; Lieutenant-Colonel C. W. Park, *Letters from Ladysmith* (Ladysmith: Ladysmith Historical Society, 1972), pp. 2, 5.

24 Park, *Letters from Ladysmith*, pp. 6–8, 20; see also GHM, PB 66, 'War Diary of Cunyngham', p. 4; SGM, 55, Chapman MSS, Maj. G. N. Chapman to his father, 13 December 1899.

25 'Letters from the Front', *Western Times*, 11 April 1900, p. 4; 'A Barnstaple Soldier on the Boer Repulse', *North Devon Herald*, 12 April 1900, p. 2; see also Devonshire and Dorset Regimental Headquarters, Box 18, letter of Drummer E. Boulden, 24 March 1900.

26 L. Childs, *Ladysmith: The Siege* (Barnsley: Leo Cooper, 1999), pp. 120, 136.

27 'A Crewkernian in Besieged Ladysmith', *Somerset County Gazette*, 7 April 1900, p. 2; 'Soldiers' Letters', *Devon Weekly Times*, 12 April 1900, p. 6.

28 'Letters from a Ladysmith Defender to Friends in Crieff', p. 3; see also 'A Brave Regiment', *Manchester Evening Chronicle*, 4 April 1900, p. 3.

29 'Interesting Letter from a Bristolian', *Bristol Observer*, 7 April 1900, p. 4.

30 'Mutinous Spirit in Highland Brigade', *John O'Groat Journal*, 19 January 1900, p. 2.

31 'Methuen Leading Men to Death' and 'Highlander's Criticism of Lord Methuen', *Strathearn Herald*, 13 and 20 January 1900, pp. 3 and 2; 'The Order to Retire', *Glasgow Evening News*, 9 January 1900, p. 2.

32 'Written on the Battlefield', *Glasgow Evening News*, 11 January 1900, p. 5; see also 'A Salford Highlander's Picture of the Magersfontein Fight', *Manchester Evening News*, 25 January 1900, p. 5.

33 'Some Highlanders' Comments', *Western Morning News*, 11 January 1900, p. 8; 'An Escape at Magersfontein', *Wells Journal*, 11 January 1900, p. 5.

34 'A Scots Guardsman's Defence of Lord Methuen', *Glasgow Evening News*, 15 March 1900, p. 3; 'Methuen and His Guards', *Morning Leader*, 23 April 1900, p. 2; 'A Tribute to Lord Methuen', *Somerset County Gazette*, 26 May 1900, p. 3; 'Home from the War', *Crediton Chronicle*, 8 June 1901, p. 5.

35 'A Crieff Soldier's Opinion of the Boers', *Strathearn Herald*, 3 March 1900, p. 2; 'Stirling Soldiers' Impressions of Campaign', *Bridge of Allan Reporter*, 13 January 1900, p. 5; Spiers, 'The Scottish Soldier in the Boer War', p. 154.

36 Pakenham, *Boer War*, pp. 209–10, 236, 368; G. Powell, *Buller: A Scapegoat? A Life of General Sir Redvers Buller 1839–1908* (London: Leo Cooper, 1994), pp. 165, 192; Field Marshal Lord Carver, *The National Army Museum Book of the Boer War* (London: Sidgwick & Jackson, 1999), p. 255; D. Judd and K. Surridge, *The Boer War* (London: John Murray, 2002), pp. 131–2, 168.

37 'Letter from a Northawton Postman Reservist' and 'Letter from the Front', *Western Times*, 26 January 1900, p. 8, and 30 January 1900, p. 6; 'The Devons at Tugela', *Devon Weekly Times*, 19 January 1900, p. 5; 'Letters from the Front', *Western Morning News*, 25 January 1900, p. 8; 'A Modbury Reservist's Adventure', *Totnes Times*,

10 February 1900, p. 5.

38 'A Molland Man at the Tugela Battle' and 'Letter from an Okehampton Man', *Western Times*, 26 January 1900, p. 2; 'Letters from the Front', *North Devon Herald*, 18 January 1900, p. 5; F. Pretorius, *The Anglo-Boer War 1899–1902* (Cape Town: Struik Publishers, 1998), p. 17; 'Letters from Ayrshire Men', *Ayr Advertiser*, 25 January 1900, p. 4.

39 'Letters from Ayrshire Men', p. 4; 'A Glasgow Reservist at the Colenso Battle', *Glasgow Herald*, 9 February 1900, p. 8.

40 'A Scottish Rifleman's Experience at Colenso', *Glasgow Evening News*, 25 January 1900, p. 3.

41 *Ibid.*; 'A Creech St Michael Man at Chieveley', *Somerset County Gazette*, 14 April 1900, p. 11; 'Solders' Letters' and 'A Tribute to Buller', *Devon Weekly Times*, 9 March 1900, p. 7, and 27 April 1900, p. 6.

42 'The Doings of the Somersets in South Africa', *Somerset County Gazette*, 7 April 1900, p. 2; 'The Boer as a Fighting Man', *North Devon Herald*, 15 March 1900, p. 8; 'A Marple Man at the Tugela Disaster', *Manchester Evening News*, 25 January 1900, p. 5.

43 'With General Buller's Relief Force', *Devon Weekly Times*, 11 May 1900, p. 7; 'The 2nd Battalion P.A.S.L.I. in South Africa', *Somerset County Gazette*, 7 July 1900, p. 3.

44 'Another Good Word for Buller', *Devon Weekly Times*, 20 April 1900, p. 6; 'The Soldiers' Confidence in Buller', *Royal Cornwall Gazette*, 8 March 1900, p. 7; 'Interesting Letters from a Bristol Sapper', *Bristol Observer*, 7 April 1900, p. 2; 'Unbounded Confidence in Buller', *Mid-Devon and Newton Times*, 10 March 1900, p. 3; 'A Creech St Michael Man at Chieveley', p. 11; 'A Perth Scots Grey's Experience', *Strathearn Herald*, 3 March 1900, p. 2; 'A Perth Soldier Before Ladysmith', *Perthshire Constitutional & Journal*, 2 April 1900, p. 3.

45 'A South Tawton Man's Experiences', *Western Times*, 12 April 1900, p. 8; Keep Military Museum, 65/101, Sgt-Maj. W. Young, diary, n.d.

46 'A Teignmothian's Opinion of Gen. Buller', *Mid-Devon and Newton Times*, 17 March 1900, p. 7.

47 'The Relief of Ladysmith' and 'With General Buller', *Somerset County Gazette*, 7 and 14 April 1900, pp. 2 and 11; 'Letter from an Ashburton Man' and 'The Devons at the Front', *Totnes Times*, 5 May and 10 November 1900, pp. 3 and 8; 'Incidents of the War', *North Devon Herald*, 30 August 1900, p. 3; 'The Devons at the Front', *Mid-Devon and Newton Times*, 10 November 1900, p. 8; 'Letter from a Devonian at the Front', *Crediton Chronicle*, 1 February 1902, p. 5.

48 'War Letters', *Cornishman*, 1 February 1900, p. 4; 'Newton Soldier's Letter', *Totnes Times*, 10 March 1900, p. 5; 'Soldiers' Letters', *Manchester Evening Chronicle*, 3 March 1900, p. 3; see also 'A Scots Guardsman with Lord Roberts', *Somerset County Gazette*, 26 May 1900, p. 3; 'An Ashburton Man at Ladysmith', *Mid-Devon and Newton Times*, 25 November 1899, p. 3.

49 'Private Hughes, of Pittenweem, on Lieutenant Tait's Death', *Fife News*, 10 March 1900, p. 3; 'A Gordon Highlander on Indian v. African Warfare', *Edinburgh Evening News*, 15 March 1900, p. 6; 'Letter from a Ross-shire Soldier at the Front', *Ross-shire Journal*, 26 January 1900, p. 7.

50 'From Hospital to Battlefield', *Highland News*, 3 February 1900, p. 6; 'Interesting Letter from a Bristolian', p. 4; 'Soldiers' Beards a Foot Long' and 'Facing Death without a Tremor', *Stroud Journal*, 23 March and 18 May 1900, pp. 3 and 3; 'A Crewe Man with the Black Watch', *Manchester Evening News*, 25 January 1900, p. 5; 'A Stoke St Gregory Man with Lord Roberts at Bloemfontein', *Devon and Somerset Weekly News*, 5 May 1900, p. 6; 'Letters from the Front', *Somerset Standard*, 12 April and 1 June 1900, pp. 6 and 7.

51 'Letter from a Glasgow Man with Gatacre's Column', *Glasgow Herald*, 26 December 1899, p. 6; 'The Battle of the Modder River', *Glasgow Evening News*, 2 January 1900, p. 2; 'Letter from the Front from a North Devon Officer', p. 4.

52 'The Boer as a Fighting Man', *North Devon Herald*, 15 March 1900, p. 8.

53 'Letters from the Front', *Falkirk Herald*, 24 March 1900, p. 5; 'Lord Roberts's March

to Bloemfontein', *Somerset County Gazette*, 26 May 1900, p. 3; 'Paardeberg Described by a Sergeant of the D.C.L.I.', *West Briton*, 22 March 1900, p. 2.

54 'A Tauntonian in the Royal Field Artillery', *Somerset County Gazette*, 13 October 1900, p. 3; 'Letters from the Front', *Falkirk Herald*, 24 March 1900, p. 5.
55 'Letters from the Front', p. 5; see also Amery (ed.), *The Times History*, vol. 3, pp. 431–3, 445–6.
56 'The Cornish Charge', *Western Morning News*, 3 July 1900, p. 8; 'On the Field', *Evening News*, 5 April 1900, p. 2; *Diary of L/Cpl. Rose*, p. 10.
57 'Paardeberg Described by a Sergeant of the D.C.L.I.', p. 5.
58 'Cornish Charge', p. 8.
59 *Ibid*. Fife, who is the most authoritative source, mentions only one charge, but he fell injured in the first line. See also 'The Charge of the Cornwalls', *Cornish Telegraph*, 28 March 1900, p. 3; 'One of "The Dukes" at Paardeberg', *North Devon Herald*, 17 May 1900, p. 3; Amery (ed.), *The Times History*, vol. 3, pp. 440–1.
60 'Their First Fight', *Morning Leader*, 6 April 1900, p. 2.
61 These parts of his letter to Colonel Aldworth's daughter were edited out of the published version: compare DCLI Museum, 'Memorials of Lt-Col. Aldworth', Lt H. Fife to Miss Aldworth, 26 March 1900, with 'Cornish Charge', p. 8.
62 Lt.-Col. L. Gordon-Duff, *With the Gordon Highlanders to the Boer War & Beyond* (Staplehurst: Spellmount, 2000), p. 73; and 'A Graphic Narrative', *Manchester Evening Chronicle*, 12 April 1900, p. 3.
63 'A Graphic Narrative', p. 3; and *Diary of L/Cpl. Rose*, pp. 12–13.
64 SGM, 187, Gardner MSS, Lt R. M. S. Gardner to F and M, 26 February 1900; 'A Tauntonian in the Oxfordshire Light Infantry', *Devon and Somerset Weekly News*, 17 May 1900, p. 6.
65 'The "Somerset County Gazette" at the Front', *Devon and Somerset Weekly News*, 17 May 1900, p. 6; 'A Galmington Man in the D.C.L.I.', *Somerset County Gazette*, 28 April 1900, p. 3; 'Second Gloucesters at Bloemfontein', *Cheltenham Chronicle*, 28 April 1900, p. 3; Pretorius, *The Anglo-Boer War*, p. 24.
66 'A Tauntonian in the Duke of Cornwall's', *Somerset County Gazette*, 2 June 1900, p. 3; *Diary of L/Cpl. Rose*, pp. 16–19.
67 'Mounted Infantry Everywhere', *Morning Leader*, 17 April 1900, p. 2.
68 'Letter from the Front', *Argyllshire Herald*, 29 September 1900, p. 3; see also 'Letters from the Front', *Southern Guardian*, 25 August 1900, p. 3; 'Letter from a Seaforth', *Inverness Courier*, 31 July 1900, p. 5.
69 'A Tauntonian in the Royal Field Artillery', p. 3.
70 Gordon-Duff, *With the Gordon Highlanders*, p. 101; *Diary of L/Cpl. Rose*, pp. 29–30; 'The Cornwalls at Pretoria', *Cornish Times*, 28 July 1900, p. 5; '"Not at All Fair"', *Stroud Journal*, 10 August 1900, p. 3; 'Fighting on Mealies', *West Briton*, 26 July 1900, p. 6.
71 'The Battle of Almond's Nek', *Southern Times*, 14 July 1900, p. 3; 'Letters from the Front', *Southern Guardian*, 28 July 1900, p. 3; 'The 2nd Dorsets in South Africa', *Dorset County Chronicle*, 26 July 1900, p. 12.
72 'Battle of Almond's Nek', p. 3; 'Letters from the Front', *Somerset Standard*, 27 July 1900, p. 7.
73 Lord Roberts to Lord Lansdowne, 7 June 1900, in A. Wessels (ed.), *Lord Roberts and the War in South Africa 1899–1902* (Stroud, Gloucestershire: Sutton Publishing Ltd for the Army Records Society, 2000), p. 97.
74 'Twixt Veldt and Kopje: Hairbreadth Escapes', 'A Letter from the Front' and 'Twixt Veldt and Kopje: An Exciting Ride', *Inverness Courier*, 12 June, 7 September and 9 November 1900, pp. 3, 3 and 3.
75 'The Cameron Highlanders', *Inverness Courier*, 2 October 1900, p. 3.
76 'The Marauding Boers', *Ross-shire Journal*, 30 November 1900, p. 8; 'Letter from Lieut. J. Bryan', *Gloucestershire Chronicle*, 5 January 1901, p. 7; see also 'Chasing the Boers', *Crediton Chronicle*, 24 August 1901, p. 8.
77 'Chasing De Wet', *Western Morning News*, 18 March 1901, p. 8.
78 'Letter from Captain Peacock', *Somerset County Gazette*, 22 December 1900, p. 8;

SLIA, 214, N. C. Farrance, 'The Prince Albert's (Somerset Light Infantry) in South Africa 1899–1902: The Letters of Captain F. M. Peacock from the 2nd Battalion' (Bristol, n.d.), p. 47; on shooting, see *One Man's Boer War 1900 The Diary of John Edward Pine-Coffin*, ed. S. Pine-Coffin (Bideford: Lazarus Press, 1999), pp. 67–75, 84–92, 102, 114–16.

79 'Letters from Sergt. Husband, of the P.A.S.L.I.', *Somerset County Gazette*, 28 July 1900, p. 3; see also 'The 2nd Somersets in South Africa', *Devon and Somerset Weekly News*, 21 March 1901, p. 6, and 'A Tauntonian at Heidelberg', *Somerset County Gazette*, 25 August 1900, p. 3.

80 'From East London to Komati Poort', *North Devon Herald*, 23 May 1901, p. 3.

81 'Graphic Description of the Fall of Dewetsdorp', *Stroud Journal*, 18 January 1901, p. 7; see also Amery (ed.), *Times History*, vol. 5, pp. 29–32.

82 'Letter from a Redruthian at the Front', *Cornubian and Redruth Times*, 29 March 1901, p. 7.

83 'The 2nd Somersets in South Africa', *Somerset Country Gazette*, 11 May 1901, p. 12.

84 S. B. Spies, *Methods of Barbarism? Roberts and Kitchener and Civilians in the Boer Republics, January 1900–May 1902* (Cape Town: Hunan & Rousseau, 1977), pp. 50–1, 102–3, 120–1, 175.

85 ASHM, N-D4.CUN.B., Diary of Capt. Boyd A. Cunningham, 29 December 1900; see also Spiers, 'The Scottish Soldier in the Boer War', p. 156.

86 'Instances of Boer Atrocities', *Dorset County Chronicle*, 7 March 1901, p. 12; 'Experiences at the Front', *Cornish Guardian*, 30 August 1901, p. 3.

87 SLIA, 214, Farrance, 'Prince Albert's (SMLI) in South Africa', p. 98; 'Interesting Letter from the Front', *Bristol Times and Mirror*, 5 April 1902, p. 8.

88 'Boer Atrocities', *Bridport News*, 19 July 1901, p. 7; 'Our County's Share in the War', *Somerset County Gazette*, 20 July 1901, p. 12; 'A Plymouth Soldier's Story' and '"Death or Glory"', *Western Morning News*, 12 July 1900, p. 8, and 21 October 1901, p. 8; 'Letters from Lymstonians', *Devon Weekly Times*, 5 January 1900, p. 5.

89 'A Boer Stronghold', *Ayr Advertiser*, 5 September 1901, p. 7; see also 'Letter from the Front' and 'Letters from the Front', *Argyllshire Herald*, 5 May 1900, p. 3, and 20 October 1900, p. 3; 'An Indignant Gloucester', *Gloucester Journal*, 1 December 1900, p. 8.

90 'From a Sergeant of the "Dukes"', *Cornish Guardian*, 26 April 1901, p. 3; see also 'Devons at the Front', *Totnes Times*, 20 April 1901, p. 8.

91 'A Bridgwater Soldier's Letter', *Devon and Somerset Weekly News*, 6 February 1902, p. 2; 'An Ilchester Reservist's Experience in a Blockhouse', *Devon and Somerset Weekly News*, 2 January 1902, p. 7.

92 ASHM, N-DI.MacD, Pte J. MacDonald, diary, 24 June 1901, p. 21.

93 'South African Affairs', *Cornish Telegraph*, 30 April 1902, p. 5; 'A Soldier's Reply to the Pro-Boers', *Inverness Courier*, 11 June 1901, p. 3; 'An Indignant Gloucester', p. 8.

94 'What the Seaforths Are Doing', *Ross-shire Journal*, 13 September 1901, p. 7.

95 'Comforts for the 2nd Dorsets', *Dorset County Chronicle*, 24 October 1901, p. 8; see also 'Evil Done by the Pro-Boers', *Western Gazette* (Yeovil), 29 November 1901, p. 2; 'At the Front', *Argyllshire Herald*, 9 November 1901, p. 3, and 'A Soldier on Pro-Boers', *Ayr Advertiser*, 5 September 1901, p. 7.

96 'Experiences of a Barum Reservist at the Front', *North Devon Herald*, 4 January 1900, p. 5; 'A Notable Letter from the Front', *Ross-shire Journal*, 21 March 1902, p. 5.

97 'A Letter from a "Cornwall"', *West Briton*, 31 May 1900, p. 4.

98 'A Soldier's Reply to the Pro-Boers', p. 3.

99 'South African Affairs', p. 5; 'The Boer Refugees', *Bristol Times and Mirror*, 26 July 1901, p. 8.

100 'Concentration Camps' and 'Medical Work in Boer Camps', *Bristol Times and Mirror*, 16 January 1902, p. 8, and 21 September 1901, p. 8.

101 'A Bristol Soldier on British "Barbarities"', *Bristol Observer*, 24 August 1901, p. 8.

102 'Interesting Letter from the Front', p. 8.
103 'Linesman' (Lt M. H. Grant), *Words by an Eyewitness* (Edinburgh: Blackwood, 1902), pp. 274–5; see also 'Letter from Ladysmith', *Stroud Journal*, 1 December 1899, p. 6.
104 'Letters from the Front', *Poole, Parkstone and East Dorset Herald*, 15 March 1900, p. 8; 'Back from the Front', *Bradford Daily Argus*, 12 January 1900, p. 4; 'Letters from the Front', *Northern Scot and Moray & Nairn Express*, 6 July 1901, p. 3; 'Somerset and the War' and 'Langport Men at the Front', *Somerset County Gazette*, 9 December 1899, p. 10, and 21 April 1900, p. 3.
105 If there were pro-Boers among this sample, they were not particularly conspicuous: K. Surridge, '"All You Soldiers Are What We Call Pro-Boer": The Military Critique of the South African War 1899–1902', *History*, 82 (1997), 582–600.
106 'The Boer as a Fighting Man', p. 8.
107 'The Somersets in South Africa', *Somerset County Gazette*, 10 August 1901, p. 12; 'Seaforth Volunteers Wanting Home', *Ross-shire Journal*, 22 March 1901, p. 5.
108 'Letter from the Front', *Bath Weekly Argus*, 24 May 1902, p. 12.
109 'A Gordon on the Capture of Cronje', *Manchester Evening News*, 19 April 1900, p. 5.

EPILOGUE

Letter-writing by the late Victorian soldiery was not merely more voluminous than previously recognised (though still an activity of a minority of the rank-and-file) but was a highly significant undertaking in its own right. Like the less extensive efforts in sketching, diary-keeping and poetry, this correspondence reflected a desire to record and interpret major historical events. Active service in Africa involved travel to exotic locations, campaigns over difficult terrain, often in extreme climatic conditions, and the prospect of testing personal courage, weaponry and disciplined skills against a diverse array of enemies. Soldiers knew that these enemies usually had advantages in numbers and in their knowledge of their own terrain (only partially offset by the willingness of local auxiliaries to assist in scouting, transport and combat), and that all these enemies had specific military skills (even the much-maligned Egyptians who had professional training and aptitudes in engineering and gunnery). While British soldiers relished the prospect of prevailing over these foes, with the possibility of earning promotions and medals, they realised, too, that African service was fraught with risks, not least of losing far more of their number from sickness and disease than from combat. In short, British soldiers appreciated that any service in Africa represented a challenge to their command, organisation, discipline and fighting skills.

In assessing the value of letter-writing by regimental officers and other ranks three caveats have to be acknowledged: first, the correspondents often wrote from a limited body of knowledge and a very narrow perspective; second, they sometimes erred in their recollections and in their estimates of enemy numbers, casualties incurred, distances travelled and the duration of events; third, their letters normally reached Britain after the publication of official despatches and the reports of war correspondents. None of these caveats was absolute, and in the earlier campaigns from southern Africa, where war correspondents were hardly conspicuous, the surviving letters and sketches of soldiers were even more valuable as first-hand evidence. Nevertheless, soldiers frequently recognised that family and friends probably knew as much about their particular campaign as they did themselves. When serving in Suakin, Lieutenant Lloyd often began letters to his wife with the disclaimer that she would already 'have heard all about to-day's performance'.[1] In a conflict spread out over a vast theatre, as in the South African War, Private R. Bullen (2/Gloucesters) expected that his parents in Lifton, Devon, would 'get more news than we do'.[2]

Compounding this perception were the effects of isolation in remote locations: Private James Glasson (2/DCLI), when protecting a bridge at Bethulie in the Orange Free State, about 100 miles from the nearest town, complained: 'We don't know any news here. Have not seen a paper for three weeks, and then there is no news of the war but what is sent out from London.'[3] Private R. Munro (2/Black Watch), when based at the desolate garrison of Winburg, yearned for mail and newspapers from home as 'it is weary waiting in such a dismal hole as this is'.[4] Soldiers moving into action were not much better informed. On the eve of Magersfontein, a Highland officer conceded: 'We get very little news here'; or, as Lance-Corporal A. Taylor (1/HLI) added, 'no news . . . whatever about the war elsewhere, as there are a lot of spies about'.[5] Another comrade in the Highland Brigade later acknowledged: 'We know nothing of the plans of operations, but quietly go where we are ordered in profound ignorance . . .'.[6] Even Captain John E. Pine-Coffin, a Devonian who commanded the 2/Loyal North Lancashire Mounted Infantry, repeatedly bemoaned the lack of news: as he noted in his diary, 'all ordinary traffic stopped by Lord Kitchener'.[7]

Admittedly the South African War was unique in its scale, dispersal of units and protracted guerrilla warfare. In earlier campaigns, soldiers found it easier to comment on the capture of Kumase or the burning of Cetshwayo's kraal or the relief of Gordon. Moreover, they often had personal tales to recount, promotions and medals to celebrate,[8] and marches, garrisons, duties and battles to describe. If they wrote primarily to reassure, impress or entertain friends and family, they provided a personal perspective on campaigning that the official despatches and articles of war correspondents could never emulate. In sending home letters, poetry, sketches and sometimes diaries (see chapter 1), soldiers sought not only to describe their impressions of active service in Africa but to interpret events which the press had already reported. Lance-Corporal Rose (2/DCLI) feared that the 'people at home little know what we are going through', and Lance-Corporal T. Rice, RE, insisted that 'the horrors of war can't be imagined' except by those involved.[9] Misunderstanding the enemy, argued Sergeant J. E. Hitchcock (2/Coldstream Guards), simply compounded this incomprehension: 'the feeling in England is that they [the Boers] are a lot of harmless farmers, but they are worse than savages, and armed as well as us'.[10]

Many soldiers took a keen interest in how their exploits were reported in the newspapers but had ambivalent feelings about the war correspondents. While regimental officers often enjoyed their company (see chapter 8), bemoaned their absence (chapter 6) or grieved over the death of the more respected correspondents (notably the Hon. Hubert Howard, killed by a British shell at Omdurman, and G. W. Steevens, whose death from typhoid in Ladysmith was described by Colonel Park as 'a terrible loss, both to the Daily Mail and the public'[11]), others remained deeply sceptical of the profession. In the Sudan Colonel Archibald Hunter objected to the presence of war correspondents, '1stly on the score of their drinking, 2d they quarrel in their cups among themselves, 3d they pester one for news & keep back one's work'. Correspondents, he affirmed, 'are never really in the know & all they can claim to give the public is the common talk & speculation of the camp'.[12] Major John M. Vallentin (2/Somerset Light Infantry) was equally unimpressed when he first encountered journalists in South Africa: 'I have been amazed how little they attempt to get hold of the truth. Numbers of them don't venture under fire, and take the account of the first man they meet as Gospel.'[13] Others suspected that correspondents would always be prevented by censorship from reporting unwelcome news. In the wake of Colenso, Rifleman Martin doubted that his father would 'get the truth through the press, as it is under Government censorship. But that frontal attack was human butchery.'[14] A Gordon Highlander also questioned whether 'the highly-paid correspondents' would examine the more mundane aspects of the South African campaign such as the 'state of the transport', particularly the lack of carts and the inadequate victualling of the mules and horses. Lord Roberts's march to Bloemfontein, he noted, was 'marked by carcasses of mules and horses that have died through overwork and no food . . .'.[15]

In fact, the Remount Department incurred so much press criticism that Major C. H. Tippet, the officer commanding remounts for the Aliwal district, wrote a lengthy defence of his staff and explained how they treated sore, debilitated, lame and maimed horses. By expressing his concern about misrepresentation in the press,[16] Tippet reflected part of a double-edged fear of the military – supposedly unjustified criticism of their own units (not least after the many abject surrenders in South Africa[17]) and excessive praise heaped on others. The press coverage of the Gordon Highlanders, real or imagined, aroused intense resentment. After the early engagements in Natal, a Devonian sergeant maintained: 'The Gordons are not in it now. It is all the Devons here, but I suppose in England it is the "Gordons did this and the Gordons did that" but don't you believe it.'[18] Many Highlanders took umbrage after reading the reports of Magersfontein: Private J. Ruddick read 'in the papers that the Gordons were in the line of fire. Well that is nonsense. We, the Black Watch, were in the line of fire'; a private of the Argyll and Sutherland Highlanders insisted: 'We did our work, and well, so why should the Gordons get all the praise'; and Private Alex Williamson (2/Seaforths) simply reckoned that the Gordons did not deserve 'as much' praise 'as they are getting'.[19] The Gordons defended themselves, professing surprise at the envy of their comrades and insisting that they had 'done their share of the work, and have done it well';[20] they even earned some accolades from soldiers in other units, especially after the charge at Doornkop.[21] In short, soldiers wrote at least in part to correct perceived misrepresentations, or oversights in the press, setting the record straight from their point of view.

Soldiers were even more concerned when they read newspaper articles, speeches by politicians or critical letters from home that seemed to them unfair, ill-informed, or unjust. Inevitably these comments tended to occur during the more controversial campaigns, such as the Anglo-Zulu War or the South African War (although there was uproar over press reports criticising the treatment of the dervish wounded after Omdurman).[22] The commanding officers, particularly Chelmsford, Buller and Methuen, bore much of the condemnation, and, despite similar misgivings by certain soldiers (notably the Highlanders towards Methuen after Magersfontein), many soldiers resented retrospective criticisms, especially from civilians at home. Sergeant Evan Jones (2/24th) deplored the condemnation of Chelmsford's strategy by 'Conservative as well as Liberal journals' on the basis of little information and without even hearing 'what he had to say'. Jones maintained: 'I shall always remain convinced that he did everything for the best. We, the 24th, ought to know what he is made of. There is not a man in the 24th that would not fight and most willingly die for him . . .'.[23] Buller evoked similar feelings, even when he was dismissed from the army after an indiscreet speech in October 1901. Private Arthur Bowden, a Devonian reservist, claimed:

> Everyone in the Army sympathises with General Buller . . . his troops had every confidence in him during his attempts to relieve Ladysmith, and after a reverse he had only to make a speech to them, and they were willing to do anything, for, I believe, the universal opinion among the men was: If Buller can't do it no one can. It is easy for people to point out his mistakes now, but at the time they could not tell him what to do. He is one of the best generals we ever had, and will always be remembered by the rank and file of the Army.[24]

If these sentiments were possibly less representative than their authors imagined, they reflected not only the enduring bonds of discipline, loyalty and respect – bonds that had to be preserved in wartime (hence the prompt removal of the Highland Brigade from Methuen's command) – but an assumption that only those who had served under a commander could assess his qualities. In an era of highly personalised commands when even staff officers, quite apart from regimental officers or other ranks, were not fully apprised of command decisions,[25] this assumption was profoundly mistaken. It was widely held, nonetheless, and may explain the deep resentment of external criticism.

Soldiers, though, had other objectives in letter-writing, not least those letters that found their way into the public domain. Officers and other ranks were hardly indifferent to the shortcomings of their kit and equipment, particularly those deficiencies exposed in African campaigns. Complaints about boots, swords, medical supplies, tardy supply columns and jamming machine-guns were all too frequent, compounded by criticisms of the transport in Egypt, whale-boats and camels in the Nile expedition, and horses, rifles and guns in the South African War. Although British expeditionary forces were generally well organised, and none foundered on account of failures in transport and supply, the complaints of soldiers, endorsed by many war correspondents and sometimes investigated at parliamentary level, helped to keep these issues under review. Even Wolseley, in trying to defend the swords used in Suakin before a parliamentary committee, admitted that 'sensational writing' had raised interest in the issue.[26]

A few soldiers also believed that their conduct on active service, if fully reported, would elevate their status in civilian society. At a time when army enlistment had little appeal and soldiers were being shunned in public places,[27] this was an understandable concern, particularly for the reservists who had left their families and civilian jobs to return to active service. Private William Henwood (2/DCLI) was convinced that his comrades, particularly 'us Reserve men, with good characters' had earned 'a great name' for themselves in South Africa, and that this should enhance their reputation at home: 'I don't think a reserve man should be looked down upon as he used to be in days gone by.'[28] Private Willis (2/Devons) agreed; he testified to the strains of reverting to military service and appreciated the commendations of 'our General' (presumably Buller) on 'the way we went into battle. We reservists feel it more than the regulars.'[29] Several chaplains testified to the 'excellent voluntary services both on Sundays and weekdays' in South Africa, the resilience and camaraderie of the soldiers in adversity, the sufferings of the sick and wounded borne with humour and fortitude, and the 'reverence and tenderness' when funerals occurred.[30] However the indiscretions of British soldiers, not least their looting, hardly enhanced their image: 'You should see the troops', wrote Private W. Chonlarton (1/Argylls), 'skirmish round looking for sheep, goats, or cows. We have them killed, cut up, stewed, and almost eaten in an hour, just like cannibals. It is pure warfare we are having now.'[31] Even worse were the reports of boredom as the war dragged on and the less publicised accounts of drunkenness and licentious behaviour.[32]

Relations with native peoples were a feature of all campaigns as expeditionary forces required assistance in labouring, transportation, carrying messages through enemy lines, gathering intelligence and providing supplies (as soldiers were always ready to supplement their rations by bartering for extra foodstuffs; see chapter 6). Natives sometimes fought alongside British forces, albeit with differing degrees of enthusiasm, as the Fantes, Swazis and Sudanese battalions demonstrated, and appreciation of their services varied accordingly. The capacity of ordinary soldiers to forge good relations with friendly natives en route or near camp sites, such as Korosko, was well documented, and their sexual liaisons, if rarely mentioned in print, found confirmation in the numbers hospitalised with venereal disease in Egypt and in Kitchener's famous refusal to quarter the Seaforth Highlanders in Assouan 'where there are 3,000 Sudanese ladies'.[33] Relations with native bearers, labourers and traders were often more brutal, especially if soldiers felt that they had been cheated. Physical intimidation of 'these black fellows', including threats to punch them 'on the nose', as described by Lance Corporal J. A. Cosser in Natal, could facilitate transactions: 'They run about here naked and look horrible, but they are very frightened of the soldiers', and punishments, if possibly less systematic than those meted out by the Boers, certainly included the flogging of 'niggers', as periodically mentioned in Pine-Coffin's diary.[34]

When military correspondents disparaged natives, they both reflected and reinforced popular stereotypes about blacks in Britain, not least when they had the backing of Wolseley himself.[35] This writing, though, has to be placed in context. Many of the complaints about native auxiliaries occurred along the line of march when expeditionary forces depended upon native support but found that progress across difficult terrain, and often in adverse climatic conditions, was slow, frustrating and beset with breakdowns. Further protests arose whenever the natives deserted in the face of the enemy, not least the 300 of the Natal Native Contingent who fled from Rorke's Drift. Yet some soldiers remained philosophical: Acting Commissary W. A. Dunne and Private Henry Hook, VC, praised the natives for their assistance in building the defences at Rorke's Drift, while Chard responded to their flight by simply compressing the overextended perimeter. The limitations of these ill-equipped auxiliaries, led by commanders who could barely speak their language, were all too obvious: as Colonel Pearson remarked, they had little to offer in the firing line and were best employed in scouting and pursuit. As he made this assessment in commending the *gallantry* of some native scouts who had died trying to hold their ground against a Zulu *impi*, he was proffering a military judgement and not a racial slur.[36] By the late 1890s, when the British

[185]

fought alongside a properly trained, equipped and led Egyptian Army, many lauded the contribution of the Sudanese and Egyptian soldiers in the battles of Atbara and Omdurman (see chapter 8).

Regular soldiers had mixed feelings, too, about other sources of auxiliary support. In the South African War where they desperately needed reinforcements, they praised the specialist skills of the Lovat scouts, the zeal of the CIV, and the improvement in Volunteer Service Companies once they became acclimatised and were trained by regular officers and NCOs.[37] Less appreciated were the rates of pay and preferential terms of service enjoyed by the volunteers and the accolades accorded them by the press: 'The papers', wrote Lieutenant John Bryan from Gloucester, 'are at present full of nothing but C.I.V. We are getting a bit tired of it out here'.[38] The Imperial Yeomanry aroused even more ire: Pine-Coffin regarded them as a 'useless lot' and 'too slow' in their patrolling and skirmishing with the enemy, while a Bristolian officer maintained: 'It is rather hard for men who have borne the heat and burden of the day from October 1899 onwards to see raw boys, who can neither shoot, ride, nor look after their horses, receive five shillings [25p] a day, while they only get, say, 1s 2d (6p).'[39] Several soldiers drew attention to disasters involving the yeomanry, such as the seizure of the camp at Tweefontein (25 December 1901) and Methuen's defeat at Tweebosch (7 March 1902), and a Seaforth observed: 'We call the Yeomanry De Wet's bodyguard or McConnachie's [sic] Scouts as they think of nothing else but their stomachs.'[40]

Soldiers were somewhat more appreciative of the services of colonial auxiliaries, not only locally raised bodies such as the Imperial Light Horse and Major M. F. Rimington's Guides, but contingents from Canada, Australia and New Zealand. Apart from reservations about the discipline of some colonial units, officers frequently lauded their skills. As Corporal Jewell (New Zealand Mounted Rifles) informed his sister in Cheltenham: 'General French has complimented us on many occasions on our coolness under fire and our horsemastership. He said we could gallop across country where English cavalry could only walk; we were the best scouts he had ever employed; and we always brought in something – either prisoners, horses, sheep, cattle, or valuable information'.[41] Yet the political significance of their contribution, which was evident even when the first Australians served in Suakin (see chapter 6), far exceeded their skills and limited numbers. Private Tom Wood (2/DCLI) admitted: 'I had no idea of the greatness of the British Empire until I came out here. It is surprising to see men here from all parts of the world, always ready to uphold the Union Jack, and to support each other in any danger.'[42] Imperial ideology, if less conspicuous in correspondence from Zululand,[43] had become more apparent in letters from

South Africa, where Staff-Sergeant Wallace H. Wood (Army Medical Staff Corps) argued that 'this is the beginning of an empire which will be the means of preventing in the future such wars as this; as no country in the world, knowing the Empire is one in deed as well as in name, will ever dare to throw down the gauntlet to us'.[44]

Most correspondents focused on more immediate matters, especially their travails in African conditions. Inevitably short-service soldiers on expeditionary forces described their experiences, especially any 'baptisms of fire', somewhat differently from those who had already seen action or spent several years in Indian, Mediterranean or African garrisons. Doubts about the reliability of short-service soldiers and reservists diminished after the Egyptian campaign, but debates persisted about the influence of old soldiers, whom Methuen regarded as 'grumbling brutes' and his 'curse' in Bechuanaland.[45] If large numbers of seasoned soldiers had to be incorporated into under-strength units earmarked for expeditionary service (and this was a recurrent failing of the Cardwell system), tensions could occur. Lance-Sergeant Grieve argued that the 1/Seaforths, when bound for the Sudan in 1898, 'is not what it used to be – that lot that joined us in Malta have played the mischief with it'.[46] Once campaigns were underway, writers dwelt upon other themes, notably the fate of comrades under fire, pride in the performance of their own units, praise or criticism of specific commanders, and adaptation to the varying demands of colonial warfare.

As all these wars were wars against nature as much as, if not, at times, more than, against their adversaries, soldiers commended both their naval support, with generally excellent relations between the two services at operational and tactical levels,[47] and the endeavours of their supporting units. The Royal Engineers were to the fore in most campaigns, clearing paths and camp sites in the tropical rain forest, building forts and roads in Zululand, repairing boats on the Nile, supervising railway construction and the erection of telegraph lines in the Sudan, and undertaking a multitude of duties, often at great risk, in South Africa. Sapper R. Gomer recalled how his company with its 6 horses, 20 mules and 406 oxen was one of the first into the Orange Free State, building bridges, running ferry boats on steel cables and cutting roads out of river banks, while 17th Company (RE) having erected the pontoon bridges across the Tugela, was the first unit to scale Spion Kop at night, in a vain attempt to construct defences on the top. 'Out of my Company', wrote a survivor, 'we lost the Major commanding and three sappers, a lieutenant and four sappers wounded.'[48] A Tauntonian baker, Corporal Frank Williams (Army Service Corps) described the prodigious task of baking for Methuen's division, with 100 bakers producing

30,000 loaves, sometimes 35,000 loaves, each day. These 1.5lb loaves were baked in 55 'Aldershot' ovens, each accommodating 108 loaves, and the work was undertaken 'all day in the burning sun, made worse by the heat of the ovens'.[49] Forces on the lines of communications brought forward the food, ammunition and other supplies, guarded the stores at fortified bases and supplied the troops at the front. Another Somerset soldier, Private E. S. Stagg, writing from Estcourt in Natal, wrote: 'We are at it day and night. We never know what it is to sleep with our boots off, and we always have our rifles by our sides . . . We are very dissatisfied with our lot.'[50] Private W. J. Brown (RAMC) soon found himself in a similar predicament, working 'day and night, and the nursing sisters the same', in a nearby hospital at Chieveley. It was 'something awful to see the wounded coming in' and 'miserable' to work 'under canvas' in the heat and thunderstorms.[51] If the medical arrangements foundered when typhoid swept the camp at Bloemfontein, the army recovered and depended, as ever, upon its support services to function effectively.

Given the risks of men succumbing to disease and fever, especially when confined in cramped conditions, British expeditionary forces usually sought early and decisive battles. Soldiers rightly worried about languishing in camps or the vulnerability of their slow-moving convoys whether in southern Africa or the Sudan (see chapters 2 and 6), and so generally relished the prospect of engaging the enemy. They described fighting in a various formations: the awkwardness of the 'square' when moving through thick bush or over broken ground, the maximised fire-power of the 'line' at Omdurman, and the movement towards more widely deployed formations, with close artillery support, in South Africa. If wedded to the strategic offensive, British forces often fought most effectively on the defensive, exploiting their advantages in fire-power (even if a few actually regretted the absence of hand-to-hand combat at Omdurman).[52] Soldiers praised the disciplined mobility of the Zulu, the courage of the Mahdists, and the shooting and field-craft of the Boers, with perceptive comparisons made by veterans like Percy Scrope Marling, VC, who fought the Boers, the Egyptians and the Mahdists all before his twenty-third birthday (and fought the Boers again in the South African War), or Robert Charles Coveny who fought in the Asante, Egyptian, Suakin and Nile campaigns before being killed at the battle of Kirbekan. In rating the Hadendowa Arabs as their most formidable foe (see chapter 5), they testified to the enduring legacy of the heroic, warrior ethos. This ethos found reflection in other campaigns when soldiers lauded the fighting qualities of the Asante, the Zulu, the Pedi and the black Sudanese, but also in their contempt for the Egyptians in 1882 and criticism of the Boers for their reluctance on many (though by no means all) occasions to engage in hand-to-hand combat.[53]

Bitter experience, however, ensured that the more discerning realised that these campaigns would not always be resolved by the clash of arms. Political pressures had intruded in 1881 and 1885, prompting the vows of vengeance for Gordon in 1898 and the exultation in the relief of Ladysmith on Majuba day. 'We gave them Majuba day!' wrote Corporal A. Hawkins (2/Devons), so helping 'to rub off the disgrace of what Gladstone did when he held the place in 1881'. He would continue fighting 'to the last for the honour of my country',[54] a refrain that recurred in the letter-writing from the various campaigns. Private A. Spear (1/Devons) was equally blunt in berating his father, who was a Liberal: 'You can see now what your Grand Old Man has done for England. We should not have been in this war if Gladstone had not given in to the Boers at Majuba in such a disgraceful way.'[55] Whether making a point, raising an issue or fulminating over grievances, real or imagined, these correspondents were reflecting their feelings as soldiers on active service and commenting on many aspects of the campaigning experience. Whenever they did so in more than a perfunctory manner, they left an invaluable record of uncensored eye-witness accounts, even if it is a record that has to be placed in context and interpreted with care.

Notes

1 NAM Acc 7709/43, Lloyd MSS, Lloyd to his wife, 20 March and 5 April 1885.
2 'From Soldiers at the Front', *Launceston Weekly News*, 10 March 1900, p. 6; see also 'News from a Somerset', *Somerset County Gazette*, 13 January 1900, p. 3.
3 'With the Dukes', *Cornish Telegraph*, 23 May 1900, p. 3; see also 'Letters from Newton Men', *Mid-Devon and Newton Times*, 24 March 1900, p. 3.
4 'Letter from One of The Black Watch', *Bridge of Allan Reporter*, 16 June 1900, p. 8.
5 'Letter from an Officer of The Black Watch', *Northern Scot and Moray & Nairn Express*, 30 December 1899, p. 6; 'Another Interesting Letter from a Muthill Man', *Strathearn Herald*, 13 January 1900, p. 3.
6 'What Campaigning Means', *Stirling Observer*, 28 March 1900, p. 7.
7 *One Man's Boer War*, ed. S. Pine-Coffin, p. 182.
8 'The Zulu War', *Aberdare Times*, 13 April 1879, p. 4; 'Soldiers' Letters', *Cornishman*, 10 May 1900, p. 5; 'An Exonian's Letter', *Devon Weekly Times*, 30 March 1900, p. 7; 'Letters from the Front', *Falkirk Herald*, 24 March 1900, p. 5.
9 *Diary of L/Cpl Rose*, ed. H. White, p. 31; 'Letter from a Bow Royal Engineer', *Western Times*, 13 March 1900, p. 6.
10 'A Woodbury Man at the Front', *Devon Weekly Times*, 12 January 1900, p. 7.
11 Cecil, 'British Correspondents and the Sudan Campaign of 1896–98', in Spiers (ed.), *Sudan*, p. 115; Harrington and Sharf, *Omdurman 1898*, p. 114; Park, *Letters from Ladysmith*, p. 34.
12 LHCMA, Maurice MSS, 2/1/4, Hunter to Maurice, 15 February 1898; on other military critics of the press, see Cecil, 'British Correspondents and the Sudan Campaign of 1896–98', pp. 110–13.
13 SLIA, F 61, J. M. Vallentin, 'Siege of Ladysmith, 1899 -1900', 24 March 1900, p. 5.

14 'Letters from South Africa', *Nairnshire Telegraph*, 24 January 1900, p. 3; see also 'The Campbells Are Coming', *Evening News*, 13 January 1900, p. 2.

15 'A Wail from a Gordon Highlander', *Manchester Evening News*, 24 April 1900, p. 6.

16 'Major Tippet at the Front', *Bristol Times and Mirror*, 12 March 1902, p. 8.

17 'Private A. Hetherington', *Falkirk Herald*, 20 October 1900, p. 6.

18 'Letters from the Front', *Western Morning News*, 6 February 1900, p. 8.

19 'A Crieff Soldier's Opinion of the Boers', *Strathearn Herald*, 3 March 1900, p. 2; 'Soldiers' Letters', *Manchester Evening Chronicle*, 15 February 1900, p. 3; QOHC, 92–135, Williamson MSS, Pte A. Williamson to Nell, 15 January 1900; see also 'A Soldier's Letter from Modder River', *Edinburgh Evening News*, 15 February 1900, p. 4.

20 'An Indignant Gordon', *Edinburgh Evening News*, 17 February 1900, p. 4 and 'Letter from the Front', *Ayr Advertiser*, 16 August 1900, p. 4.

21 'Letter from the Front', *Somerset Standard*, 31 August 1900, p. 7; 'West Australian Sergeant's Impression', *Manchester Evening Chronicle*, 29 March 1900, p. 3; Pakenham, *The Boer War*, pp. 425–6.

22 Cecil, 'British Correspondents and the Sudan Campaign of 1896–98', pp. 120–3.

23 'The Zulu War', *Aberdare Times*, 13 September 1879, p. 4; for a full account of his letter, see Emery, *Red Soldier*, pp. 252–4.

24 'Letter from a Devonian at the Front', *Crediton Chronicle*, 1 February 1902, p. 5.

25 Spiers, *The Late Victorian Army*, pp. 299–300; I. F. W. Beckett, 'Kitchener and the Politics of Command', in Spiers (ed.), *Sudan*, pp. 35–53.

26 PP, *Reports on Alleged Failures of Cavalry Swords and Pistols at Suakin*, C 5633 (1889), XVII, p. 4; see also *Report from the Select Committee on Commissariat and Transport Services (Egyptian Campaign)*, C 285 (1884), X, and Spiers, *The Late Victorian Army*, pp. 239, 256, 324.

27 'A Soldier at a Weymouth Temperance Hotel', *Somerset County Gazette*, 17 March 1900, p. 3; Skelley, *Victorian Army at Home*, pp. 247–9; Spiers, *The Late Victorian Army*, pp. 128–33.

28 'Reserve Men Try to Earn Respect', *Cornishman*, 28 June 1900, p. 8; see also 'A Cronje Memoriam Card', *Manchester Evening Chronicle*, 19 May 1900, p. 3.

29 'Christmas at Colenso', *North Devon Herald*, 25 January 1900, p. 5.

30 'Devonport Chaplain's Experiences', *Western Morning News*, 30 August 1900, p. 8; 'Tommy Atkins: A Tribute from the Rev. George Hood', *Bristol Times and Mirror*, 4 January 1902, p. 12.

31 '"Roughing It"', *Manchester Evening Chronicle*, 27 March 1900, p. 3.

32 'The Late Major Jervis-Edwards', *Western Morning News*, 7 August 1901, p. 8; W. Nasson, 'Tommy Atkins in South Africa', in P. Warwick (ed.), *The South African War: The Anglo-Boer War 1899–1902* (London: Longman, 1980), pp. 123–38.

33 NAM, Kitchener-Wood MSS, Acc. No. 6807/234, Sir H. Kitchener to Sir E. Wood, 8 March 1898 and Cooper MSS, Acc. No. 6112/595, 'Classified Return of Sick in Hospital at Alexandria & Cairo on 10th June 1898' (where venereal disease caused more hospitalisations than any other factor, accounting for 130 of the 351 cases); 'Korosko' *The 79th News*, 198 (April 1932), 173.

34 'Sheffield Soldiers in Zululand', *Sheffield Daily Telegraph*, 17 May 1879, p. 3; *One Man's Boer War*, pp. 114, 116; see also Nasson, 'Tommy Atkins in South Africa', pp. 130–3.

35 G. J. Wolseley, 'The Negro as a Soldier', *Fortnightly Review*, 50 (1888), 689–703; see also D. A. Lorimer, *Colour, Class and the Victorians: English Attitudes to the Negro in the Mid-Nineteenth Century* (Leicester: Leicester University Press, 1978), pp. 160–1.

36 Bennett, *Eyewitness in Zululand*, p. 95; 'Survivors' Tales of Great Events', *Royal Magazine* (February 1905), 339–48; PRO, WO 32/7737, Chard to Glyn, 25 January 1879; PP, *Further Correspondence, SA*, C 2260, p. 19.

37 'An Exeter Footballer's Experiences', *Western Times*, 8 May 1900, p. 8; 'Letter from Sergt. Hamilton', *Argyllshire Herald*, 5 May 1900, p. 3; 'With the C.I.V.', *Western Morning News*, 12 July 1900, p. 8; Spiers, 'The Scottish Soldier in the Boer War', pp. 163–4.

38 'Letter from Lieut. J. Bryan', *Gloucestershire Chronicle*, 5 January 1901, p. 7; see also 'Seaforth Volunteers Wanting Home', *Ross-shire Journal*, 22 March 1901, p. 5 and 'Letter from a Bridgwater Artilleryman', *Devon and Somerset Weekly News*, 5 May 1900, p. 6.

39 *One Man's Boer War*, pp. 84, 120, 140; 'An Officer on Our "Mistakes" in South Africa', *Bristol Times and Mirror*, 31 July 1901, p. 8.

40 'Maconachie's' was a tinned meat and vegetable stew: Aggett, *The Bloody Eleventh*, vol. 2, p. 340. 'A Seaforth's Letter', *Aberdeen Journal*, 20 December 1900, p. 5; see also 'Methuen on His Defeat', *Gloucestershire Echo*, 12 April 1902, p. 4; 'The Twee-fontein Disaster', *Edinburgh Evening News*, 25 January 1902, p. 2.

41 'With the New Zealanders', *Gloucester Journal*, 20 January 1900, p. 7; see also Judd and Surridge, *The Boer War*, ch. 4 and Spiers, 'The Scottish Soldier in the Boer War', p. 164.

42 'A Tauntonian in the DCLI', *Devon and Somerset Weekly News*, 30 August 1900, p. 6.

43 Lieven, 'The British Soldiery and the Ideology of Empire: Letters from Zululand', *JSAHR*, 80 (2002), 143.

44 'Facing Death without a Tremor', *Stroud Journal*, 18 May 1900, p. 3.

45 WRO, Methuen MSS, WSRO 1742/8565, Methuen to his wife, 16 March 1885.

46 NAM, Grieve MSS, Acc. No. 7906/139, Grieve to Tommie, 16 February 1898.

47 'A Newton Man in the Naval Brigade Which Saved Ladysmith', *Mid-Devon and Newton Times*, 16 June 1900, p. 8.

48 'The Work of the Royal Engineers', *North Devon Herald*, 5 April 1900, p. 2; 'The Battle of Spion Kop', *Somerset County Gazette*, 3 March 1900, p. 2.

49 'Army Bakeries in South Africa', *Somerset County Gazette*, 21 April 1900, p. 3.

50 'The Duties of the Somerset Light Infantry', *Somerset County Gazette*, 27 January 1900, p. 3.

51 'Letters from the Front', *Somerset Standard*, 27 April 1900, p. 7; see also 'With the R.A.M.C.', *Western Morning News*, 25 January 1900, p. 8.

52 Lieutenant-Colonel C. à Court Repington, *Vestigia* (London: Constable, 1919), p. 151; Barthorp, 'A Letter from Omdurman', *Soldiers of the Queen*, 89 (1997), 4.

53 'Wounded Devons' Stories of Elandslaagte', *Devon Weekly Times*, 5 January 1900, p. 5; 'The Point of a Bayonet', *Somerset County Gazette*, 10 March 1900, p. 2; 'Letter from the Front', *Argyllshire Herald*, 16 June 1900, p. 3.

54 'More Letters from the Front', *Mid-Devon and Newton Times*, 5 May 1900, p. 3.

55 'A Soldier and a Politician', *Somerset County Gazette*, 3 March 1900, p. 3.

SELECT BIBLIOGRAPHY

Primary sources

Argyll and Sutherland Highlanders Museum
  Crauford correspondence, N-C91.1
  Cunningham diary, N-D4.CUN.B.
  MacDonald diary, N-DI.MacD
  Wolrige Gordon diary, N-C91.GOR.
Black Watch Archive
  Barwood diaries, 0203/1
  Coveny, 'Letters from Egypt and the Sudan', 0204
  Newspaper cuttings, 0683
  Record of Service of the 42nd Royal Highland Regiment, 0080
  Scott-Stevenson letter, 0641
British Library Asia Pacific and Africa Collections
  White papers, MSS Eur F108/91
Devonshire and Dorset Regimental Headquarters, Exeter
  Boulden correspondence, Box 18
Duke of Cornwall's Light Infantry Museum, Bodmin
  Memorials of Lt-Col. Aldworth
Gloucestershire Record Office
  Commeline correspondence 1879, D 1233/45/26
  Marling correspondence, D 873/C110
Gordon Highlanders Museum
  Balfour, 'A Diary kept During the Siege of Ladysmith', PB 605
  Denne papers, PB 64
  Hawkins papers, PB 1832
  McRae papers, PB 173
  Macready diary, PB 175
  Meiklejohn, 'Rough account of the action at Elandslaagte,
  21 October 1899', PB 182,
  Seton-Karr diary 1882, PB 228
  'War Diary of Lt-Col. W. Harry Dick Cunyngham (2 Bn),
  1899', PB 66
Hatfield House Muniments
  Salisbury papers
Keep Military Museum, Dorchester
  Young diary, 65/101
King's Own Royal Regimental Museum, Lancaster
  Woodgate journal, KO LIB 137
Liddell Hart Centre for Military Archives, King's College London
  Maurice papers
National Archives (Public Record Office)
  Cardwell papers, PRO 30/48
  War Office, WO 32/7737; WO 33/26; WO 33/34; WO 33/38; WO 33/42; WO 33/44; WO
  106/264,
National Army Museum
  Anstruther correspondence, Acc. No. 5705/22
  Cameron correspondence, Acc. No. 8305/55
  Churchward correspondence, Acc. No. 7003/25
  Coghill correspondence, Acc. No. 7112/39/4
  Cooper papers, Acc. No. 6112/595
  Danby correspondence, Acc. No. 7003/2
  Ferguson correspondence, Acc. No. 6807/269

Grieve correspondence, Acc. No. 7906/139
Hooper TS diary, Acc. No. 2001/03/73
Kitchener-Wood correspondence, Acc. No. 6807/234
Lloyd correspondence, Acc. No. 7709/43
Mason correspondence, Acc. No. 8401/62/2
Meiklejohn, 'The Nile Campaign', Acc. No. 7704/36/3
Skinner diary, Acc. No. 7909/15
Spraggs diary, Acc. No. 7706/14
Tuck diary, Acc. No. 7005/21
National Library of Scotland
Blackwood papers, MSS 4001–940
Northamptonshire Regimental Museum Collection
Roe TS diary, 397
Queen's Own Highlanders Collection
Baynes, Capt. K. S., *Narrative of the Part Taken by the 79th Queen's Own Cameron Highlanders in the Egyptian Campaign* (private, 1883)
Williamson correspondence, 92–135
Royal Archives
Duke of Cambridge papers
Royal Engineers Library
'Recollections of Lt Thomas Ryder Main', Acc. No. 11315
Royal Gloucestershire, Berkshire and Wiltshire Regiment Museum, Salisbury
Cameron, 'Action at Tofrik', 004/17
Edwards letter, R 4659
Finn letter, 004/24
Holman, 'The Battle of Tofrik or McNeill's Zeriba', 009/7
'R. Marine Surgeon's views on the campaign', 004/28
Royal Pavilion Libraries and Museums, Brighton and Hove City Council
Wolseley Collection
Royal Regiment of Wales Museum, Brecon
Morris papers, ZC/2/1
Symons, 'Report on Isandhlwana', 1879, 6/A/4
Royal Welch Fusiliers Regimental Museum
Digest of Service: Historical Register, 2nd Battalion Royal Welch Fusiliers, 407
Soldiers of Gloucestershire Museum
Duncan correspondence
Gardner correspondence, 187
Willcock correspondence
Somerset Light Infantry Archive, Taunton
Farrance, 'The Prince Albert's (Somerset Light Infantry), in South Africa 1899–1902
The Letters of Captain F. M. Peacock from the 2nd Battalion' (Bristol, n.d.), 214
Vallentin, 'Siege of Ladysmith, 1899–1900' (24 March 1900), F 61
Waddy, 'Impressions of Zululand, 1875 to 1879', ARCH/332
Staffordshire Regiment Museum, Lichfield
Astell, 'Diary of Dongola Expedition 1896'
Bent, 'From Korti to Huella in a Whaler', 7648
Sudan Archive Durham University
Farley, 'Some Recollections of the Dongola Expedition', 304/2
Hunter correspondence, D//S 13
West Sussex Record Office
Trafford, 'A Diary of the Sudan campaign, 1884–5', RSR, MS 1/85
Wiltshire and Swindon Record Office
Methuen correspondence, WSRO 1742

Parliamentary papers

Ashantee Invasion Latest Despatches from Sir Garnet Wolseley, No. 6 (1874), XLVI

Further Correspondence Respecting the Affairs in South Africa, C 2260 (1878–9), LIII; C 2482 (1880), L; C 2740 (1881), LXVI; C 2866 (1881), LXVII; C 2950 (1881), LXVII

Further Correspondence Respecting the Affairs of Egypt, C 3969 (1884), LXXXVIII

Further Correspondence Respecting the Affairs of the Transvaal and Adjacent Territories, C 4432 (1884–85), LVII

Further Correspondence Respecting the Ashantee Invasion, No. 5 (1873)

Gold Coast. Further Correspondence Respecting the Ashantee Invasion, Nos 5, 6 and 8 (1874), XLVI

Report from the Select Committee on Commissariat and Transport Services (Egyptian Campaign), C 285 (1884), X

Reports on Alleged Failures of Cavalry Swords and Pistols at Suakin, C 5633 (1889), XVII

Newspapers

Aberdare Times
Aberdeen Journal
Abergavenny Chronicle
Aberystwyth Observer and Merionethshire News
Abingdon and Reading Herald
Alnwick and County Gazette
Arbroath Guide
Argyllshire Herald
Army and Navy Gazette
Auckland Times and Herald
Ayr Advertiser
Bath Weekly Argus
(Batley) Reporter
Birkenhead and Chester Advertiser
Birmingham Daily Post
Blackburn Times
Bradford Daily Argus
Bradford Daily Telegraph
Bradford Observer
Brechin Advertiser
Brecon County Times
Bridge of Allan Reporter
Bridport News
Bristol Observer
Bristol Times and Mirror
Broad Arrow
Bury Times
Carnarvon and Denbigh Herald
Cheltenham Chronicle
Chichester Express
Citizen
Colchester Chronicle
Cornish Guardian
Cornishman
Cornish Telegraph
Cornish Times
Cornubian and Redruth Times
Coventry Herald and Free Press
Coventry Standard
Crediton Chronicle
Crieff Journal
Daily Chronicle
Daily News
Daily Telegraph
Derby Mercury
Derbyshire Times
Devon and Somerset Weekly News
Devon Weekly Times
(Dewsbury) Reporter
Dorset County Chronicle
Dover Express
Dover Telegraph
(Dundee) Weekly News
Eastern Province Herald
East of Fife Record
(Edinburgh) Daily Review
Edinburgh Evening News
Evening News
Evening Standard
Falkirk Herald
Fife Herald
Fife News
Fleetwood Chronicle
Folkestone Chronicle
Gainsborough Leader
Glasgow Evening News
Glasgow Herald
Glasgow News
Gloucester Journal
Gloucestershire Chronicle
Gloucestershire Echo
Grantham Journal
Graphic
Grimsby News
Hampshire Chronicle

Hampshire Independent
Hampshire Observer
Hampshire Telegraph and Sussex
    Chronicle,
Hastings and St Leonards News
Hereford Journal
Hereford Times
Highland News
Horncastle News and South Lindsey
    Advertiser
Ilkley Gazette
Illustrated London News
Illustrated Weekly (Bradford) Telegraph
Invergordon Times
Inverness Courier
Irish Times
John O'Groat Journal
Kentish Chronicle
Kentish Gazette
Kinross-shire Advertiser
Lancaster Guardian
Launceston Weekly News
Leamington, Warwick, Rugby and
    County Chronicle
Leeds Mercury
Leicester Chronicle and Leicestershire
    Mercury
Lichfield Mercury
Liverpool Mercury
Manchester Courier
Manchester Evening Chronicle
Manchester Evening News
Manchester Guardian
Manchester Weekly Times
Methodist Times
Mid-Devon and Newton Times
Midland Counties Express
Montgomeryshire Express
Morning Advertiser
Morning Leader
Morning Post
Nairn County Press and Advertiser
Nairnshire Telegraph
Natal Mercury
Natal Witness
Newcastle Courant
Northampton Mercury
North Devon Herald
North Wales Express
North Wales Guardian
Northern Scot and Moray & Nairn
    Express
Northern Weekly
Nuneaton Chronicle
Oswestry Advertizer and
    Montgomeryshire Mercury

Oxford Times
Perthshire Constitutional & Journal
Pictorial World
Poole, Parkstone and East Dorset
    Herald
Portsmouth Times and Naval Gazette
Reading Mercury, Oxford Gazette,
    Newbury Herald & Berks County
    Paper
Ross-shire Journal
Rothesay Express
Royal Cornwall Gazette
Rugby Advertiser
Salford Journal
Salisbury Journal
Scotsman
Sheffield Daily Telegraph
Somerset County Gazette
Somerset County Herald
Somerset Standard
Southern Guardian
Southern Times
South Wales Daily News
South Wales Daily Telegram
South Wales Evening Telegram
South Wales Weekly and Daily Telegram
Staffordshire Advertiser
Stirling Observer and Midland Counties
    Advertiser
Strathearn Herald
Stroud Journal
Surrey Mirror
Surrey News
Sussex Daily News
Tamworth Herald
The Times
The Times of Natal
Tiverton Times
Totnes Times and Dartmouth Gazette
Transvaal Argus
Uttoxeter New Era
Warwick and Warwickshire Advertiser
Weekly Mail
Wells Journal
West Briton
Western Daily Mercury
Western Gazette (Yeovil)
Western Mail
Western Morning News
Western Times
Wigan Observer and District Advertiser
(York) Evening Press
York Herald
Yorkshire Gazette
Yorkshire Post and Leeds Intelligencer
Yorkshire Telegraph

SELECT BIBLIOGRAPHY

Secondary sources

Addison, P. and Calder, A. (eds.), *Time to Kill: The Soldier's Experience of War in the West, 1939–1945* (London: Pimlico, 1997).

Agbodeka, F., *African Politics and British Policy in the Gold Coast 1868–1900* (London: Longman, 1971).

Aggett, W. J. P., *The Bloody Eleventh: History of The Devonshire Regiment*, vol. 2: *1815–1914* (Exeter: Devonshire and Dorset Regiment, 1994).

Alford, H. S. L. and Dennistoun Sword, W., *Egyptian Soudan: Its Loss and Recovery* (London: Macmillan, 1898).

Amery, L. S. (ed.), *The Times History of the War in South Africa 1899–1902*, 7 vols. (London: Sampson Low, Marston, 1900–9).

Anglesey, Marquess of, *A History of the British Cavalry 1816 to 1919*, 8 vols (London: Leo Cooper, 1973–97).

'An Officer' (Pritchard, Lt H. L.), *Sudan Campaign 1896–1899* (London: Chapman & Hall, 1899).

Bellairs, Lady, *The Transvaal War* (Edinburgh: Blackwood, 1985).

Bennett, Lt-Col I. H. W., *Eyewitness in Zululand: The Campaign Reminiscences of Colonel W. A. Dunne, CB, South Africa, 1877–1881* (London: Greenhill Books, 1989).

Biddulph, Sir R., *Lord Cardwell at the War Office* (London: John Murray, 1904).

Blackburn, D. and Caddell, Capt. W. Waithman, *Secret Service in South Africa* (London: Cassell & Co., 1911).

Bond, B. (ed.), *Victorian Military Campaigns* (London: Hutchison, 1967).

Boyden, P. B., *Tommy Atkins' Letters: The History of the British Army Postal Service from, 1795* (London: National Army Museum, 1990).

Brackenbury, H., *The Ashanti War*, 2 vols. (Edinburgh: Blackwood, 1874).

Brooks, R., *The Long Arm of Empire: Naval Brigades from the Crimea to the Boxer Rebellion* (London: Constable, 1999).

Callwell, Sir C. E., *Small Wars: A Tactical Textbook for Imperial Soldiers* (London: HMSO, 1896; reprinted, London, Greenhill Books 1990).

Carter, T. F., *A Narrative of the Boer War: Its Causes and Results* (London: John MacQueen, 1900).

Carver, Field Marshal Lord, *The National Army Museum Book of the Boer War* (London: Sidgwick & Jackson, 2000).

Castle, I., *Majuba 1881: The Hill of Destiny* (London: Osprey, 1996).

Cecil, H. and Liddle, P. H. (eds.), *Facing Armageddon: The First World War Experienced* (London: Leo Cooper, 1996).

Chandler, D. and Beckett, I. F. W. (eds.), *The Oxford Illustrated History of the British Army* (Oxford: Oxford University Press, 1994).

Child, D. (ed.), *The Zulu War Journal of Colonel Henry Harford, CB* (Pietermaritzburg: Shuter & Shooter, 1978).

Childers, Lt-Col. S., *The Life and Correspondence of the Right Hon. Hugh C. E. Childers, 1827–1896*, 2 vols. (London: John Murray, 1901).

Claridge, W. Walton, *A History of the Gold Coast and Ashanti*, 2nd edn, 2 vols. (London: Frank Cass, 1964).

Clark, S. (ed.), *Invasion of Zululand 1879: Anglo-Zulu War Experiences of Arthur Harness; John Jervis, 4th Viscount St Vincent; and Sir Henry Bulwer* (Johannesburg: Brenthurst Press, 1979).

—— (ed.), *Zululand at War: The Conduct of the Anglo-Zulu War* (Johannesburg: Brenthurst Press, 1984).

Cromer, Earl of, *Modern Egypt*, 2 vols. (London: Macmillan, 1908).

Cunynghame, GCB, Gen. Sir A. T., *My Command in South Africa, 1874–1878* (London: Macmillan, 1879).

Curling, Henry, *The Curling Letters of the Zulu War: 'There Was Awful Slaughter'* ed. A. Greaves and B. Best (Barnsley: Pen & Sword Books, 2001).

Dennis, P. and Grey, J. (eds.), *The Boer War: Army, Nation and Empire. The 1999 Chief of Army/Australian War Memorial Military History Conference* (Canberra: Army History Unit, 2000).

Downham, J., *Red Roses on the Veldt: Lancashire Regiments in the Boer War, 1899–1902* (Lancaster: Carnegie Publishing, 2000).

Droogleever, R. W. F., *The Road to ISANDHLWANA: Colonel Anthony Durnford in Natal and Zululand 1873–1879* (London: Greenhill Books, 1992).

Emery, F., *The Red Soldier: Letters from the Zulu War, 1879* (Johannesburg: Jonathan Ball, 1977).

—— *Marching Over Africa: Letters from Victorian Soldiers* (London: Hodder & Stoughton, 1986).

Featherstone, D., *Khartoum 1885* (London: Osprey, 1993).

—— *Tel El-Kebir 1882: Wolseley's Conquest of Egypt* (London: Osprey, 1993).

Gleichen, Count, *With the Camel Corps Up the Nile* (London: Chapman & Hall, 1888).

Gooch, J. (ed.), *The Boer War: Direction, Experience and Image* (London: Frank Cass, 2000).

Gordon-Duff, Lt.-Col. L., *With the Gordon Highlanders to the Boer War and Beyond* (Staplehurst: Spellmount, 2000).

Grenfell, Lord, *Memoirs of Field-Marshal Lord Grenfell* (London: Hodder & Stoughton, n.d.).

Guy, J., *The Destruction of the Zulu Kingdom* (London: Longman, 1979).

Hamilton, E. W., *The Diary of Sir Edward Walter Hamilton 1880–1885*, ed. D. W. R. Bahlman (Oxford: Clarendon Press, 1972).

Hamilton, Gen. Sir I., *Listening for the Drums* (London: Faber & Faber, 1944).

Hamilton-Browne, Col. G., *A Lost Legionary in South Africa* (London: T. Werner Laurie, 1912).

Harrington, P. and Sharf, F. A. (eds.), *Omdurman 1898: The Eye-Witnesses Speak. The British Conquest of the Sudan as Described by Participants in Letters, Diaries, Photos, and Drawings* (London: Greenhill Books, 1998).

Hart-Synnot, Maj.-Gen. Fitzroy, *Letters of Major-General Fitzroy Hart-Synnot*, ed. B. M. Hart-Synnot (London: E. Arnold, 1912).

Hodgson, P., *The War Illustrators* (London: Osprey, 1977).

Holland, B., *Life of the Duke of Devonshire*, 2 vols. (London: Longmans, Green & Co., 1911).

Holme, N., *The Noble 24th: Biographical Records of the 24th Regiment in the Zulu War and the South African Campaigns 1877–1879* (London: Savannah, 1999).

Hope, R., *The Zulu War and the 80th Regiment of Foot* (Leek: Churnet Valley Books, 1997).

Jackson, F. W. D., *Isandhlwana: The Sources Re-Examined* (The Barracks, Brecon: South Wales Borderers and Monmouthshire Regimental Museum, 1999).

Jackson, T., *The Boer War* (London: Channel 4 Books, 1999).

Judd, D. and Surridge, K., *The Boer War* (London: John Murray, 2002).

Keown-Boyd, H., *A Good Dusting: The Sudan Campaigns 1883–1899* (London: Leo Cooper, 1986).

Knight, I. (ed.), *There Will Be an Awful Row at Home About This*, special publication no. 2 (Victorian Military Society, 1979).

—— *Brave Men's Blood: The Epic of the Zulu War, 1879* (London: Guild Publishing, 1990).

—— (ed.), *'By Orders of the Great White Queen': Campaigning in Zululand through the Eyes of the British Soldier, 1879* (London: Greenhill Books, 1992).

—— *The Sun Turned Black: Isandlwana and Rorke's Drift - 1879* (Rivonia: William Waterman, 1995).

—— *Great Zulu Battles 1838–1906* (London: Arms & Armour Press, 1998).

—— *The National Army Museum Book of the Zulu War* (London: Sidgwick & Jackson, 2003).

Laband, J., *The Battle of Ulundi* (Pietermaritzburg: Shuter & Shooter, 1988).

—— (ed.), *Lord Chelmsford's Zululand Campaign 1878–1879* (Stroud, Gloucestershire: Alan Sutton for the Army Records Society, 1994).

Lee, J., *The Modernisation of Irish Society, 1848–1918* (Dublin: Gill & Macmillan, 1973).

Lehmann, J., *The First Boer War* (London: Jonathan Cape, 1972).

Liddell, Col. R. S., *The Memoirs of the Tenth Royal Hussars* (London: Longmans Green, 1891).

'Linesman' (Grant, Lt. M. H.), *Words by an Eyewitness* (Edinburgh: Blackwood, 1902).

Lloyd, A., *The Drums of Kumasi: The Story of the Ashanti Wars* (London: Longmans, 1964).

Lorimer, D. A., *Colour, Class and the Victorians: English Attitudes to the Negro in the Mid-Nineteenth Century* (Leicester: Leicester University Press, 1978).

MacKenzie, J. M. (ed.), *Popular Imperialism and the Military 1850–1950* (Manchester: Manchester University Press, 1992).

McCalmont, Sir Hugh, *The Memoirs of Major-General Sir Hugh McCalmont KCB, CVO*, ed. Sir C. E. Callwell (London: Hutchinson, 1924).

Marling, P. S., *Rifleman and Hussar* (London: John Murray, 1931).

Marter, Maj. R., *The Capture of Cetywayo* (Wokingham: R. J. Wyatt, n.d.).

Matthew, H. C. G., *Gladstone, 1875–1898* (Oxford: Clarendon Press, 1995).

Maurice, Maj.-Gen. Sir F. and Grant, Captain M. H., *History of the War in South Africa*, 4, vols. (London: Hurst & Blackett, 1906–10).

Maurice, Col. J. F. *Military History of The Campaign of 1882 in Egypt* (London: HMSO, 1887).

Meredith, J. (ed.), *Omdurman Diaries 1898* (Barnsley: Leo Cooper, 1998).

Miller, S. M., *Lord Methuen and the British Army: Failure and Redemption in South Africa* (London: Frank Cass, 1999).

Morris, D. R., *The Washing of the Spears* (London: Jonathan Cape, 1966).

Neillands, R., *The Dervish Wars: Gordon and Kitchener in the Sudan 1880–1898* (London: John Murray, 1996).

Norris-Newman, C. L., *In Zululand with The British Throughout the War of 1879* (London: W. H. Allen, 1880).

Nutting, A., *Gordon: Martyr and Misfit* (London: Constable, 1966).

Oatts, Lt-Col. L. B., *Proud Heritage: The Story of the Highland Light Infantry*, 4 vols. (London: Thomas Nelson, 1959).

Omissi, D., *Indian Voices of the Great War: Soldiers' Letters, 1914–18* (London: Macmillan, 1999).

Pakenham, T., *The Boer War* (London: Weidenfeld and Nicolson, 1979).

—— *The Scramble for Africa* (London: Weidenfeld and Nicolson, 1991).

Park, Lt-Col. C. W., *Letters from Ladysmith* (Ladysmith: Ladysmith Historical Society, 1972).

Paton, Col. G. *et al.* (eds.), *Historical Records of the 24th Regiment, from its Formation, in 1689* (London: Simkin Marshall, 1892).

Peach, V., *By Jingo! Letters from the Veldt* (Totnes: Totnes Community Archive, 1987).

Philip, J., *Reminiscences of Gibraltar, Egypt, and the Egyptian War, 1882* (Aberdeen: D. Wyllie & Son, 1893).

Pine-Coffin, J. E., *One Man's Boer War 1900 The Diary of John Edward Pine-Coffin*, ed. Susan Pine-Coffin (Bideford: Lazarus Press, 1999).

Pollock, J., *Kitchener: The Road to Omdurman* (London: Constable, 1998).

Powell, G., *Buller: A Scapegoat? A Life of General Sir Redvers Buller 1839–1908* (London: Leo Cooper, 1994).

Preston, A. (ed.), *In Relief of Gordon: Lord Wolseley's Campaign Journal of the, Khartoum Relief Expedition 1884–1885* (London: Hutchinson, 1967).

—— (ed.), *Sir Garnet Wolseley's South African Journal, 1879–1880* (Cape Town: A. A. Balkema, 1973).

Pretorius, F., *The Anglo-Boer War 1899–1902* (Cape Town: Struik Publishers, 1998).

Reade, W., *The Story of the Ashantee Campaign* (London: Smith, Elder & Co., 1874).

Repington, Lt.-Col. C. à Court, *Vestigia* (London: Constable, 1919).

Sandes, Lt.-Col. E. W. C., *The Royal Engineers in Egypt and the Sudan* (Chatham: Royal Engineers Institution, 1937).

Skelley, A. R., *The Victorian Army at Home: The Recruitment and Terms and Conditions of the British Regular, 1859–1899* (London: Croom Helm, 1977).

Small, E. Milton (ed.), *Told from the Ranks* (London: Andrew Melrose, 1877).

Spiers, E. M., *The Late Victorian Army 1868–1902* (Manchester: Manchester University Press, 1992).
—— (ed.), *Sudan: The Reconquest Reappraised* (London: Frank Cass, 1998).
Spies, S. B., *Methods of Barbarism? Roberts and Kitchener and Civilians in the Boer Republics, January 1900–May 1902* (Cape Town: Hunan & Rousseau, 1977).
Stanley, H. M., *Coomassie and Magdala: The Story of Two British Campaigns in Africa* (London: Sampson Low, 1874).
Steevens, G. W., *With Kitchener to Khartum* (London: Blackwood, 1898).
Sutherland, G., *Policy-Making in Elementary Education, 1870–1895* (London: Oxford University Press, 1973).
Symons, J., *England's Pride: The Story of the Gordon Relief Expedition* (London: Hamish Hamilton, 1965).
Thompson, P. S., *The Natal Native Contingent in the Anglo-Zulu War 1879* (Natal: University of Natal, 1997).
Trench, C. Chevenix, *Charley Gordon: An Eminent Victorian Re-Assessed* (London: Allen Lane, 1978).
Trustram, M., *Women of the Regiment: Marriage and the Victorian Army* (Cambridge: Cambridge University Press, 1984).
War Office (Intelligence Branch), *Narrative of the Field Operations Connected with the Zulu War of 1879* (London: Greenhill Books, 1989).
Ward, S. G. P., *Faithful: The Story of the Durham Light Infantry* (Edinburgh: Thomas Nelson, 1964).
Warwick, P. (ed.), *The South African War: The Anglo-Boer War 1899–1902* (London: Longman, 1980).
Wavell, Field Marshal Sir A., *Soldiers and Soldiering* (London: Jonathan Cape, 1953).
Wessels, A. (ed.), *Lord Roberts and the War in South Africa 1899–1902* (Stroud: Sutton Publishing for the Army Records Society, 2000).
White, H. (ed.), *The Diary of 2874 L/Cpl. A. W. Rose 2nd D.C.L.I.: His Experiences in the South, African War 9th October, 1899–28th December 1901* (Bodmin: DCLI Museum, n.d.).
Wilkinson-Latham, R., *From Our Special Correspondent: Victorian War Correspondents and Their Campaigns* (London: Hodder and Stoughton, 1979).
Yorke, E., *Rorke's Drift 1879: Anatomy of an Epic Zulu War Siege* (Stroud: Tempus, 2001).
Ziegler, P., *Omdurman* (London: Collins, 1973).
Zulfo, I. H., *Karari: The Sudanese Account of the Battle of Omdurman* (London: Frederick Warne, 1980).

Articles

A. O. G., 'From Cairo to Trinkitat with the Suakin Field Force', *Royal Engineers Journal*, 14 (1 April 1884).
—— 'From Cairo to Trinkitat and El Teb with the Suakin Field Force', *Royal Engineers Journal*, 14 (1 May 1884).
'Ashantee War. Extract from a letter from Lieut. H. Jekyll, R.E.', *Royal Engineers Journal*, 4 (2 March 1874).
'Balloon Work on Active Service', *Royal Engineers Journal*, 15 (1 June 1885).
Barthorp, M., 'A Letter from Omdurman', *Soldiers of the Queen*, 89 (June 1997).
Blackburn, Captain J. E., 'From Gemai to Debbeh in a "Whaler"', *Royal Engineers Journal*, 15 (2 February 1885).
Conway, A., 'Welsh Soldiers in the Zulu War', *National Library of Wales Journal*, 11:1 (1959).
'Diary of an Officer with the Khartoum Expedition', *Royal Engineers Journal*, 15 (1 January 1885).
Emery, F., 'At War with the Zulus 1879', *Royal Engineers Journal*, 96 (1982).
'Extracts from the Diary of Lieut. H. H. L. Malcolm, 79th, Q. O. Cameron Highlanders, during the Egyptian War, 1882', *79th News*, 202 (April 1933).

Fraser, Major T., 'Majuba', *Royal Engineers Journal*, 11 (1 June 1881).

'Gold Coast. – Abstract from a letter from Lieut. H. Jekyll, R.E.', *Royal Engineers Journal*, 4 (1 February 1874).

Green, Colonel A. O., 'Cairo', *Royal Engineers Journal*, 28 (1898).

Harness, Lieutenant-Colonel A., 'The Zulu Campaign from a Military Perspective', *Fraser's Magazine*, 101 (1880).

Harris, Major J. (ed.), 'The Nile Expedition of 1898 and Omdurman – The Diary of Sergeant S. W. Harris, Grenadier Guards', *Journal of the Society for Army Historical Research*, 78 (2000).

Harvie, I., 'The Raid on Essaman, 14 October 1873: An Account by Lieutenant Edward Woodgate of an Operation during Wolseley's Ashanti Expedition', *Journal of the Society for Army Historical Research*, 77 (1999).

Hume, Brigadier-General J. J. F., 'A Narrative of the 94th Regiment in the Boer War, 1880–81', *The Ranger*, 4:8 (1925).

'Korosko', *The 79th News*, 198 (April 1932).

Lawson, Lieutenant H. M., 'Desert Notes from Korti to El Goubat', *Royal Engineers Journal*, 15 (1 April 1885).

Lieven, M., 'The British Soldiery and the Ideology of Empire: Letters from Zululand', *Journal of the Society for Army Historical Research*, 80 (2002).

Mackworth, Major A. W., 'The Field Telegraph Corps in Egypt', *Royal Engineers Journal*, 12 (1 December 1882).

Manifold, Lieutenant M. E. G., 'The Field Telegraph, Dongola Expedition, 1896', *Royal Engineers Journal*, 27 (1897).

McIntyre, W. D., 'British Policy in West Africa: The Ashanti Expedition of 1873–4', *Historical Journal*, 5:1 (1962).

McNeill, Brigadier-General A. J., 'Further Reminiscences', *Caber Feidh: The Quarterly Magazine of the Seaforth Highlanders*, 6:46 (1933).

Montague, W. E., 'Besieged in the Transvaal: The Defence of Standerton', *Blackwood's Magazine*, 130 (1881).

R. L. A., 'A Diary of the Fashoda Expedition', *The 79th News*, 42 (1 March 1899).

Schölch, A., 'The "Men on the Spot" and the English Occupation of Egypt in 1882', *Historical Journal*, 19:3 (1976).

Smith, Captain S., 'Diary of Work Performed by the 8th Company, R.E., in Egypt', *Royal Engineers Journal*, 13 (1 January 1883).

'Some Recollections of the Zulu War, 1879: Extracted from the Unpublished Reminiscences of the late Lieut-General Sir Edward Hutton, KCB, KCMG', *Army Quarterly*, 16 (1928).

Spiers, E. M., 'The British Army: Recent Writing Reviewed', *Journal of the Society for Army Historical Research*, 63:256 (1985).

Stearn, R., 'Bennet Burleigh, Victorian War Correspondent', *Soldiers of the Queen*, 65 (June 1884).

Stewart, J. W., 'A Subaltern in the Sudan, 1898', *The Stewarts*, 17:4 (1987).

'Suakin, 1885, Field Operations', *Royal Engineers Journal*, 16 (1 May 1886).

Surridge, K., '"All You Soldiers Are What We Call Pro-Boer": The Military Critique of the South African War 1899–1902', *History*, 82 (1997).

'Survivors' Tales of Great Events', *Royal Magazine* (February 1905).

'The Defence of Potchefstroom', *Journal of the Royal Scots Fusiliers*, 3 (1930).

'The Defence of Potchefstroom, December, 1880–March 1881: Leaves from the Diary of 2/Lieut James R. M. Dalrymple-Hay, 21st Foot', *Journal of the Royal Scots Fusiliers*, 2 (1929).

'The Fall of Khartoum: Notes from an Officer's Diary during the Campaign, 1898', *Pall Mall Magazine*, 17 (January–April 1899).

Tylden, Major G., (trans.), 'Majuba, 27th February 1881: A Contemporary Boer Account', *Journal of the Society for Army Historical Research*, 17 (1938).

—— 'The Sekukuni Campaign of November–December 1879', *Journal of the Society for Army Historical Research*, 29 (1951).

—— 'The British Army and the Transvaal, 1875 to 1885', *Journal of the Society for Army*

Historical Research, 30 (1952).

Ward, S. G. P. (ed.), 'The Scots Guards in Egypt, 1882: The Letters of Lieutenant C. B. Balfour', *Journal of the Society for Army Historical Research*, 51 (1973).

—— (ed.), 'The Diary of Colonel W. D. Bond, 58th Regiment', *Journal of the Society for Army Historical Research*, 53 (1975).

Winsloe, R. W. C., 'The Siege of Potchefstroom', *Macmillan's Magazine*, 47 (1883).

Wolseley, G. J., 'The Negro as a Soldier', *Fortnightly Review*, 50 (1888).

INDEX

Lightning Source UK Ltd.
Milton Keynes UK
UKOW05f0929131216
289866UK00005B/122/P